Lost Souls

D1296746

Lost Souls

The Philosophic Origins of a
Cultural Dilemma

David Weissman

STATE UNIVERSITY OF NEW YORK PRESS

Published by
State University of New York Press, Albany

© 2003 State University of New York

All rights reserved

Printed in the United States of America

For information, address State University of New York Press,
90 State Street, Suite 700, Albany, NY 12207

Production by Marilyn P. Semerad
Marketing by Anne M. Valentine

Library of Congress Cataloging-in-Publication Data

Weissman, David, 1936–
    Lost souls : the philosophic origins of a cultural dilemma / David Weissman.
    p. cm.
    Includes bibliographical references and index.
    ISBN 0-7914-5755-9 (alk. paper) — ISBN 0-7914-5756-7 (pbk. : alk. paper)
    1. Mind and body. I. Title.

B105.M53W45 2003
128'.2—dc21
                                                            2002042640

10 9 8 7 6 5 4 3 2 1

To my brother and sister

Contents

Illustrations

Acknowledgments

I am grateful to my wife, Kathy, for this book's title and cover art; to Marshall Spector and Elaine Sternberg for critical comments; to Jean Van Altena for editing the manuscript; and to Gary Foreman for preparing the illustrations.

Introduction

Philosophy's dominant trajectory, fixed long ago, is severely disrupted by evidence that mind is the activity of body. We see this effect in our ambivalent responses to an English local council. A retirement home sought compensation for burying dead residents. The council declined, advising the home to write off its costs as "business waste."[1] We hesitate. Why are dead bodies treated with so little respect? Because our worth derives from the virtues and powers of mind, not body. We have value as we live, not as cadavers. Why linger over them? Because bodies are sanctified by virtues their minds once expressed. We are different from used milk cartons. But are we? How shall we defend human dignity if mind's singularity—including all its powers for thought and feeling—derive from the neural complexity of human bodies?

Philosophers share this quandary with the moral community, though its severity eludes us. We regard dualism as a stubborn problem: how do neurons generate colors, tastes, sounds, and consciousness? We ignore the historical developments that made dualism a postulate for established philosophic views about knowledge and value. This posture—half impatient of dualism, half dependent on it—is unstable. Engineers build machines that mimic thought and perception. Physiologists map these activities in the brain. There is little about mind that cannot be explained in physical terms. Nothing that is unexplained—principally the awareness of perceptual data—supports the exalted status ascribed to mind when its separability from body was confidently affirmed. Questions once avoided are suddenly urgent. How do knowledge and feeling emerge as we engage other people and things? What justifies human self-esteem as we tinker with the molecules and chips that may replace us?

Plato, Descartes, and Kant are the principal points of reference for assumptions that are no longer viable. Whitehead directs us. He described philosophy's trajectory as a series of footnotes to Plato. Wanting to avert the implication that Platonic tradition is scattershot, we alter the metaphor and imagine a Nevada highway. Apparently straight when observed from a height, it is visible only from ridge to ridge when seen from cars moving along it. Philosophy, too, has an occluded view of itself, because its Platonic origins are distorted by later interpretations. Descartes' *cogito* incorporated and privatized Plato's figure of the divided line. Later refinements, especially those of Kant, embellished mind's self-sufficiency while making it the ground for being and intelligibility. Psychocentrism and subjective idealism were complementary results. Now, when our Platonism derives from Descartes and Kant, their mentalism is sabotaged by the physiology Descartes inspired. The cogito dissolves because of nearly comprehensive evidence that mind is the activity of body. Platonism endures— norms abide amidst the flux—but the road deviates. Cartesian, Kantian extensions are plowed over or abandoned. Nothing is lost: bodies think and feel, regulate themselves, cooperate, and create. Only our orientation is reversed: having previously located all of intelligibility and being within mind, we, like Aristotle, locate minds in the natural world.

My historical narrative is brief. Chapters one and two discuss the principals of the story: Plato, Plotinus, Augustine, Proclus, and Descartes. Chapter three elaborates five issues that are fundamental to Descartes' version of the line—including epistemic and ontological foundationalism, self-knowledge, intelligibility, the geometrical character of the physical world, and mind's self-valorization. It also considers an array of ideas recast in the light of his foundationalism. Chapter four describes the reformulations of Descartes' ideas by Kant, Nietzsche and Heidegger, Carnap and Quine. Should we prefer their aversion to metaphysics or their egregiously metaphysical psychocentrism? Chapter five argues that Descartes' reading of Plato is subverted by contemporary elaborations of his physiology. We often suppose that philosophic views are abandoned, never falsified. The developments recounted here challenge our complacency. The cogito cannot be the source of intelligibility and the ground for all being if working models of mental functions and empirically tested theories confirm that mind is the activity of a physical system. Chapter six considers the implications for several disputed questions. Only some are featured topics in philosophy journals—truth, for example. All are critical for the reorientation at hand. Disputes focused by these issues churn. Their irresolution is evidence of the deeper crisis they express: the demise of assumptions that directed us for three and a half centuries. Chapter seven weighs the costs. It considers Platonic and

Cartesian ideas that we shall want to reformulate if we no longer believe with Nietzsche that we are "under an invisible spell," fated "always [to] revolve once more in the same orbit."[2]

These chapters rethink philosophy's past, resources, and prospects. We misconstrue this history when Kant and Descartes obscure its evolution. They emphasized the self-sufficiency of individual, self-inspecting minds, each a theater where thinkable reality is reduced to the matters occurring on stage or screen before an audience of one. Starting from the self-sufficiency of the cogito or the transcendental ego, proclaiming that all intelligibility lies within thought, we fail to understand that these are the claims of an imploded neo-Platonism. This is the tradition of the Great Chain of Being.[3] Founded by Plato, embellished by Plotinus, it describes the descending orders of reality as they emanate from the One. The One is simple and timeless. Emanation is the flow of determinations created when the One undergoes a succession of internal differentiations—from intelligibles (Plato's Forms) to World-soul (a whole that expresses itself in finite minds, living and inert bodies). This story was vitiated by its excesses. What can we know of the One or its emanations, the Forms and World-soul? What remains when Plato's Good, the Sun to all Being and source for the Plotinian One, is discounted as a myth? Only the reduced, but better known light of consciousness turned on itself. Finite, self-sufficient thinkers—each having innate ideas of the Forms or able to schematize any possible experience—survived th e inflated cosmology bequeathed by Plotinus, Augustine, and Proclus.

Philosophy has a different trajectory if we acknowledge that humans are mechanical systems constrained by laws we discover but do not make, laws that regulate our causes, constituents, and circumstances. Is it possible to think well of ourselves if our materials or genes are not so different from those of chimpanzees? Descartes and Kant helped sustain the illusion that such questions can be ignored. Now, when Cartesian matter cannibalizes Cartesian mind,[4] understanding and morale require different answers.

Readers may be unfamiliar with some of the thinkers discussed. Believing that they should have these authors' views without mediating commentary, I quote critical passages. The Table of Contents provides a detailed outline of the argument.

Chapter One

Plato's Divided Line

1. The Line

Plato's allegory of the cave distinguishes three orders of intelligibility: there are shadows on the cave's rear wall, cast by statues carried between a fire and the wall, and the things outside the cave imitated by the statues.[1] His divided line is a more complex and abstract expression of these differences:

> Conceive . . . that there are these two powers I speak of, the Good reigning over the domain of all that is intelligible, the Sun over the visible world. . . . [Y]ou have these two orders of things clearly before your mind: the visible and the intelligible? . . . Now take a line divided into two unequal parts, one to represent the visible order, the other the intelligible; and divide each part again in the same proportion, symbolizing degrees of comparative clearness or obscurity. Then one of the two sections in the visible world will stand for images. By images I mean first shadows, and then reflections in water or in close-grained, polished surfaces, and everything of that kind, if you understand. . . . Let the second section stand for the actual things of which the first are likeness, the living creatures about us and all the works of nature or of human hands. . . . Will you also take the proportion in which the visible world has been divided as corresponding to degrees of reality and truth, so that the likeness shall stand to the original in the same ratio as the sphere of appearances and belief to the sphere of knowledge? . . . Now consider how we are to divide the part which stands for the intelligible world. There are two sections. In the first the mind uses as images those actual things which themselves had images in the visible world; and it is compelled to pursue its inquiry by starting from assumptions and

5

travelling, not up to a principle, but down to a conclusion. In the second the mind moves in the other direction, from an assumption up towards a principle which is not hypothetical; and it makes no use of the images employed in the other section, but only of Forms, and conducts its inquiry solely by their means.[2]

And:

[T]he Sun is not vision, but it is the cause of vision and also is seen by the vision it causes. . . . It was the Sun, then, that I meant when I spoke of that offspring which the Good has created in the visible world, to stand there in the same relation to vision and visible things as that which the Good itself bears in the intelligible world to intelligence and to intelligible objects. . . . Apply this comparison, then, to the soul. When its gaze is fixed upon an object irradiated by truth and reality, the soul gains understanding and knowledge and is manifestly in possession of intelligence. But when it looks towards that twilight world of things that come into existence and pass away, its sight is dim and it has only opinions and beliefs which shift to and fro, and now it seems like a thing that has no intelligence.[3]

An example focuses these claims. Imagine a life-preserver hanging from a yardarm and reflected in a pond:

Figure 1.1. The Lower Part of the Divided Line: Physical Objects and Their Appearances.

The life-preserver and its reflection are the two levels below the divided line. They exhaust materiality, and provide all the content for perception. Aristotle described such things as primary substances and their perceptual effects. They are the only realities he acknowledged.[4] We move beyond the divided line when the form of things perceived is abstracted from their instantiations:

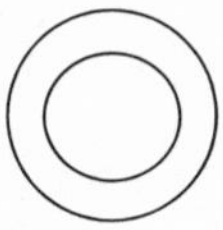

Figure 1.2. Geometricals.

Abstraction also facilitates the fourth and last step. We simplify the concentric circles, reducing them to one:

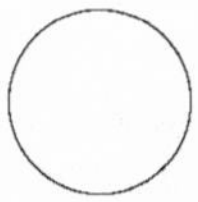

Figure 1.3. A Form.

These figures, representing its four sections, confirm that the line is more than allusive. Figure 1.4 supplies other details:[5]

subject matters	states of mind	method	value
Forms: i. the Good ii. Others	Knowledge: i. Intuitive ii. Discursive	i. Rational intuition ii. Dialectic	
Mathematicals	Mathematical knowledge	Deduction	
Physical objects	True opinion or belief	Perception	
Images	Opinion or belief	Imagination	

Figure 1.4. The Divided Line.

The arrows representing *value* indicate that all activity intends the Good (the upward-pointing arrow), and that lower orders derive their character from it (the downward arrow). Every next lower order is a further privation of the Good: there is little character or value in the back of the cave.

Thought as awareness—*nous*—is insufficiently represented. It appears only once in figure 1.4—under *method*, as rational intuition — though it has successively attenuated expressions at every lower level of the line. For everything that is, is as perceived. Figure 1.4 should be three-dimensional, with successive degrees of awareness (from more or less confused perception through deduction to rational intuition) represented by a plane parallel to the plane of the line. This alignment would express the isomorphism of perception and its object: rational intuition, like the Forms, is eternal; imagination and sensation are as corruptible and changeable as things imagined or seen.

2. The Line's Transmission

A. *Plotinus*

Plotinus was the principal source of information about Plato for Augustine, though he was subsequently neglected or unknown until Ficino's translations of the *Enneads* in the late fifteenth century. These remarks about him emphasize considerations that were decisive for Descartes.

Plotinus's restatements of the divided line describe the ascent from sensibles to intelligibles:

> All human beings from birth onward live to the realm of sense more than to the Intellectual. Forced of necessity to attend first to the material, some of them elect to abide by that order and, their life throughout, make its concerns their first and their last....And those of them that pretend to reasoning have adopted this as their philosophy; they are like the heavier birds which have incorporated much from the earth and are so weighted down that they cannot fly high for all the wings Nature has given them. Others do indeed lift themselves a little above the earth; the better in their soul urges them from the pleasant to the nobler. . . . But there is a third order —those godlike men who, in their mightier power in the keenness of their sight, have clear vision of the splendour above and rise to it from among the cloud and fog of earth and hold firmly to that other world, looking beyond all here, delighted in the place of reality, their native land, like a man returning after long wanderings to the pleasant ways of his own country.[6]

The three orders of this passage somewhat parallel the three orders of Plato's cave: Plato writes of images, the statues they represent, and the things represented by the statues. These are metaphors, respectively, for images or impressions, material things, and the Forms. Plotinus conflates the first two orders by merging sensations with the material things perceived. He emphasizes the ascent to the intelligibles, but fails to distinguish mathematicals from the Forms. We expect him to repair this omission in a later *Ennead*, saying, after the *Republic*, that mathematicals are located above the divided line, and, after the *Timaeus*, that geometricals—triangles especially—are the structural basis for every qualitative infusion of space.

Plotinus does write of mathematicals; but not in the way anticipated, given his Platonism:

> Number must be either the substance of Being or its Activity; the Life-Form as such and the Intellectual-Principle must be Number. Clearly Being is to be thought of as Number collective, while the Beings are Number unfolded: the Intellectual-Principle is Number moving within itself, while the Living-Form is Number container of the universe. Even Being is the outcome of the Unity and since the prior is unity the secondary must be Number.[7]

And:

> Next we come to Being, fully realized, and this is the seat of Number; by Number Being brings forth the Beings; its movement is planned to Number; it establishes the numbers of its offspring before bringing them to be. . . . As a unity, it suffers no division, remaining self-constant. . . . Thus Number, the primal and true, is Principle and source of actuality to the Beings.[8]

Plotinus writes copiously of number but says little of geometricals, because the transition from One to the diversity of many is a central mystery of his theory. The issue is joined when he affirms that the multitude of intelligibles (Forms) emanates from an undifferentiated One, and that the material world emanates from the intelligibles, each sometimes having many instances. Number—the one and the many—is, therefore, critical for the explication of Plotinus's three orders—the One, Being, and Soul. The status of geometricals is less plain, because Plotinus all but avers that space is a delusion: "How can the Soul take magnitude even in the mode of accident?" he asks, given that Soul is "immaterial and without magnitude." He amplifies:

> But how account, at this, for extension over all the heavens and all living beings? There is no such extension. Sense-perception, by insistence upon which we doubt, tells of Here and There; but reason certifies that the

> Here and There do not attach to that principle; the extended has partici-
> pated in that cosmos of life which itself has no extension. . . . If, then, the
> divided and quantitatively extended is to participate in another kind, is to
> have any sort of participation, it can participate only in something undi-
> vided, unextended, wholly outside of quantity. Therefore, that which is
> to be introduced by the participation must enter as itself an omnipresent
> indivisible.[9]

This is the consequence of saying that extension is the Soul's manner of
exhibiting Nature to itself. Here, where extension is merely an appearance, geometricals are best described numerically: "continuous quantity
is measured by the discrete."[10] For space is a "counterfeit unity, an
appearance by participation."[11] It is a Soul's obscure representation of
the Forms:

> It is therefore by identification that we see the good and touch it, brought
> to it by becoming identical with what is of the Intellectual within our-
> selves. In that realm exists what is far more truly a cosmos of unity. . . .
> And what is there to hinder this unification? . . . We may be told that this
> unification is not possible in Real Beings; it certainly would not be possi-
> ble, if the Reals had extension.[12]

Plato implied in the *Timaeus* that space is a reality coordinate
with Forms that are more or less perfectly inscribed in it: "This new
beginning of our discussion of the universe requires a fuller division
than the former, for then we made two classes; now a third must be
revealed. . . . What nature are we to attribute to this new kind of
being? We reply that it is the receptacle, and in a manner the nurse, of
all generation."[13] Nothing in this implies that space is merely an
appearance, or that geometricals are not its fundamental structuring
principles. Plato has made a *deus ex machina*—the Demiurge—responsible for space's creation. Plotinus is more rigorously Platonic: space,
he thinks, is a degenerate mode for exhibiting such things as participate in the Forms.

His ontology is also rigorously Platonic, as when he affirms the
duality of eternal mind and instrumental body:

> We may treat of the Soul as in the body—whether it be set above it or
> actually within it—since the association of the two constitutes the one
> thing called the living organism, the Animate. Now from this relation,
> from the Soul using the body as an instrument, it does not follow that the
> Soul must share the body's experiences: a man does not himself feel all
> the experiences of the tools with which he is working. . . . But, we ask,
> how possibly can these affections pass from body to Soul? Body may
> communicate qualities or conditions to another body: but—body to
> Soul? Something happens to A; does that make it happen to B? As long

as we have agent and instrument, there are two distinct entities; if the Soul uses the body it is separate from it.[14]

Soul is never diminished by its utilitarian relation to body, for like knows like so that Soul ascending to the Forms is, like them, eternal and incorruptible.

Soul's status is nevertheless problematic. For we need to ascertain the relation of All-soul, the animator of material being at large, to individual souls, the movers of particular bodies. Plotinus answers that each individual soul has all of the Forms within it, not merely a selection:

> (T)he We is constituted by a union of the supreme, the undivided Soul—we read—and that Soul which is divided among (living) bodies. For, note, we inevitably think of the Soul, although one and undivided in the All, as being present to bodies in division, in so far as any bodies are Animates, the Soul has given itself to each of the separate material masses; or rather it appears to be present in the bodies by the fact that it shines into them; it makes them living beings not by merging into body but by giving forth, without any change in itself, images or likenesses of itself like one face caught by many mirrors.[15]

Just as the Form of sail is altogether in every sail,[16] so are all the Forms imprinted in every soul. Each is, in principle, an autonomous knower: none need rely on any other for knowledge of one, several, or many Forms:

> (T)o localize thought is to recognize the separate existence of the individual soul. But since the soul is a rational soul, by the very same title by which it is an All-Soul, and is called the rational soul, in the sense of being a whole (and so not merely 'reasoning locally'), then what is thought of as a part must in reality be no part but the identity of an unparted thing.[17]

Every particular soul is both conscious of its content, and conscious of itself:

> (S)elf conversing, the subject is its own object, and thus takes the double form while remaining essentially a unity. The intellection is the more profound for this internal possession of the object. This principle is the primally intellective since there can be no intellection without duality in unity. . . . [T]here must be a unity in duality, while a pure unity with no counterbalancing duality can have no object for its intellection and ceases to be intellective: in other words the primally intellective must be at once simplex and something else.[18]

Plotinus may have believed that Plato would agree, though Plato does not say that the embodied shards of soul reflect on themselves while intuiting the Forms. Accordingly, self-consciousness—the self-perception that attends every perception of the Forms—is a personalizing emphasis that distinguishes him from Plato. What is the status or role of the I hereby discovered? Plotinus explains that such thinking—self-thinking—is productive. "Thus the act of production is seen to be in Nature an act of contemplation, for creation is the outcome of a contemplation which never becomes anything else, which never does anything else, but creates by simply being a contemplation."[19] Self-consciousness is self-creation. "All the forms of Authentic Existence spring from vision and are a vision"[20]: I am, because of perceiving that I am.

Plotinus is also sensitive to those intensifications of self occurring during meditations that abstract us from bodily states:

> In order, then, to know what the Divine Mind is we must observe Soul and especially its most God-like phase. One certain way to this knowledge is to separate first, the man from the body—yourself, that is, from your body; next to put aside that Soul which moulded the body, and very earnestly, the system of sense with desires and impulses and every such futility, all setting definitely towards the mortal: what is left is the phase of the Soul which we have declared to be an image of the Divine Intellect, retaining some light from that source, like the light of the sun which goes beyond its spherical mass, issues from it and plays about it.[21]

Descartes will say that nothing is better known to mind than the mind itself.[22] Plotinus anticipates him: "[W]e are most completely aware of ourselves when we are most completely identified with the object of our knowledge."[23]

Selfhood expresses itself in self-control:

> In childhood the main activity is in the Couplement [of Soul to materiality], and there is but little irradiation from the higher principles of our being; but when these higher principles act but feebly or rarely upon us their action is directed towards the Supreme; they work upon us only when they stand at the mid-point. But does not the We include that phase of our being which stands above the mid-point? It does, but on condition that we lay hold of it: our entire nature is not ours at all times but only as we direct the mid-point upwards to downwards, or lead some particular phase of our nature from potentiality or native character into act.[24]

This implies free will:

> We begin with evil acts entirely dependent upon the souls which perpetrate them—the harm, for example, which perverted souls do to the good and to each other. Unless the fore-planning power alone is to be charged with the vice in such souls, we have no ground of accusation, no claim to redress: the blame lies on the Soul exercising its choice. Even a soul, we have seen, must have its individual movement.[25]

These passages confirm that Plotinus anticipated the principal features that Descartes later ascribed to the cogito: souls are individualized, inscribed with innate ideas of the Forms, self-aware, endowed with free will, and distinguishable from the bodies they animate. Soul elevates us: we control bodily impulses, while seeking knowledge, not merely opinion. Why seek knowledge? Because having it locates soul within the exalted domain from which it derives. In Plotinus, as in Plato and Descartes, there is tension wherever intellect is joined to materiality. Soul rises:

> Imagine, then, the state of a being which cannot fall away from the vision of this [the Eternal] but is for ever caught to it, held by the spell of its grandeur, kept to it by virtue of a nature itself unfailing—or even the state of one that must labour towards Eternity by directed effort, but then to rest in it, immovable at any point, assimilated to it, co-eternal with it, contemplating Eternity and the Eternal by what is Eternal within the self.[26]

Body falls:

> The souls peering forth from the Intellectual Realm descend first to the heavens and there put on a body; this becomes at once the medium by which as they reach out more and more towards magnitude (physical extension) they proceed to bodies progressively more earthy. Some even plunge from heaven to the very lowest of corporeal forms; others pass, stage by stage, too feeble to lift towards the higher the burden they carry, weighed downwards by their heaviness and forgetfulness.[27]

Reason draws us up; bodily impulses drag us down. The self-conscious, self-controlled thinker is haplessly bound to its body:

> (T)he steersman of a storm-tossed ship is so intent on saving it that he forgets his own interest and never thinks that he is recurrently in peril of being dragged down with the vessel; similarly the souls are intent upon contriving for their charges and finally come to be pulled down by them; they are fettered in bonds of sorcery, gripped and held by their concern for the realm of Nature.[28]

Bodies are firmly material. Indeed, their materiality is sometimes understood in mechanical—physiological—terms: "The vehicles of touch are at the ends of the nerves . . . the nerves start from the brain. There brain therefore has been considered as the centre and seat of the organism as a living thing."[29] Materiality is, nevertheless, ambiguous, for Plotinian matter is not a separate principle or entity existing alongside, or allied to soul (whether All-soul or individual souls). Recall that space and time are introduced—as degenerate modes for perceiving the intelligibles—when All-soul expresses itself materially. Accordingly,

Plotinus's dualism is qualified: it is better described as the variable state or change of state appropriate to the degree of reality things embody.[30]

What could Descartes have learned of the divided line from Plotinus? The *Enneads* describe all of it, except for the geometricals.

B. *Augustine and Proclus*

The line's essential features were emphasized by Augustine in the Latin West, and by Proclus in the Hellenistic East: both write of an ascent from sensory experience to the Forms; both suppose that cosmic reason (nous) is fractured and personalized when Forms are instantiated in our finite minds and in nature. Augustine and Proclus agree that we are autonomous, self-conscious thinkers with responsibility for, and control of, ourselves. Augustine's concerns were focused by his Christianity: how do individual souls redeem themselves by repressing impulse while rising to the perception of God?[31] Proclus was more philosophically ambitious. No matter if space is delusory from the standpoint of Being and the Forms: this is the arena where bodies integrate their parts and interact. Anticipating Descartes, he provided for the geometricals passed over when Plotinus emphasized number: geometry is essential to nature because bodies are extended.[32]

The divided line is each one's keel:

> And thus by degrees I was led upward from bodies to the soul which perceives them by means of the bodily senses, and from there on to the soul's inward faculty, to which the bodily senses report outward things— and this belongs even to the capacities of the beasts—and thence on up to the reasoning power, to whose judgment is referred the experience received from the bodily sense. And when this power of reason within me also found that it was changeable, it raised itself up to its own intellectual principle, and withdrew its thought from experience, abstracting itself from the contradictory throng of fantasms in order to seek for that light in which it was bathed. Then, without any doubting, it cried out that the unchangeable was better than the changeable. From this it follows that the mind somehow knew the unchangeable, for, unless it had known it in some fashion, it could have had no sure ground for preferring it to the changeable. And thus with the flash of a trembling glance, it arrived at *that which is*.[33]

Twelve hundred years separate Descartes from Augustine and Proclus. Are they his sources or only his antecedents? Consider Descartes' revisions of Plato's figure, then some possible answers.

Chapter Two

Descartes' Revisions
of the Line

1. Platonic Themes

A. Knowledge versus Belief

The first *Meditation* reminds us that opinion is less than knowledge, and that the beliefs surveyed—in everyday life and science—are opinion only: "[R]eason already persuades me that I ought no less carefully to withhold my assent from matters which are not entirely certain and indubitable than from those which appear to me manifestly to be false, if I am able to find in each one some reason to doubt, this will suffice to justify my rejecting the whole."[1] Belief is less than knowledge, because casual assent to received "truths" is no substitute for the inspection—the intuition—of ideas set before the mind.[2] This is Descartes' standard, as it was Plato's: we take the measure of things by looking up the divided line to essences or Forms known with certainty, not down the line to the objects and enthusiasms of popular belief.

The myth of Cartesian skepticism starts here, in Descartes' method of universal doubt. Wanting to distinguish knowledge from belief, he exaggerates the difference between them, as when he insists that all our beliefs about contingencies could be false. We wrongly infer that Descartes doubts the truth of most ideas we have of the world: typically, they are true contingently if at all. This misconstrues Descartes' aim. He requires that we distinguish beliefs about contingencies—they may be mistaken—from necessary truths—their negations are contradictory. His skepticism is heuristic only. For opinions are often reliable. They are innocuous, unless confused with knowledge. The apparent skepticism of the first *Meditation* is staged: systematic doubt emphasizes the distinction—graphic in the divided line—between knowledge and opinion.

B. Mind-Body Dualism

The difference of knowledge and opinion parallels the contrast between knowing mind and perceiving body. Like knows like, implying that mind inspects eternal ideas, grasping their content without distortion, when isolated from bodily effects. Compare data seen or heard. They vary with changes in eyes or ears, implying that the instability of perceptual judgments is an effect of body's instability. Dualism, for Descartes and Plato, is a strategy that makes knowledge possible. Minds liberated from bodies can have rational intuition and knowledge. Minds coupled to bodies are distorted and distracted. They perceive and believe, but cannot know.

The duality of thinking mind and body is one of four ways that body is traditionally set apart from a significant human activity or condition. Life, morality, and immortality are also said to have bases distinct from body. Descartes' dualism provides for three of these at once. The separability of thought and body implies immortality, because body's corruption doesn't affect the mind,[3] and because Descartes assumes that a mind knowing eternal essences is also eternal. More, he affirms (see below) that the self-valorizing thinker is the highest good, other things being good or bad because of their effects on it. Live and let live—in the style of Mill's *On Liberty*—is the principle underlying the ethical theory this view promotes. Only the duality of body and its animating principle is unaffected by the duality of thought and body. For Descartes was not a vitalist. Body, including all its states and activities, is, he says, a mechanical system.41

2. Four Alterations: Descartes Amends Plato's Figure in These Critical Ways

A. Imaginings and Material Particulars Merged as Empirical Differences

Plato distinguished images from the physical objects that are their causes, as images on the walls of a cave are cast by statues carried before a fire. Descartes reduces these two to one. The wax experiment of the second *Meditation* emphasizes the shifting appearances of the sensible world.[5] Explaining one set of images (those on the cave walls) by referring them to physical objects (carved figures) makes no deep ontological point if the figures too are altered by heat or pressure. *Everything* below the line is a more or less ephemeral appearance. We look elsewhere for its stable foundation.

B. Forms Replaced by Geometricals

Plato divided the area above the line into two parts: mathematicals and the Forms. Forms are instantiated in myriad primary and secondary properties (impenetrability, weight, color, and sound, for example). Descartes proposed that qualitative differences reduce to the spatial properties of figure, magnitude, and motion. This eliminates the qualitative Forms, leaving mathematicals to fill the space between the horizontal line and the Good:

> [B]efore examining whether any such objects as I conceive exist outside of me, I must consider the ideas of them in so far as they are in my thought, and see which of them are distinct and which confused. In the first place, I am able distinctly to imagine that quantity which philosophers commonly call continuous, or the extension in length, breadth, or depth, that is in this quantity, or rather in the object to which it is attributed. Further, I can number in it many different parts, and attribute to each of its parts many sorts of size, figure, situation and local movement, and, finally, I can assign to each of these movements all degrees of duration. . . . I counted as the most certain those truths which I conceived clearly as regards figures, numbers, and the other matters which pertain to arithmetic and geometry, and, in general, to pure and abstract mathematics.[6]

The third *Meditation* is subtitled in part, "*Of the essence of material things.*" This passage is Descartes' cryptic way of saying that mathematical natures (hence kinematics) are necessary and sufficient to explain the diverse appearances of things. Extending the tradition of Pythagoras, the *Timaeus*, Iamblichus, and Proclus, we dispense with qualitative Forms and their derivative, Aristotelian essences.

There is also this corollary: Plato said that Forms are distorted when instantiated, because matter is unstable.[7] But matter cannot distort the instances of Forms, if matter is identical with clear and distinct geometrical ideas.

C. The Cogito *Substituted for the Good*

Plato's figure is much simplified. There is no division below the line. The mathematicals fill a larger space above it. Now, when they, with the Good, are the only entries above the line, Descartes makes the first of two momentous changes: he substitutes the cogito for the Good.

Plato's Good, like the Sun, grounds the being and intelligibility of every other thing: each of them is created and made visible by its light.[8] Essentialism and instrumentalism are derivative criteria: athletes and warriors are good because of being instances of their kind; knives are good if they cut. Both criteria presuppose the Good that makes difference intelligible. and both apply to particular things or regions. Neither can be used to appraise the goodness of the whole, because the whole of Being is neither the instance of a kind, nor an instrument for some purpose beyond itself. Having no point of reference beyond the whole, we appraise it by taking the measure of some factor within it. Plato supposed that the goodness of the whole is the harmony of its parts, as the good of the state is the harmony of its citizens.[9]

Each of these four points survives when Descartes substitutes the cogito for the Good. Good ideas are the undistorted instances of their kind; instruments are good because of serving our aims; the whole is good if ordered; and I—the cogito—am good because of being the self-illuminating—self-conscious—ground of the rest. Nothing else exists if it is not in me as one of my qualifications. None of them is good or bad except as it is good or bad for me: "I observe . . . that the objects which stimulate the senses do not excite different passions in us because of differences in the objects, but only because of the various ways in which they may harm or benefit us, or in general have importance for us."[10]

The *us* in this passage is particular: I appraise utilities as they are good or bad for me. I am their final cause and measure, and, in this respect, their self-valuing, unconditioned Good.

D. The Line Ensouled

Descartes now makes a final change: he supposes that all the line is incorporated within the cogito. All intelligibility is here, within me. I think the geometricals, using them to explain the perceived sensibles (as implied by the wax experiment). I who embody the line am its final cause, its self-elected, unconditioned Good: other things—the states qualifying me—are good or bad as they affect me. Where *esse est percipi*,[11] I am the ground and condition for everything that is or can be.

These are claims more often made on God's behalf. The justification for making them of the cogito is deferred to section 4.

3. The Line Redrawn with Descartes' Emendations

Descartes' emended line is simpler than the original (figure 2.1).

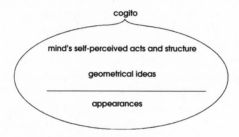

Figure 2.1. The Divided Line Redrawn.

Geometricals are the standard for clarity and distinctness among mind's contents, because some of their relations cannot be denied without contradiction. Appearances, occurring below the dividing line, are empirical data. Discerning their immanent, geometrical forms would explain their generation. Mind, possessed of its own light, strives to see one in the other. And always, mind perceives its own structure and acts, interests and desires. Every content thought or perceived is appraised: is it good or bad for me?

Notice the explicit anomaly: Descartes joins the universality and necessity of geometrical ideas to the particularity of the cogito. I never lose track of myself while contemplating universals, because I can't think of them without thinking of me and my interests.

4. The Equivocal Status of God and Space: The Richer and Leaner Theories

Locating all of the line within the cogito plainly violates two of Descartes' claims: he says that God, not the cogito, is the ground of being and intelligibility; and that space is a distinct substance, not merely the projection or assembly of geometrical ideas. I explain this discrepancy by proposing that there are competing metaphysical theories in the

Meditations. The ontologically richer theory invokes God and space as well as the cogito to account for our knowledge of external, material things: God guarantees the truth of geometrical essences, if mind certifies that its ideas of them are clear and distinct. This is Descartes' way of justifying the impression that we have knowledge of things existing apart from us. The leaner theory acknowledges only the cogito. Knowledge is achieved when mind confirms the clarity and distinctness of its ideas.[12] Clarity and distinctness are sometimes the intuitionist requirement that matters exhibit their character as they are inspected while standing before the mind: mind's own states—its thinking and passions, for example—are known because perceived. Other times, clarity and distinctness are a logical criterion: it is clearly and distinctly perceived that ideas are necessary when their negations are contradictions, as it would be contradictory that I think but do not exist. The leaner theory shrinks the domain of things known to those that satisfy this truth test: namely, the cogito and its clear and distinct ideas. There is no extra-mental reality—no extra-mental space—in which truths have application. (We nevertheless infer that the domain of their application is not restricted to one mind only. We extrapolate, describing the domain of their application as *rational space.* This, the domain of thought, is the Cartesian equivalent of Platonic nous. It comprises the aggregate of individual thinkers, each one knowing or capable of knowing the same necessary truths.) Which theory provides for the divided line? Both do, though one locates it within God, the other within the cogito. Why did Descartes advance these two, apparently contrary views? Did he bury his true beliefs about mind's self-sufficiency to avert the Inquisition, making God the linchpin of his story? Or is the leaner theory merely the part extracted by successors who stripped Descartes' views of their speculative assumptions about God and extra-mental space? The historical question is unresolvable, because the *Meditations* can be read in either way. It culminates in the second *Meditation* with mind's self-discovery, or in the third with the argument that an infinite God is the necessary ground for finite minds and their every knowledge claim.[13]

Evidence for the richer theory is pervasive in Descartes' texts. God is the necessary ground for contingent beings, the source of all motion, and the guarantor of clear and distinct ideas. Still, the issue isn't settled, because mind's self-discovery is evidence of its self-sufficiency—I exist as long as I perceive that I do, for nothing could make it seem that I am not when I perceive that I am.[14] The method of universal doubt—doubt every claim whose truth mind cannot determine for itself—is also evidence for the leaner theory. For mind's truth test, clarity and distinctness, is either presentational or logical: I don't need God to guarantee my ideas if the matters perceived are set directly before me without distorting mediation (mind's own structure, for example), or if my ideas are true because their negations are contradictions. The richer theory affirms that God guarantees the truth of clear and distinct ideas in an extra-mental space. The leaner theory abjures this guarantee, because it dispenses with everything extra-mental, including God and space.

There is only the uncertainty provoked by Descartes' contention that God could have created a world in which the principle of noncontradiction is suspended:[15] one could not prove the necessity of one's beliefs by determining, in such a world, that their negations are contradictions. We can ignore this claim if we have already abandoned the richer theory, and with it the God so empowered. Or we establish the leaner theory and mind's autonomy in this other way. Assume the richer theory, but suppose that God has suspended the principle of noncontradiction. We thinkers are perpetually misled, for we believe that we have discovered necessary truths when we have not. This outcome subverts the richer theory. For it implies that God is a deceiver, hence imperfect and not God. Accordingly, we assume as before that the principle is not suspended. Proving our judgments necessary—because their negations are contradictions—we affirm their truth without needing God to guarantee them.

Notice that suspending the principle of noncontradiction entails that the principles of identity and excluded middle are also suspended. Everything that is should also not be; nothing should have a distinguishing identity because every property is and is not posited of it; contradictories should be everywhere intermingled rather than mutually exclusive. Having no evidence of this breakdown, we infer the steady application of all three principles. God and his guarantee are superfluous, because these principles (or noncontradiction alone) are sufficient to establish the necessity of candidate truths. Space, too, is dispensable, because geometrical truths are all we can know of it.[16] The ontology of the leaner theory—the self-sufficient cogito—is reaffirmed.

It is relevant to practical life and science, though not to Descartes' Platonic views about knowledge and opinion, that this ontology is frustrated by its meager implications for knowledge. For the range of necessary truths accessible to a priori reflection is much narrower than Descartes supposed. His principal examples of necessity, the theorems of Euclidean geometry, are restricted to its flat space; they don't obtain in possible worlds where space is curved. Only the principles of noncontradiction, identity, and excluded middle, hence the truths of arithmetic, are necessary in the strong sense that they apply to all possible worlds. Nor do we enlarge the array of confirmed necessities by scrutinizing empirical data to discern their immanent geometrical essences, as Descartes proposed in his wax experiment. He supposed that thought would discern a geometrical structure responsible for the divers forms of the wax (when heated or cold), and that altering this form in imagination would expose its structural limits, limits that could not be superseded without violating—contradicting—its geometrical essence. Yet, altering a suspected form generates a contrary, not a contradiction (as compressing a circle creates an ellipse, not a contradiction). Descartes' project is also confounded by the infinity of geometrical forms that might have generated any particular effect. Compare the fragment of a shape with the many figures having this fragment as a part. We might prove necessary truths about every such figure, but not that one or another is responsible for the data at issue. There is, finally, this obstacle to Descartes' passion for necessities. The objects of inquiry are contingent only, or contingent to any depth we can discern: which is preferred, tea or coffee? Jejune contingencies are the principal content of experience. The cogito would likely inspect them; but it could find nothing in them worthy of knowledge.

These are some reasons for saying that the cogito has very limited authority as validator of its ideas. This is, nevertheless, the engine tuned by Descartes' successors. Prizing mind's self-sufficiency, they fortify it or reduce its burdens. God is the switchboard operator in Malebranche's occasionalism,[17] but he is excused from every intervention when Hume argues that causality is only contiguity.[18] Space disappears as an extra-mental domain when Descartes' successors assimilate it to the cogito. Leibniz reduces space to a confusedly perceived ordering principle. [19] Kant describes it as the form of external intuition[20] Almost no prominent philosopher after Descartes affirms that space is the extra-mental arena or matrix in which the physical world is arrayed. Newton thought otherwise, but this is evidence that realist physics and idealist philosophy have different trajectories.

Descartes was equivocal: he invoked the richer theory whenever there were tasks that mind could not do for itself. His successors rejected his posits—God and space—because they understood the promise of the leaner theory. Elaborating mind's powers, hence its autonomy as world-maker, became their principal task. It is the leaner theory that distinguishes Descartes and the lineage he inspired

5. Skepticism

The skepticism of the first *Meditation* is a ploy used to set knowledge against opinion. There is nothing timid about the richer theory, and nothing explicitly skeptical when the leaner theory emphasizes mind's self-sufficiency, not its doubts about God and the extra-mental world. Still, the issue lingers, because we are rightly suspicious of the motive for affirming mind's self-sufficiency: namely, the fear that judgments about extra-mental states of affairs are always fallible, never validated. How shall we avoid this skeptical snare on the way to establishing the possibility of knowledge? The leaner theory is Descartes' solution. We eliminate the gap between thought and its objects—hence error—if all being is located within the space where it is faultlessly seen.[21] Everything known is mind's qualification.

6. Descartes' Sources

How shall we explain Descartes' appropriation of the divided line? There are three alternatives: he learned of Plato's line from Plotinus, Augustine, or Proclus; his views resemble theirs, but are otherwise unrelated; or Descartes read Plato's basic works, including the *Republic* and the *Timaeus*.

Similarity without influence is all my argument requires. Still, this alternative is implausible. It ignores the considerable evidence that both Augustine and Proclus were powerfully influential in the thought of Descartes' time. Antoine Arnauld reminded Descartes—in a friendly set of objections to the *Meditations*—that his argument for the cogito recapitulates Augustine.[22] Still, Augustine cannot be Descartes' only source, because Augustine's use of Plotinus is restricted by his religious aims: to affirm God's existence and nature, to describe a practice that makes God accessible, and to affirm human free will, thereby relieving God of responsibility for evil.[23] And, critically, Augustine knew Plato by way of Plotinus, so that he, like Plotinus, has nothing to say of geometry.[24]

Proclus was more systematic than Augustine, and he is the possible source for such claims as these: (i) Proclus emphasized the self-sufficiency of derivative realities, including souls,[25] and (ii) the essential unity of every distinct being.[26] (iii) He described thought thinking itself: "Every intellect in activity knows that it thinks; for the character of thinking is not distinct from thinking that it thinks."[27] (iv) Proclus distinguished thinking and its object from the thinker:

> Non-discursive thought in Neo-Platonism is usually studied in Plotinus. This misses the important differences in Proclus. The Athenian School took the Iamblichean analysis of *nous* further. Proclus distinguishes three senses of non-discursive thought. There is the intellect thinking of itself in the act of thinking (the thinker), intellect having as its object the process

of thinking, and intellect having a substantial object of thought. So there are three levels, each with its appropriate intellect and thoughts.[28]

(v) Proclus alleged that subordinate intellects have innate ideas of all the Forms.[29] (vi) Proclus' "canon"—the idea that there must be as much reality in the cause as there is in the effect—is familiar in Descartes' "new" argument for God's existence in the third *Meditation*.[30] (vii) Space is acknowledged as the domain of bodies, not merely as a delusory mode of perception: "The place of things is a pure body extended in three dimensions. There is a place for all the corporeal universe, which is cosmic space. Space, the true place, is a body of light."[31] (viii) There is no void, because space pervades all of nature.[32] (ix) Geometry, as kinematics, is the science of space. Proclus "is a pioneer of dynamical geometry, the geometry of the moving point, *locus*. A single point generates complex curves by following at the same time many different simple trajectories in space."[33] Vortices may be the simplest trajectories for moving points. The elision of mathematics—especially geometry—with physics is almost complete.[34] (x) Proclus rejected Aristotle's substantial forms. His elements link "mathematics with dynamics. . . . [They] are delineated geometrically, but they exhibit active powers."[35] The elements are "quanta, particles of quantity, not pure qualities."[36] They are triangles joined to create the Platonic solids (the only regular figures inscribable in spheres), figures of four, six, eight, and twenty sides. (xi) Body is inert. All activity is generated by nous.[37] (xii) Our finite minds cannot penetrate the higher causes of the phenomena, we perceive. We are restricted to hypotheses that may make good sense of the phenomena though the entities they postulate are fictions.[38]

Each of these claims prefigures an idea in Descartes, though there are few or no citations of Proclus in Descartes' writings (none in the indexes to the Tannery and Adam volumes of his *Oeuvres*). The apparent debt to him is uncanny, E.R. Dodds suggests a plausible link. Proclus's *The Elements of Theology* was recast in Christian form within a generation of his death by someone writing as "Dionysius the Areopagite." "Descartes owed much to his contemporary and intimate friend the theologian Gibieuf, who was steeped in ps. Dion[ysius]."[39]

Descartes may not have read Plotinus, Augustine, or Proclus. He may never have spoken of them or Pseudo-Dionysius to Gibieuf. These are plausible sources for his ideas, but the evidence can also be explained in this other way: Descartes could have learned of the divided line and all that is Platonic in these other notions by reading Plato. His references to him are rare and unsystematic; but here the chance of correlation rather than derivation is vanishingly likely. Is it plausible that Descartes did not read Plato's *Republic*, *Parmenides*, or *Timaeus*, the bedrock of European science and education? His reformulation of the divided line is strong internal evidence to the contrary. Add the Augustinianism of his milieu, and the similarity of his views with those of Proclus. The latter two alternatives—direct and indirect contact with Plato's texts—are likely true, though the first alone would be sufficient for our purpose: Descartes' formulation parallels the one of the divided line, even if he did not consciously rework it. Recall Heidegger's description of this lineage: "inhuman fidelity to the most covert history of the West."[40]

Descartes' reluctance to detail his sources is well known. The usual explanation cites his vanity, though his motive in this case may be philosophic and dialectical, not psychological. We usually suppose that his targets in the *Meditations* are the conceptual fixtures of medieval Aristotelianism—substantial forms and prime matter, for example. Could it also be true that the *Meditations* is a critique of the neo-Platonists? Descartes' mathematical physics is death to the qualitative forms of the one, but his retreat into the cogito and his emphasis on truth and certainty cripple the exotic speculations of the other. Neo-Platonists had elaborated Plato's figures and myths into doctrinaire claims about the One (= the Good), the intelligibles, World soul, finite souls, nature, and its finite modes (bodies), all with myriad cosmetic refinements. Neo-Platonism was a cascade of subtleties. It had lost most of its credibility by Descartes' time, but not so long before as to escape his ascetic call to order. Hence the irony when Descartes resurrects Platonism on the basis of the one surviving element of the neo-Platonic ontology. What can be known with certainty when all its graded orders have evaporated or collapsed? Only the solitary, self-critical thinkers that were a late but best-known emanation from the One and the Forms. Tacitly renouncing neo-Platonic excess, Descartes fails to acknowledge his role as spokesman for a Platonism made sober and testable because private.

All this is interpretation, given the near absence of references to Plato or Platonists in Descartes' texts. What stops us from explaining a theory by citing myths or metaphors that may have been incidental to its development? Conceding the possibilities for abuse, I suggest that a surmise like mine is least vulnerable when the idea at issue is widely known and espoused, often by people who believe it innocuous, safe, and true. Descartes' use of the line satisfies this standard. The Platonism he assumed was regarded in his time as the uncontested intellectual birthright of European thought. Plotinus, Augustine, and

Proclus were the waterwheel for these views in the centuries before Descartes. He is their sponsor in modern times. More strongly, his emendation of Plato's line has organized Western philosophic thinking for nearly four hundred years, a point confirmed by the thinkers— Kant, Nietzsche and Heidegger, Carnap and Quine—considered in chapter Four.

No one is barred from proposing a different metaphor to explain the evolution of philosophic thought before and after Descartes. But let that alternative meet three tests: Does it have the allusiveness and historical weight of Plato's figure? Does it apply as tidily to the details of Descartes' ideas? Is it conspicuous still in the writings of his successors? No figure but Plato's line has these virtues.

Chapter Three

Consequences

What are the effects of incorporating the divided line within the cogito? Here are five considerations explicit or implied in Descartes, and still dominant in our time. Each consolidates mind's role as ground, final cause, or measure of the ideas and impressions qualifying it.

1. Foundationalism

A. Epistemic and Ontological Foundationalism

Recall the tentative conclusion to which Descartes has brought us at the end of the third paragraph of the second *Meditation*.[1] Everything but mind's existence is dubitable: mind would exist if nothing else did. He asks, "[W]hat am I?," and answers, "A being that thinks," one that discerns clear and distinct ideas within itself. Foundationalism has one or the other of two emphases: ideas, or the thinker that entertains them. It is *epistemic* or *ontological*.

Epistemic foundationalism is two things. Better known in our time is the program for replacing obscure ideas with complexes that are constructed or derived from clarified simples. This directive is plainly expressed in Rule Five of Descartes' *Rules for the Direction of the Mind*:

> The whole method consists entirely in the ordering and arrangement of the objects on which we must concentrate our mind's eye, if we are to discover some truth. We shall be following this method exactly if we first reduce complicated and obscure propositions step by step to simpler

*ones, and then, starting with the intuition of the simplest ones of all try
to ascend through the same steps to a knowledge of all the rest.*[2]

"This one rule," Descartes continues, "covers the most essential points
in the whole of human endeavour."[3] Reconstructed ideas are presented
and seen. They show their content and form (like the simple sentences
of Wittgenstein's *Tractatus*[4]) nothing hidden or disguised.[5] We understand circularity, for example, because of inspecting the clarified idea of
it, or because it is defined discursively but essentially as a closed line
every point on which is equidistant from a point not on the line. The
abstracted image is superior to the definition, because one grasps the
idea—the essence—without the mediating words.

This is the second and more fundamental aspect of epistemic
foundationalism, the point made above when Descartes emphasizes
that we seek intuition of the simplest natures. They are presented and
seen. Plato's divided line anticipates this claim by distinguishing intuitive from discursive knowledge, placing one above the other. Why this
priority? Because intuition precludes error:

> We can best learn how mental intuition is to be employed by comparing
> it with ordinary vision. If one tries to look at many objects at one
> glance, one sees none of them distinctly. Likewise, if one is inclined to
> attend to many things at the same time in a single act of thought, one
> does so with a confused mind. Yet craftsmen who engage in delicate
> operations, and are used to fixing their eyes on a single point, acquire
> through practice the ability to make perfect distinctions between things,
> however minute and delicate. The same is true of those who never let
> their thinking be distracted by many different objects at the same time,
> but always devote their whole attention to the simplest and easiest of
> matters: they become perspicacious.[6]

Rational intuition—the presentation and grasp of ideas—is thought's
aim and the condition for knowledge. This is plainest when I perceive
myself, clearly and distinctly, without mediation. Compare discursive
knowledge: it is less reliable than intuition because the words used to
formulate our ideas separate us from the things signified.[7] Intuition is
more secure, because things known are presented without distorting
mediation and seen. There is also this corollary: epistemic foundationalism of the first kind dissolves confusion by replacing obscure ideas
with complexes whose elements satisfy foundationalist demands of the
second kind—simple ideas and the complexes formed of them are
inspected and seen.

Descartes' intuitionism is, nevertheless, weaker than Plato's in the
respect that nous perceiving the Forms is said to grasp both *that* and

what they are. Descartes distinguished meaning and truth, because innate ideas are a source of meanings, though truth is problematic: how can we ascertain the truth of thoughts or sentences within the mind if their referents obtain, inaccessibly, beyond it? Descartes solved the problem by proposing a truth test that mind can apply without having to go beyond itself—as it cannot—to confirm the extra-mental reference of its ideas. His solution was clarity and distinctess construed as a logical test. This is the requirement that ideas should count as true only if necessary (because their negations are contradictions). Necessary truths apply everywhere, hence beyond mind in space. Yet, this is not a complete solution. It is true necessarily that two plus two are four: but this truth, applying everywhere, doesn't entail that there are four particulars anywhere. This is the reason for invoking God's guarantee: mind ascertains the necessary truth of its ideas without being able to create material conditions that satisfy them.

The separation of ideas and their referents—truth's diremption from meaning (*that* from *what*)—is the implication of Descartes' richer theory, and the motive for the leaner one. The richer theory postulates realities to which mind has no direct access (including God and space). The leaner theory responds defensively: it says that no method or entity (God, for example) guarantees truths about an extra-mental world. Accordingly, the autonomy claimed for the cogito can be regarded in either of two ways: as the ground or expression of its power, or as a claim made defensively when we limit knowledge (hence the things of which we can have it) to claims a thinker can certify.

The value that drives epistemic foundationalism is *certainty*: it requires that ideas exhibit their meaning and truth as they stand before an inspecting mind. The richer theory postulates that truth is correspondence, and that God instantiates essences clearly and distinctly perceived. The leaner theory renounces these speculative inferences and encourages mind's retreat into itself. It reformulates truth as the coherence relation of ideas, thoughts, or sentences. Rules Six and Eleven prescribe our conservative aim and practice:

> *In order to distinguish the simplest things from those that are complicated and to set them out in an orderly manner, we should attend to what is most simple in each series of things in which we have directly deduced some truths from others, and should observe how all the rest are more, or less, or equally removed from the simplest.*[8]

> *If, after intuiting a number of simple propositions, we deduce something else from them, it is useful to run through them in a continuous and completely uninterrupted train of thought, to reflect on their relations to one another, and to form a distinct and, as far as possible, simultaneous*

> *conception of several of them. For in this way our knowledge becomes much more certain, and our mental capacity is enormously increased.*[9]

Truths are the ideas of intuited simples,[10] including extension, shape, and motion; intellectual operations, such as judgment and will; and those which are common to intellectual and material things—namely, existence, unity, and duration.[11] Or truths are the successive ideas or sentences in a skein that starts in clear and distinct simple ideas or propositions, before advancing deductively in steps.

Is the leaner theory deficient, because it emphasizes truth vehicles—ideas or propositions—while ignoring the extra-mental states of affairs that are their truth conditions? One may answer in the way suggested above: necessary truths apply universally; it is incidental if they have no instances (there are necessary truths about circles though there may be no circles). This response is unconvincing, because it so plainly fails to explain the "moral" certainties of everyday experience:[12] we seem to perceive and engage an array of particulars. Having necessary truths is good but not sufficient; theory should acknowledge or provide for particulars that instantiate such truths. How could the leaner theory supply these particulars? Descartes' version of the cogito is too rudimentary to provide an answer. He intimates the embellishments required when he remarks that dreams and imaginings contrive realistic particulars.[13] But they are invoked, in the first *Meditation*, to sabotage our confidence in perception, not as evidence that mind might create experience without the support of things perceived. Descartes moves back and forth between the richer and leaner theories, as his argument invokes or dispenses with extra-mental things. There was no cure for his indecision until Kant introduced his transcendental psychology. It vindicated the leaner theory in two, correlated arguments: mind creates the experience of stable, interacting particulars by virtue of its own powers, not because we know or interact with the things re-presented in experience. (See chapter Four, section 1.)

Such arguments, some explicit in Descartes, some formulated by his successors, reverse several of Plato's emphases. Plato conflated meaning and truth: one who perceives the Forms knows—in either order—what they are by knowing that they are, or that they are by knowing what they are. Descartes affirmed that meaning is prior to truth, and that existence is a function of truth. For nothing does or can exist if there is not or cannot be a true idea of it. The leaner theory expresses this a priori, prescriptivist bias: nothing exists if mind cannot testify that it does.

This outcome is one solution to the implicit dilemma of Plato's line: we perpetually struggle to climb out of our selves, though we never escape the web of our thinking. We fail, because our aim is misconceived. Requiring knowledge, hence the certainty that comes with mind's direct inspection of its objects, we ridicule every knowledge claim that lacks this sanction. Never knowing the extra-mental world in this intuitionist way, we are lashed back and forth by contrary motives: we want intuitionist certainty, but need reliable claims about states of affairs that are not directly inspectable. Never convinced that we meet this standard—as Descartes wanted certainty, and doubted everything short of it—we retreat into a perfected idealism. Where nothing apart from mind can be thought or known, let mind prescribe and create: truth and meaning—hence existence and character—are its products.

Ontological foundationalism is the hypothesis that some states, properties, or activities are the basic furniture of existence. Anything that is not one of them is a complex constructed from them, or their qualification. Ontological foundationalism may be monistic or pluralistic: everything (matter, for example) has the same basic properties; or there is a fissure in being, hence things of two or more kinds.

Descartes' psychocentrism (like materialism) is monistic. It alleges that self-sufficient mind is the ground for every other being. The cogito exists necessarily each time it perceives itself, though its existence is contingent: it need not exist. The existence of other things is all the more conditional: they exist as mind's inspectable qualifications. This, the ontology of Descartes' leaner theory, is unequivocally solipsistic. I may believe that there are other minds like mine, but this is a gesture to common sense, one for which there is no provision in the second *Meditation*. The leaner theory stops every inference to entities or alleged states of affairs having an existence and character independent of the ways we think of them. Yet, mind's alleged self-sufficiency is implausible: someone would have to tell what mind must do to create the experience of an extra-mental world. Kant's first Critique was a baroque answer.

B. Mind's Structure

Descartes identified mental substance with mental activity, not with a mental agent. Mind is what it does. Considered historically, mind is the succession of its acts. Its structure at any moment is the order of dependency among its functions (see figure 3.1).

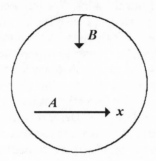

Figure 3.1. Mind's Structure.

A is first-order consciousness—imagining or perceiving, for example. *x* is its object. *A* does not occur in the absence of an *x*, because *A* is intentional: there is no intention without something intended. Every occurrence of *A* and every *x* is set before *B*, second-order consciousness. *B* is self-perceived: I am, or can be aware of everything occurring within me, including this awareness of myself. *A* and *B* are mutually conditioning: neither can occur in the absence of the other. So, *A* cannot exist in the absence of *B*'s testimony that it exists (because nothing exists, according to Descartes, if we cannot know that it is). Equally, *B* presupposes *A*: it, too, exists as discerned, though it cannot discern itself in the absence of *A* or *x*. *B*'s attention is always divided (or comprehensive): inspecting any *x*, the cogito does or can perceive itself, as *A* and as *B*.

Mind is the crucible, or theater, where experience is made thinkable. Its resources are primitive, but suggestive to someone who believes that mind expresses its self-sufficiency by articulating and inspecting whatever stands before it. First-order awareness is receptive: the sensory data present to it are content for awareness and analysis. What is more, they provoke our awareness of the innate ideas that second-order awareness uses to clarify and organize percepts. Self-consciousness also has control of the will, as when it affirms or denies that ideas are clear and distinct. Unstated but implied is the assumption that self-consciousness is a unifying power, one that binds the disparate elements of thought and perception.[14]

Foundationalism evokes pylons drilled into something firm. Descartes' ontology, like Plato's line, revises our orientation. Mind is Being. It needs no ulterior ground, because consciousness is always in touch with itself. Here—in self-consciousness—is the foundation of the leaner theory. Other things—powers, especially—lie within, or hang like a pendant from it. Experience is Becoming. All its intelligibility derives from the differentiations and relations prescribed by mind's ideas, or, as Kant will say, its schematizing rules. Remember the Forms as they supply nous with a thinkable manifold.

2. Self-knowledge

Plato believed that thought has no structure but that of the Forms perceived: it is aware of the Forms, but not of itself. Descartes' cogito is self-conscious. "I am, I exist," he says, "that is certain. But how often? Just when I think."[15] These sentences obscure mind's complexity. For the thinking signified is first-order awareness—perceiving, conceiving, or willing, for example—though nothing can be said to exist if there is not evidence of its existence. Accordingly, first-order awareness cannot be known to occur—and, by the parity of being and knowledge,[16] cannot occur—if it is not witnessed by second-order consciousness. This is Descartes' anticipation of Berkeley's *esse est percipi*.

Self-confirming self-inspection extends the project of intelligibility: wanting to make all of Being perspicuous, the cogito turns on itself. Why doesn't self-preoccupation outrun our concern for other things? Because mind can know itself only in the illumination supplied when it thinks of them: subjectivity is offset by content that usually points beyond us to alien things thought or perceived. How do we avoid the infinite regress of successively higher-order acts of self-reflection? Descartes assumes that there is no regress: second-order awareness is entirely illuminated in the moment of inspecting first-order acts and their objects.

His investigation distinguishes mind's character from its existence while seeming to give existence priority over character. What I am is apparently incidental when Descartes affirms that "I am, I exist each time I that I pronounce it, or that I mentally conceive it."[17] For I cannot affirm it as true, and I would not be, if it were not clear and distinct that I am. This phrase—"and I would not be"—is strange until we realize, as above, that nothing exists, myself included, if it is not known to exist. But more conspicuously now, mind's character is not incidental to its existence. For there is no way to determine that I am without exercising mind's character as a thinker. I am a being that exists by virtue of its awareness of other things: I cannot discover that I am without deploying this awareness in an act of self-awareness. Indeed, existence is secondary to character in the respect that nothing exists if it cannot be perceived. Accordingly, the *what* and *that* of my being are complementary: everything I am is self-perceivable; nothing that I am would be if I were not.

This double emphasis feeds our narcissism. For we cannot think of other things without also thinking of ourselves. Arguments that once sought God as the ground for all Being—God as the necessary or infinite ground for contingent, finite beings—now turn on the cogito. This new emphasis is immodest but advantageous, because mind perpetually seeks and finds confirmation of its existence and character. (Compare the speculative, unverifiable claims about a God known analogically, as the infinite to the finite.) Still, the conduct of our inquiry is uncertain. How shall I turn myself over and around so that all my acts, powers, and architecture are plainly seen? Descartes avers that mind's structure is immediately accessible. Introspect, he says: nothing is better known to mind than mind itself.[18] He describes his findings: "But what then am I? A thing which thinks. What is a thing which thinks? It is a thing which doubts, understands, [conceives], affirms, denies, wills, refuses, which also imagines and feels."[19] These results are generic and incidental to the particularities of Descartes' experience. They remind us, by omission, that self-description can go either of two ways: to a generic account of mind's valencies, acts, and structure, or to the specificity of its content.

Self-reflection is truest to the spirit of the divided line when the contents discerned are necessary truths. Achieving this perception requires that mind be active, proving that an idea is necessary because its negation is a contradiction. But now, when necessity is established, mind rises beyond the activity of proof and affirmation to contemplation. Acknowledging the truth of ideas it has demonstrated—saying *yes* when logic precludes saying *no*—mind enjoys its truths, simultaneously perceiving its own quiescence. This compares to the active, strategic calculations of a mind made practical by its associated body. Plato emphasized that thought moves up and down the divided line, sometimes rising to truth, other times descending to practicality. Descartes' emendation reduces body to mere appearance. Yet, his *Passions of the Soul* emphasize that he, too, defers to bodily needs and interests: "The function of all the passions consists solely in this, that they dispose our soul to want the things which nature deems useful for us."[20] Self-reflection turns from necessary truths to one's needs and values. Granting that I am the Good, what is good for me? Platonic nous has no content or personality distinct from the Forms. The cogito must acquire personality. Particularizing self-reflection must generate the thick selfhood distinguished by interests, perspectives, and aims. A mind contemplating necessary truths seems out of time. Practical thinking obliges mind to revise its projects and rethink its past, until it has no future.

3. *A Priori* Intelligibility

Plato supposed that Being is the fixed identity of kinds. His Forms are refined, abstracted properties that supply content for thought, and character for corruptible, material particulars. These two considerations—thought and reality—are a point of equivocation within our notion of *intelligibility*. The ambiguity is benign, because the two are complementary: the character (hence difference) of things is content for discriminating thought.

Plato didn't believe that these two domains are separable or even distinguishable: everything in the Forms registers within intuitive thought. This equivalence—in the world if and only if in thought—is expressed in the assumption that truth is identity: things are seen as they are—hence thought and known—when thought knows the Forms by perceiving them within itself. There is no gap between knower and known, hence no margin for error.

Descartes altered these assumptions by personalizing thought. No longer a cosmic illumination, the one Sun is fractured into myriad self-illuminating shards or—so far as each of us can see—illumination is reduced to the scope of a single cogito.[21] Before, each of us could hope to locate him or herself within the orderly world. Now—after Descartes' leaner theory—the world is compressed, filling only the circle of each one's consciousness. E.R. Dodds quotes Coleridge saying of Proclus what is also true of Descartes: "The most beautiful and orderly development of the philosophy which endeavours to explain all things by an analysis of consciousness, and builds up a world in the mind out of materials furnished by the mind itself."[22] Practical encounters confirm that we live in a world we haven't made. Descartes' leaner theory affirms the contrary: suppressing the evidence of error, frustration, and death, we say that intelligibility is located, without remainder, in us. It may seem that restricting intelligibility to one or many minds (assuming others) entails that thinkers may disagree about the character of things conceived. This doesn't happen, if every mind has the same innate ideas, and if none affirms any complex idea that is not clear and distinct, hence true necessarily. Thinking the same ideas, making the same judgments, guarantees uniformity.

The problem lies elsewhere, in the self-sufficiency Descartes ascribes to mind. Both the richer and the leaner theory assume that all mind's information is innate. They agree that nothing further is learned from contacts with the external world, because the idea of every possible difference or relation is already present in mind, though unnoticed or unconscious. Perceiving other things is nevertheless critical, because the obscurity of sensory data provokes us to recall the clear and distinct ideas within us. The leaner theory exaggerates this bias: all of Plato's line has been loaded into our finite minds; there is no intelligible domain apart from the cogito, hence no source of information that might revise or abet what is there already.

Mind's self-sufficiency is undiminished when the cogito is appropriated by empiricist realists such as Locke. He supposes that intelligibility derives from the similarities and differences observed in sensory data, not in innate ideas. This looks to be a window into the thinkable extra-mental world, but it is not. For that world cannot be the measure of our percepts (though it is their source), because we have no extra-perceptual access to extra-mental causes: we cannot test the accuracy of our percepts by comparing them to their causes (the look of a face to the face itself). The gap between "nominal" and "real" essences is unbridgeable.[23] Berkeley generalizes this admission to the difference between primary and secondary properties (shape or mass versus taste or color): we have no reason to believe that images or ideas of primary properties are like their referents if resemblance or isomorphism cannot be established for ideas of secondary properties. Nothing, says Berkeley, is like an idea but another idea.[24] The only intelligibles mind discerns are those it passively perceives or actively constructs.

The richer theory soldiers on. Closing the gap between mind and the extra-mental world by invoking God's guarantee, it avers naively that mind's intelligibles—its clear and distinct ideas—have application there. But this is problematic when generalization, extrapolation, and analogy enable mind to think clearly and distinctly about many things that may have no instances in the extra-mental world: angels and infinite numbers, for example. There are also discernible, intrapsychic states—attitudes, desires, moods, and feelings—that exist only within us. And there are the disputed cases—modalities and generalities—that are plainly represented in thought, though we are uncertain of their place in the larger world. The leaner theory inherits this baggage without being able to extenuate mind's responsibility for any of it. Every thinkable difference and relation—whether material, mental, logical, or moral—can have, it says, no other venue.

Accommodating this array within mind requires that we specify the faculty responsible for each of these differences: thought or imagi-

nation, for example. Descartes lists these faculties;[25] and, more signifi-
cantly, he distinguishes first- from second-order awareness. All the features appropriate to materiality are the objects or content of first-order
thought and perception. Some feelings—anger and pain, for example—
may also be perceived without reflection, though attitudes and moods
often provoke it. More complex ideas and feelings—generalities, the
modalities, and duty—are introduced when second-order awareness
comments on matters perceived unreflectively. Mind's autonomy is pro-
gressively secured as theorists ascribe enhanced powers to mind's faculties and the two orders of awareness. But there is a cost. Kant,
especially, burdens the cogito to a degree that cannot be exaggerated:
all intelligibility is mind's qualification or product. Worse, self-sufficiency is isolation: mind's conscious light is the arena and boundary of
the thinkable world.

Inspecting every content and all its structure, the cogito responds
to isolation by feeding on itself. This is more than anxiety, for mind
would cease to be were it not self-aware. Why not settle on a particular content, letting attention shift between it and mind itself? Because
roaming attention has two effects: mind discovers its complexity by
surveying the diversity of its acts; but more, attention gives life to
activities that would cease to be if they were not perceived. Think of a
student who vows to read all the books in the college library.
Discerning himself while devouring them, he incorporates and perceives everything thinkable.

This is the motive for complementary investigations: scrutinize
the array of possible differences in first-order content while looking at
the same time for constancies or differences in mind's activities. The
mind so occupied is more than a careful observer. Moving from passivity to analysis, it discerns form in first-order content (or imposes it),
while perceiving differences in itself. Accordingly, two of Descartes'
books have priority for the foundationalism he espouses. The *Rules*
describes our procedure as we ascend the line from obscurity to clarity.
The *Meditations* discovers the cogito.

Mind is Plato's cave: it moves from darkness to light by analyzing—clarifying—its ideas. Plato and Descartes agreed that clarified
ideas resolve themselves into separate, crystalline simples or structures.
Neither supposed that analyses would differ because of the biases and
stipulations of their authors. Suppose, however, that biases—different
analytic strategies—do intrude, so each rendering of the intelligibles—
whether ideas or sentences—is more art than science. This implies the
idiosyncrasy of analysis, and the bar to accord.

4. The Geometrical Character of the Physical

Descartes' richer theory identifies matter with space. The leaner one identifies matter with geometrical ideas. The richer theory derives from the *Timaeus*. Plato speculates that space is a receptacle, and that its elementary contents are the four regular polyhedra—figures of four, six, eight, and twenty sides—constructed from plane triangles. Platonic solids comprise their geometrical properties only. Yet, things constructed of them are said to alter their relative positions, thereby implying space, these things, and motion. This is also the inventory of Descartes' richer theory: things whose only properties are geometrical alter their relative positions, principally in vortices.

This hypothesis is unsatisfactory as it stands, and weaker than it needs to be. It is unsatisfactory, because it ignores mass, the factor intimated by our notions of weight and impenetrability. Plato and Descartes ignore mass, presumably because they don't understand its derivation from factors they cite. Pythagoreans believed that figures are hard bodies, implying that mass is something additional to space and geometry. Should we extend the list of material properties by adding mass, calling it a variable independent of the others? This was Newton's solution: his inventory of independent variables includes mass, motion, space, and time, though mass may be the effect of accelerated motion in a geometrized space. This is the unfinished trajectory that goes from Pythagoras through Plato, Iamblichus, Proclus, and Descartes to Einstein. One who remarks that space is distended around a gravitational body may suppose that this is body's effect on space, implying body's priority over space. Einstein's general relativity entails, to the contrary, that mass varies with acceleration in curved space:

> Descartes was not so far from the truth when he believed he must exclude the existence of an empty space. This notion indeed appears absurd, as long as physical reality is seen exclusively in ponderable bodies. It requires the idea of the field as the representative of reality, in combination with the general principle of relativity, to show the true kernel of Descartes' idea; there exists no space "empty of [gravitational] field."[26]

Mass is covariant with this field, so that all the tangle of materiality may have only this to explain it. How shall we understand that mass is a product of motion, when normally we suppose that masses are the things moving? Ignoring the exact physics—and the particles of sugar—think of cotton candy whipped into being apparently from nothing but air.

Descartes' leaner theory is more severely challenged. It affirms that space and motion reduce to the truths of a geometrized physics. These are all we know of space—hence, of matter. Their existence is just the posit of these truths. Two issues hereby implied are easily conflated. First is our suspicion that a mathematicized physics confuses materiality with our mathematical representations of it: has Descartes conflated being with knowledge? Second is this question about matter: is it generated by motion in a gravitational, spacetime field? The first question is narrowly philosophical: is it plausible that all of Being is restricted to a mind that thinks itself and its qualifications? The other question has no answer apart from the dialectic of physical theory and experiment. Let physicists amplify, then falsify or confirm that motion in spacetime is sufficient to generate matter. Accordingly, the first of these questions is the only one pertinent here: does materiality reduce to the formulae of mathematical physics? (A parallel: does history lived reduce to history written?)

Descartes' leaner theory has only this response: such things as qualify the cogito exist in either of two ways. They are set before the mind and inspected, or they are posited by its truths. Positing is a rhetorical gesture: it adds nothing to the ontology of ideas or sentences set before the mind. Space and time, for example, are said to exist because phenomena are perceived to have spatial or temporal spread or position (hence Kant's description of them as forms of intuition). Or they exist because of being posited by ideas or sentences judged true: we infer from truths to the existence or character of the states of affairs they signify. (This is amplified below in chapter Four, section 2B, as the distinction between the formal and material modes of speech.) Such ideas show their structure to a discerning inspection; or they are true because of being entailed. *Knowledge* is defined accordingly:

> [L]et us now review all the actions of the intellect by means of which we are able to arrive at a knowledge of things with no fear of being mistaken. We recognize only two: intuition and deduction. . . . [I]ntuition is the indubitable conception of a clear and attentive mind which proceeds solely from the light of reason. Because it is simpler, it is more certain than deduction.[27]

Knowledge and being are convertible, for Descartes as for Parmenides and Plato: they are one. The leaner theory provides for space merely by confirming the truth of ideas or sentences that characterize the spatial character of the material world. Such truths posit their truth conditions. There is no other access to space, or need for it.

5. The Self-valorizing Ego

Plato's Good—like the Sun—creates other things and makes them visible. The cogito, too, is our primary source of light. More, I who discover that I am, affirm that my being is a good for me, though my goodness is as much aspiration, as achievement. I earn my place at the top of the line by the choice of my projects and instruments. I prize virtue, taking care that everything I am or do may enhance it. Descartes' description mixes Stoic virtues with his appropriation of Plato's line:

> The goodness of each thing can be considered in itself without reference to anything else, and in this sense it is evident that God is the supreme good, since he is incomparably more perfect than any creature. But goodness can also be considered in relation to ourselves, and in this sense I do not see anything which we can deem good unless it somehow belongs to us and our having it is a perfection. Thus the ancient philosophers, unenlightened by the light of faith and knowing nothing about supernatural beatitude, considered only the goods we can possess in this life; and what they were trying to discover was which of these is the supreme, that is the chief and greatest good. In trying to decide this question, my first observation is that we should not consider anything as good, in relation to ourselves, unless we either possess it or have the power to acquire it. Once this is agreed, it seems to me that the supreme good of all men together is the total or aggregate of all the goods—that of the soul as well as those of the body and of fortune—which can belong to any human being; but that the supreme good of each individual is quite a different thing, and consists only in a firm will to do well and the contentment which this produces.[28]

Two kinds of good are affirmed or implied here: the cogito is a self-elected good-in-itself; other things are good or bad instrumentally because of their effects on it. Where there are several or many minds, each ranks its instruments in accord with its aims. We are impelled concurrently in two directions (see figure 3.2).

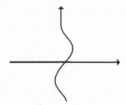

Figure 3.2. Two Vectors.

The horizontal arrow plots the course of daily life; the vertical arrow signifies the drive to enhance oneself, intellectually, aesthetically, or morally. The hard, straight line of the horizontal exaggerates the difference: both arrows sometimes twist and falter.

The good, as Descartes describes it, is private, never communal. There may be other minds—they may be aggregated—but there are no corporate realities, hence no corporate goods for families, friendships, sects, or states.

6. Descartes' Legacy

Descartes' heirs affirmed mind's self-sufficiency by embellishing one or more of the five points above. But their focus was often more narrow. Here are eleven issues they considered. Each is formulated in terms Descartes commended. The first three (A–C)—existence, God, and mind as thinking substance—are broadly metaphysical. The fourth (D)—a hierarchy of mutually-conditioning orders—is rarely discussed, but critical for Descartes and his successors. The next four (E–H)— ideas or percepts, ideas as rules, meaning, and truth—are essential to the apriorism Descartes encouraged. Modalities (I) are both structural, hence metaphysical, and an opening to will and value (J and K). All but one of these issues—God—is exploited by the thinkers discussed in chapter Four.

A. Existence

Existence is the prize of Descartes' self-discovery: " 'I am, I exist, that is certain. But how often? Just when I think. For it might possibly be the case if I ceased to think, that I should likewise cease altogether to exist.' "[29] All but explicit is the implication that I must witness my being in order to exist. First-order awareness requires authentication by self-affirming self-awareness: being-in-itself is fragile, unknown, or perhaps nothing at all if it is not perceived by being-for-itself. Yet, how is it ascertained that one has rightly perceived the other? Only if they are merged so that the existence verified is the being of the verifier: namely, a self conscious of itself.

Why is existence emphasized as the elementary fact about us, not merely assumed as a necessary condition for mind's distinctive powers— will, responsibility, or reason, for example? Because Descartes' self-discovery is the anchor for every other claim. Am I uncertain about God's existence, or stymied by competing theories about matter? My being is the unimpeachable ground for those speculations: I exist whether or not other things also exist.

B. God

God, not the cogito, is the ontological ground of Descartes' richer theory. He is the infinite One; finite thinkers are creatures of his will and shards—partitions—of him. Malebranche, Leibniz, and Berkeley agreed that God is the epitome of Being and source of its lesser expressions.[30] Yet, this persuasion wasn't universal. Even Descartes seems to have had his doubts. The second *Meditation* implies that the cogito's existence depends on nothing additional to its self-perception: the idea of it is clear and distinct, hence a necessary truth. Moreover, Descartes' idea of God is disconcerting: there is no positive idea of God's infinity, but only the negative one of a quantity "than which nothing greater can be conceived."[31] Critics objected that this idea of God is merely an extrapolation from our self-perception. So, Descartes described God as a thinker "immense, incomprehensible, and infinite,"[32] with a will that is, in principle, identical with human will.[33] Secular thinkers shunned these anthropomorphisms. Kant is emblematic. He ignored the richer theory, emphasizing mind's sufficiency.[34]

C. Mind as Thinking Substance

Descartes' richer theory acknowledges substances of three kinds, God, finite minds, and space (material particulars are its modes). His leaner theory reduces the three to one: namely, mind itself. Its two modes are consciousness and self-consciousness: things are known when they are set before the first while surveyed by the second, as when ideas are clarified under the scrutiny of self-consciousness. Awareness focused by content is generically the activity that Descartes recast in Aristotelian terms: thought is said to be the activity of a substance having essential functions (including thought, perception, and will). Yet, mind's substantiality is uncertain, because Descartes failed to characterize the thinker in any terms but those appropriate to its activity: namely, its modes of consciousness. Descartes obscured this ambiguity, sometimes by inferring from thought to a thinker, other times by eliding thought with a thinker.[35]

The product of this ambiguity is a substance having remarkable powers. Suppose that mind ascertains its functions by perceiving the structure—including innate ideas and the orders of awareness—that qualifies it to know other things and itself. The cogito hereby establishes its priority in two respects. (i) It is the existential ground for the existence of every other thing, because each of them exists only as its qualification. (ii) The demand that there be evidence confirming the cogito's own existence is generalized as the norm for every possible object of knowledge: nothing can be said to be if it is not perceived. *Esse est percipi* was Descartes' tacit slogan, before it was Berkeley's.[36]

The notion of mind as thinking substance was quickly elaborated. Leibniz remarked that consciousness is more or less intense and reflexive: some monads merely perceive, others do that while comprehending themselves.[37] Locke agreed that the only knowable phenomena are those occurring before the mind.[38] Berkeley added that nothing else does or could exist, God excepted.[39] Kant argued that mind creates the intelligibility of things known as experienced, mind being a faculty of rules, not ideas.[40] Fichte described a subject that creates its thinkable objects in the course of self-consciously directing itself.[41] Hegel described the trajectory of a being that passes beyond finite self-consciousness to the Absolute mind in which it participates.[42] This is the transition from potentiality to actuality, from obscure finite perspectives to the lucidity of a thinking that perceives all of being arrayed necessarily within itself.[43]

Descartes' leaner theory is, all the while, a burden to his successors. The more we emphasize that mind is the only substance —the ontological ground—the more we are obliged to embellish our theories, crediting mind with powers for doing the things extra-mental objects would do. Mind's interaction with the material world is a primary example. Assuming its absence leaves mind to generate experience on its own: the "things" seen or heard must be self-generated, typically by the imagination.[44] A self-sufficient, thinking substance needs all the powers Kant assigns it.

D. A Hierarchy of Mutually-Conditioning Orders

Descartes distinguished awareness from self-awareness, making the second the guarantor of the first: I think only if aware that I do. Mind's hierarchical, self-iterating structure has four primary implications. First is the reciprocity of lower and higher orders: each is conditioned by the other. There is no second-order awareness without first-order content, and no first-order awareness without higher-order confirmation of its character and existence. Second, higher-order awareness enjoys first-order content, or—because percepts are obscure—it introduces the innate ideas that clarify them.[45] Higher-order awareness may introduce these articulations without taking care to record what it does; or it makes its contributions explicit—after the fact, or in the course of making them. This second, more deliberate attitude is the posture of philosophic analysis: second-order awareness elucidates the characters or structures it has introduced into first-order content. Third is the alleged completeness and self-sufficiency of this dyad: a mind turned upon itself confirms its existence while supplying itself with content: namely, lower-order awareness and its content. Fourth, *esse est percipi*: we cannot think, imagine, or allude to anything having existence and character apart from the two orders of awareness. Such things are unperceivable and unthinkable. Kant described them as *negative noumena*.[46] But this is not a deficiency. Mind is a self-sufficient monad, without access to, or need for, anything beyond itself.

This hierarchical structure repeats itself when Descartes' mentalism is reformulated in psychological, linguistic, or logical terms. Kant invokes all four of the claims made for the cogito when his transcendental psychology distinguishes empirical content from its transcendental, conditions.[47] (i) There is reciprocity between the orders, because the empirical is content for the transcendental while the latter introduces character and order into the former. (ii) The structure immanent in first-order content is exposed by describing the work of the transcendental ego. (iii and iv) Kant alleges that nothing is intelligible apart from these orders. Philosophy tailors itself accordingly: it tells what mind does to create a thinkable experience, or it specifies the structure that transcendental activity introduces into first-order content.

More familiar in our time are Carnap's reformulation of this difference—the material and formal modes of speech[48]—and Tarski's distinction between object- and meta-languages.[49] Here, too, the four implications of Descartes' formulation are preserved. (i) Lower and higher orders are mutually conditioning or implicative. We move between them merely by adding or removing inverted commas. (ii) The formal mode, or meta-language, explicates and exhibits logical relations that are immanent but obscure or suppressed in the material mode or object-language. Knowledge isn't achieved until truth claims are clarified and justified by the higher-order analysis that exposes their logical structure, whether inductive or deductive. So, truth requires no reference beyond thought or language to extra-mental or extra-linguistic states of affairs. We establish it by asserting in the meta-language that a sentence in the object language is true,[50] or by formalizing in the meta-language the relations of sentences in the object language.[51] The first moves truth conditions for sentences from the extra-linguistic world into the object-language (the truth condition for a sentence in the meta-language is a sentence in the object-language); the second identifies truth with the inductive or deductive logical relations explicated in the meta-language. (iii) Intelligibility and truth are restricted to these hierarchies. Existence is there too (and only there), because existence is posited by truths: snow is white (the material mode) when `Snow is white' is true in the formal mode. (iv) Thought has no content, and knowledge no object apart from these orders.

The cogito, like hierarchies made in its image, is an island in the void. All lucidity is captured within its two, mutually-conditioning orders. The extra-mental world—nature—is invisible, because unthinkable. References to it are meaningless.[52] The difference of levels within these hierarchies is exactly intimated by the division of Plato's line: phenomena having obscure or immanent form lie below the line; clarified form is above it. Plato makes this a difference in being. Descartes' leaner theory relocates the difference within mind, making all the rest of being unthinkable—if any there be.

E. Which is Prior: Ideas or Percepts?

Descartes' reformulation of the divided line encourages an argument that Plato rejected: intelligibility may derive from the characters and relations of percepts; ideas may be derivative. For what does mind discover when it turns upon itself? Sensory data, the lush content of experience, are likely the first thing noticed and the referents, however obscure, for our words and ideas. We assume that Plato's line cannot survive the substitution of percepts for ideas; but this is moot when Hume casts Plato's *Sophist* in empiricist terms.[53] With impressions substituted for Forms, he tells us that ideas are their less vivacious—more obscure—copies. Impressions, like Plato's Forms, are separable, but related in the respect that they are similar or different. And, like Plato, Hume denies that mind has a character distinct from things known. There may be nothing of the line that Hume cannot incorporate, except the eternal stability of the Forms. Even this is oddly mimicked by the ephemerality of impressions: it is true eternally that each has or had a decided character: blue triangle, 3:14 P.M., January 3, 1243. Compare Leibniz. Distrusting perception, he agreed with Descartes that obscurity in our percepts requires clarifying analysis. We discover that differences and relations first perceived as synthetic and a posteriori are analytic.[54] God's ideas already have this resolution. We sometimes achieve it, as happens when we perceive that the relationship of diameter to circumference derives from the character of circularity.

Overdetermination may be claimed on either side. Ideas are overdetermined by percepts, because sensory data exhibit integration and detail that exceed the information conveyed by any thought or sentence. Or priority shifts, because we emphasize that properties perceived are often a function of conceptual context. Seeing a cloak, hat, and shoes moving down the street, we infer that this is a man, though redescribing the cloak as a dress alters the judgment. Every complex property invites this redescription, but so do many properties that are simple. Feelings described variously as pleasures or pains are notoriously susceptible to the context of description.

Both sides of this issue agree that ideas or percepts are our window onto the world, though there is this consequential difference between them: percepts are direct evidence of what is, whereas ideas signify what may be. Disputes about the priority of percepts or ideas are symptoms of two other disputes: Which is prior in knowledge, truth or meaning? Which is prior in Being, actuality or possibility?

F. Ideas Construed as Rules

People who differ about mind's principal content—ideas or percepts—often agree that mind is usually a passive witness to matters inspected. Mind analyzes or appreciates its content; but whatever content is prior, mind observes. The emphasis changes if ideas are rules, for then mind's power is transformed.

Rules may be used in either of two ways. They organize perceptual or conceptual data, as when the items on a list are alphabetized. Or, more radically, they introduce character and relations into otherwise featureless data. Unschematized data of the sort that Kant postulated are the perceptual equivalent to prime matter.[55] Their schematization expresses mind's power and autonomy. Before Kant, mind's content, whether innate or acquired, was thought to be supplied, not created. After him, there is no articulate experience that mind does not generate for itself. This is the perfected realization of Descartes' leaner theory: mind's self-sufficiency—the cogito as foundational—is all but achieved. Only the source of raw, unschematized sensory data is unexplained.

The conflation of ideas and rules is intimated when Descartes supposes that the idea of man or the sun is a rule for interpreting sensory data.[56] Leibniz is still more explicit when he describes space and time as principles for ordering the data of experience, data that God has supplied to individual monads.[57] Kant gives the notion its explicit formulation. Transcendental categories are rules for differentiating and organizing experience:[58] they require that there be quality, quantity, and relation in every thinkable world.[59] The categories are determinable and abstract: it is a transcendental requirement that every experience have a before and an after, but an empirical contingency that dawn precede dusk. Accordingly, the transcendentals require determination supplied by additional rules—empirical schemas. They differentiate and order empirical data, thereby creating the qualitative, numerical specificities of experience: sunrise and sunset.[60] Hegel generalized this use of rules by subordinating the private experiences of individual minds to the norms of social or cultural worlds: these corporate entities are created and sustained by rules they exhibit and enforce.[61] We infer that there are as many sets of rules as there are cultures, or that each culture gives distinctive expression to a common set of determinable rules.

Carnap (reconstructed semantical frameworks),[62] the later Wittgenstein (language games as forms of life),[63] Austin (performative utterances),[64]2 and logicist, formalist, and intuitionist accounts of mathematics[65] carry the emphasis on rules into our time. All agree that mind uses rules to create the experience of data or worlds, be they practical and empirical, or conceptual and abstract.

G. Meaning

Plato and Descartes would have us agree that ideas prefigure all that is or may be, and that sensory data are vague or obscure until we use ideas to articulate them. Or we have it from Locke, Berkeley, Hume, and Russell that impressions are primary, while ideas are their less forceful copies. Either way, mind sorts the primary bearers or signifiers of character and relation, while clarifying their derivatives. Both sides agree that we are more prone to obscurity than clarity. For we rarely ascend to the top of the line where mind easily surveys the intelligibles, remarking their similarities and differences. What do confused ideas signify or express? What do they mean? The intuitionism common to Plato and Descartes is the promise that clarified ideas exhibit their character or structure, hence the meanings—the essences—they signify. Analysis is the cure for obscurity: analyzed ideas show their sense.

Meaning analysts respond with a variety of strategies, from piece-meal reconstructions focused by particular topics (ordinary-language analyses or Husserl's eidetic reductions) to the holist views of those who argue that the meaning of every thought, word, or sentence is a function of its context (the situations provoking action for Dewey, linked fields of sentences for Quine). Analysts disagree about content and method, but all take their agenda from Descartes' *Rules*. Aristotle moved about the natural world cataloguing animals, stars, and the weather. He could differentiate and describe them without having to make them thinkable, because—he supposed—every such thing has an intrinsic form. Cartesians can attend only to the intelligibles at hand: they differentiate and catalogue the ideas, rules, percepts, words, or sentences that qualify awareness. These contents also have form, form that is immanent or imposed, and discerned. Thought has done all it can when these contents are clarified and ordered, for then the mean-ings exhibited are inspected and seen. We have content for the idea of triangularity if we see a triangle, or understand that each is a closed figure having three sides. Or we learn the meaning of *triangle* by dis-cerning the rules that constrain its use.

There is no chasm, in this respect, between Cartesians who argue for meaning as sense and those who argue for meaning as use. Both agree that meanings are disclosed as we rise to the higher of the two orders described above (section 6D). Clarified ideas or rules are inspected and seen, their meanings known.

H. Truth

What does *truth* signify if the *aboutness* of ideas is a misconcep-tion: if truth is not the correspondence relation of a propositional vehi-cle (a complex idea, thought, or sentence) to a state of affairs? For there are no extra-mental states of affairs against which to measure ideas if self-sufficient mind is the ground for all being. This has either of two implications. Truth is identity: I perceive the form of things—circles, triangles, or mind's own structure—as they qualify awareness and are seen. Or truth is coherence: the property of the ideas, thoughts, or sen-tences whose relations satisfy rules of inference.

Truth for Descartes' leaner theory is, alternately, identity or coher-ence. The truth of simple ideas is directly perceived. Complex ideas require the discipline of inference. Descartes emphasized deductive rules and relations, hence validity; but we promote the same result by substituting inductive rules. We say that ideas or sentences are true if they satisfy evidentiary rules that entitle us to affirm one sentence when one or several others are already affirmed. So, "This is Chicago" is true, if some other sentences—"Lake Michigan lies off-shore," "Indiana is directly east, and Wisconsin fifty miles north"—are also true.

This is truth as a relation of thoughts or sentences, not the truth of a thought or sentence satisfied by an extra-mental state of affairs. How does this notion of truth jibe with our everyday encounters? Isn't truth-telling vital to the cooperation that engages us effectively to other things and one another? Truth as coherence leaves us pawing the air, or we think of fictions: they cohere without being true. We expect truths to have extra-mental or extra-linguistic referents, though the leaner theory says there are none. For no such thing can be thought or known, if everything that exists is only a mind or its qualification.

I. Modalities

The leaner theory locates all three modalities—necessity, actuality, and possibility—within mind. Mind, itself, is the first actuality; nothing else is actual if it is not mind's qualification. Possibilities are material or logical. Material possibilities are mind's capacities for thought, perception, imagination, will, or self-reflection. Logical possibilities are the domain of intelligibility: they are expressed by thoughts or sentences that embody no contradictions. A systematic theory or narrative typically signifies many possibles, though it avoids contraries (hence contradictions) in order to satisfy the requirement that sentences or ideas should cohere. Necessities too are of two kinds. Some—the principles of identity, noncontradiction, and excluded middle—apply to every conceptualization. Other necessities are parochial. They constrain everything within a domain: the rules of etiquette or physical laws (the laws of motion have no exception in our world). The richer theory emphasizes that even the laws of logic are parochial: God could have created worlds in which they do not apply.[66] But this would have been an act of God's will, not of his thought. It is not plain that the cogito's will could do as much, or that thought could survive without its logical principles. For the leaner theory has only a few resources. The cogito, like a boat, is propelled by thought and will as it moves through the void. Sabotage thought (by sanctioning contradictions), and there is only will or whim to direct it.

J. Will

Descartes described will in these terms:

> [T]he faculty of will consists alone in our having the power of choosing to do a thing or choosing not to do it (that is, to affirm or deny, to pursue or to shun it), or rather it consists alone in the fact that in order to affirm or deny, pursue or shun those things placed before us by the understanding, we act so that we are unconscious that any outside force constrains us in doing so.[67]

Kant retained the emphasis on affirmation, but he substituted schemas or moral maxims for clear and distinct ideas. The power to give or withhold assent seems feeble when compared to the animal or creative will, the first as it wills survival,[68] the other as it sublimates aggression for the sake of wisdom or beauty.[69] This impression is mistaken: Kant made will the engine of his world-making. It affirms schemas and maxims by choosing them. It creates experience by willing the application of schemas that differentiate and order sensory data. It creates a coherent social order by willing maxims that satisfy the categorical imperative. The empirical ego (ego as it appears to itself) survives—it retains its identity in the midst of other things experienced—as long as the transcendental ego (ego as it operates on itself) consistently applies the same schemas or maxims.

Nietzsche believed that this "merely" cerebral activity is the foundation of all power:

> Suppose, finally, we succeeded in explaining our entire instinctive life as the development and ramification of one basic form of the will—namely, of the will to power, as my proposition has it; suppose all organic functions could be traced back to this will to power and one could also find in it the solution of the problem of procreation and nourishment—it is *one* problem—then one would have gained the right to determine *all* efficient force univocally as—*will to power*. The world viewed from inside, the world defined and determined according to its "intelligible character"—it would be "will to power and nothing else."[70]

Will makes thinkable worlds by choosing the rules used to differentiate and organize them. Animal power—catching or controlling a prey—is trivial by comparison.

Ontological foundationalists disagree among themselves about the desirability of a stable will. Some prefer stability in the "worlds" mind creates. Others—including the pragmatists and deconstructionists—sometimes emphasize that inconstancy is the price of mind's unconditioned spontaneity and power. Nothing can override us when we change our minds. For regularity and predictability are the barely routinized expressions of a power that always threatens to shatter stable appearances; every choice expresses mind's autonomy as onto-logical ground.

How shall we take responsibility for all we do or can do, when mind is baffled by its power and conflicted aims? Nietzsche answered pessimistically that self is only the will to power, and that its choice of world-making schemas is concurrent with its self-determination and self-discovery. Being what it creates and discerns, it has no disengaged reserve with which to control itself.[71]

What prevents Cartesian will from turning monstrous? Descartes supposed that will is restrained by its regard for clear and distinct ideas. Kant invoked the categorical imperative: will only those maxims that can be universalized without contradiction.[72] (Promising satisfies this requirement; lying violates it.) Descartes' post-Kantian successors some-times celebrate will's lack of constraint. Here is Martin Heidegger writing in 1940:

> (T)hought is "constructive.". . . "Constructive" thought is at the same time "exclusive." In this way it fixes and maintains what can support the edifice and fends off what endangers it. In this way it secures the foundation and selects the building materials. Constructive-exclusive thought is simultane-ously "annihilative." It destroys whatever stoppages and restraints hinder the constructive rising to the heights. Annihilation offers security against the pressure of all conditions of decline. Construction demands exclusion. Every constructing (as a creating) embraces destruction.
>
> Will to power, the essential complex of enhancement of power and preservation of power, brings its own essence to power, that is, to appearance in beings, by empowering itself for overpowering. Will to power is representation that posits values. Yet construction is the supreme mode of enhancement. Differentiating and conserving exclusion is the supreme mode of preservation. Annihilation is the supreme mode of the counteressence of preservation and enhancement.
>
> The question remains as to which peoples and what kinds of humanity ultimately and even initially will rally to the law of this fundamental trait and thus pertain to the early history of dominion over the earth. What Nietzsche outlined around 1881–82, when in *Daybreak* the thought of the eternal return of the same came to him, is no longer a question but has already been decided: "The time is coming when the struggle for dominion over the earth will be carried on—it will be carried on in the name of *fundamental philosophical doctrines*."[73]

This is Cartesian will, transformed by Kant and Fichte,[74] then perverted.

K. Value

The cogito is suffused with passions that have a distinct polarity:

All the preceding passions may be produced in us without perceiving in any way whether the object causing them is good or evil. But when we think of something as good with regard to us, i.e., as beneficial to us, this makes us have love for it; and when we think of it as evil or harmful, this arouses hatred in us. . . . This same consideration of good and evil is the origin of all the other passions.[75]

Everything appraised is considered from the perspective of its effects— good or bad—on oneself. Many things affect us, so that mind is perpetually agitated: it loves and hates concurrently. Mind's tumult is more apparent in Descartes' *Passions of the Soul* than in the *Discourse* or *Meditations*. The *Passions* considers attitudes and feelings aroused in the body as well as those present only or principally in the soul; the other texts express the quieter passion described as *wonder*.[76] Hungers and angers are disruptive. The joy appropriate to philosophic topics is ascetic and refined: it overrides the conflicts aroused when knowledge is wanted but feared (regarding health, for example). Three points dominate these ideas about value: (i) the intensity of our concern; (ii) the egoism that appraises every effect for evidence that it is good or bad for oneself, and (iii) the absence of regard for social systems and their goods—families and their welfare, for example. The egoism Descartes commends accurately expresses the obsessiveness and intensity of some human feelings. But there is an offsetting cost. Alone in the projects of our choice, dominated by anxiety and self-interest, we ignore these same concerns in other people. These are people who engage us in projects we value, at work, in families, and in friendships. We cannot be true to ourselves while denying our complicity in their lives. Yet, we have roles in several or many systems, not all of them harmonizable. There is scarcity and crowding, and the need to weigh the interests of some people against others—all of them valued—or to weigh their interests against our own. Conflict is guaranteed. Descartes avoided these issues. Acknowledging the authority of Crown and Church, prizing whatever stability they might assure, he did his best to be left alone.

These eleven issues are principal topics of concern when Descartes' ontological foundationalism is elaborated. Husserl summarized its agenda:

Every imaginable sense, every imaginable being, whether the latter is called immanent or transcendent, falls within the domain of transcendental subjectivity, as the subjectivity that constitutes sense and being. The attempt to conceive the universe of true being as something lying outside the universe of possible consciousness, possible knowledge, possible evidence, the two being related to one another merely externally by a rigid law, is nonsensical. They belong together essentially; and, as belonging together essentially, they are also concretely one, one in the only absolute connection: transcendental subjectivity. The "phenomenological self-explication" that went on in my ego, this explication of all my ego's constitutings and all the ojectivities existing for him, necessarily assumed the methodic form of an apriori self-explication.[77]

Mind describes its content and structure. This is all that science is or can be, for nothing is intelligible apart from mind, its ideas, aims, and values.

Chapter Four

Descartes' Heirs: Ontological Foundationalism and "The End of Western Metaphysics"

Plato affirmed that Being comprises nous and the Forms. Forms are paradigmatic differences everywhere available for expression in Becoming. The particulars instantiating them stabilize for a while, then dissolve. Plato added that our finite minds are shards of World-soul. We can distinguish among sensible particulars, because the Forms are present in us as innate ideas: we discern or prescribe character, hence identity, to things that are otherwise too obscure to achieve it. All this is softened and reinterpreted when Descartes fractures nous, describing each splinter as a mind that cannot think its ideas if it cannot reflect on itself. The transition from Being to Becoming is hereby reformulated—in epistemological terms—as the descent from clarity to confusion.

Surveying Descartes' successors for restatements of Plato's figure, we expect to find expressions for this short-list of requirements: (i) Do they locate all of intelligibility within mind? (ii) Do they affirm that there is an energy, an *eros* or will, that drives mind to rise out of obscurity—meaning confused ideas or percepts—to the luminous domain of clarified differences and relations? (iii) Do they suppose that the intelligibles known to mind—whether founded in ideas, rules, or percepts—are the basis and measure for the existence and character of every other thing? (iv) Do they say that mind can know its structure? These four marks distinguish Descartes' reformulation of Plato's line.

Each of the four is prominent in Kant. Some or all are present in the Kantians of our time—whether *romantic* or *analytic*. They agree that the world is intelligible in ways that thought prescribes, though mind stands alone: its ideas cast no shadows beyond itself.

1. Kant

Kant worried that the stability of experience would be miraculous and unsustainable if, as Hume said, "(T)here is no absolute nor metaphysical necessity, that every beginning of existence shou'd be attended with [a cause]."[1] What stabilizes a current visual array? Why does every next apple resemble the ones previously seen? One might have explained the stability of experience in either of two ways: the extra-mental things perceived are stable in themselves, or mind stabilizes its experience of them. Hume rejects both possibilities. He denies the extra-mental reality of things perceived: no extra-mental apple steadies the array of properties set within and before me. Nor can mind do it. Being "a heap or collection of different perceptions, united together by certain relations,"[2] it has no structure—no faculties—with which to stabilize "things" perceived or their relations. (We ignore Hume's inconsistent appeal to mind's "secret operation," habit, and "custom."[3]) Yet, experience is stable. Complicated arrays of data hold their form; every next wave does resemble the last. There seem to be only three ways to explain these effects: stability is a miracle tested and extended every moment; things perceived are stable; or experience is stabilized by the mind that creates it. The first option—order is an accident that could disintegrate at any moment—was unacceptable to Kant. The second and third are not mutually exclusive: stable things in the extra-mental world might be perceived by a mind that stabilizes its experience. Still, the second option is also rejected, because it requires unverifiable inferences about extra-mental states of affairs. Knowing them by way of experience, having no additional, unmediated access to them, we cannot say what they are in themselves.

Kant surmised that mind alone guarantees the stability of experience. He explains its unity, for example, by saying that mind "runs through" the "forms of intuition,"[4] thereby securing the spatial and temporal relations of sensory data. This is a first defence against the threat that experience may dissolve; but there is more to explain. Every datum has a particular character, and each participates in one or more perceptual array, each having a distinctive order or form (as sheep differ from goats). Kant explains these effects by elaborating the suggestion, intimated in Descartes and Leibniz,[5] that mind's innate ideas are rules. Rules, unlike ideas, never stand before the mind. We never-theless infer their application, given their effects. The use of certain rules—the Categories—is a necessary condition for having any experi-ence.[6] Every sensory datum must have quality, quantity, and relation: it is a datum of this or that character, it is one or many, and it relates spa-tially and temporally to other percepts. The Categories are unalterable and indispensable, but they are variables—determinables—without values. They achieve specificity when additional rules—the empirical schemas—are used to differentiate and organize experience.[7] So, the rule for distinguishing things as *red* requires (for example) its applica-tion to every third datum. Other schemas organize arrays of data, thereby creating the experience of perceiving particular objects: sheep and goat name both a class of animals and the schemas that organize percepts to create the experience of seeing sheep and goats. It is too often overlooked that the necessary application of the Categories—there is no experience without all three of them—is offset by mind's choice of schemas. They are freely altered or replaced.

The source of these data is never explained. Indeed, Kant argues

Kant provides this foundation for experience by separating two mental functions that Descartes merely distinguished: consciousness—awareness—is set apart from self-consciousness. Descartes believed that we cannot be conscious without also being self-conscious: the latter tes-tifies to the existence of the former, thereby securing it. Kant agrees by embellishing the point: there would be no awareness of particular sen-sory content, if higher-order awareness did not supply content for awareness. His first *Critique* nevertheless denies that mind perceives itself in the act of making experience. (He may have feared that experi-ence—this lamp, that flash of light—would lose credibility were we to discover ourselves making it.) Self-consciousness, now renamed the *transcendental unity of apperception* is said to be known indirectly when we infer from experience to its necessary, subjective conditions.[8] It unifies space and time, while using its rules to organize the sensory or conceptual data of which we have first-order awareness.

The source of these data is never explained. Indeed, Kant argues in ways that preclude explaining it. Causality is said to be a relation within experience only: namely, the contiguity of things in space and time.[9] Extra-mental states of affairs are *noumenal*.[10] Having no think-able features (indistinguishable, therefore, from nonbeing), they cannot be construed as causes of our sensory states. Kant's successors deplore the unanswered question: what is the source of sensory data? Fichte, Schelling, and Hegel invoke the productive imagination,[11] adding that imagination is activated by Kant's adaptation of Cartesian will. For will is the energizer of our world-making. It selects among the available schemas or maxims in order to create such experiences, such "worlds," as satisfy our desires.[12]

The cogito is transformed. No longer the measure of all that exists necessarily, it has become an elaborated, apperceptive monad.[13] The transcendental categories are common to every thinker, but their aims, empirical schemas, and self-generated sensory contents are not. Each thinker's product—its experience—is unique. Leibniz claimed that monads are windowless because each one's experience (and "world") is inaccessible to every other. Nothing in Kant relieves this isolation.[14] The chaos Hume invites is, nevertheless, averted. Experience is not a fragile skein: every event has necessarily an antecedent and a successor: each event occurs in the space and time of contiguous places and successive moments unified by the transcendental ego.

Kant's transcendental subject plainly exhibits its origins in the Cartesian cogito: self-consciousness becomes the transcendental unifier and schematizer. Nous is conspicuous too. It prescribes the conditions for intelligibility to the sensory flux, as Plato argued that ideas of the Forms resolve obscurity in our shifting sensations.[15] Kant's rules—both the Categories and empirical schemas—have an equivalent effect, but dramatically greater power. Plato allowed that the flux has a character of its own, however derivative and obscure. Kant's rules introduce differentiations and relations into sensory data that are otherwise characterless.

Every such claim further elaborates mind's self-sufficiency, thereby relieving the extra-mental world of responsibility for effects mind can produce by itself. We are encouraged to believe that everything extra-mental is noumenal and unthinkable, however strong our desire to speculate about it. The implications are equivocal: is there an extra-mental world, one we cannot think or know, or is everything beyond the mind less than noumenal because of being propertyless? Is there only nonbeing where Descartes' richer theory posits God and space?

Kant is very close to saying that mind is the arbiter of all that is or may be, and that we create such experiences as satisfy our needs and desires. For nothing opposes imagination and will as we lay down the conditions for intelligibility and satisfaction. Kant sometimes rejected this extreme—Fichtean—expression of his views. Other times, he couldn't resist the freedom it promises:

> I have been reproached . . . for defining the power of desire as the *power of being the cause, through one's presentations, of the actuality of the objects of these presentations.* The criticism was that, after all, mere wishes are desires too, and yet we all know that they alone do not enable us to produce their object. That, however, proves nothing more than that

some of man's desires involve him in self-contradiction, inasmuch as he uses the presentation by itself to strive to produce the object, while yet he cannot expect success from it.[16]

Cartesian will, vastly empowered, chooses to apply whatever schemas—projects or plans—satisfy us, short of contradiction. For there are no extra-mental circumstances to resist us. Or we are opposed—mysteriously—by the wills of other thinkers whose aims and values are different from ours.

What is the common domain where these thinkers might interact? There is none, apart from the discourse that passes among them. Even this talk is unexplained, if reality is shrunk to the limits of individual minds. Cartesians and Kantians ignore this limit because they are embarrassed by the solipsism—though not the idealism—that Descartes and Kant never shake. Or they disguise the crippling ontological assumption—the self-sufficient cogito—by arguing that language is essentially public, never private. The innate ideas or categories they ascribe to mind support communication, because each thinker is said to have the same innate ideas or rules: we should be able to express, confirm, and (perhaps) communicate the same necessary truths. Why are the arguments against private languages so often impassioned? Because Cartesians and Kantians fear that the ego's isolation is unbreachable. Deferring to language, insisting that its uses are mutually intelligible, we suppose that each of us organizes his or her experience in similar ways because of invoking the same ideas or rules. This is the first of several steps calculated to break down the isolation of individual thinkers. We add (a next step) that a public language may embody rules—including empirical schemas—that enable people to regularize their experiences of contingencies—this table, that chair—making them uniform. And we emphasize (a further step) that the choice of empirical schemas is value-driven. This explains the uniformity of experience, if thinkers having similar or complementary values choose the same empirical schemas to organize their experiences. This would be evidence that a public language has bridged the gaps among egos by instilling the same motives and schemas in each of them.

Language does sometimes have these effects. Yet, equally, your will and values might be incomprehensible to me. I might know them within the context of my experience as a dissonance—a resistance—I cannot explain. Seeing our different worlds as functions of our different desires requires that I know your will as well as my own. But I don't know the differences between our experiences and worlds, because I don't know your will directly. Nor do I have indirect access to the experience created when your values determine the choice of empirical schemas used to articulate your experience. Any argument to the contrary expresses our habitual inclination to speculate beyond the bounds of experience. Kant has described this as transcendental dialectic, an error to resist.[17] I cannot so much as infer that there are other wills with plans different from my own, or that plans enacted within those other minds inexplicably collide with mine. Kantian egos inherit all the constraints that Leibniz described: they are windowless monads.[18]

The nonbeing of the extra-mental world, the isolation of individual minds, the mutual unintelligibility of their wills and experiences—these are issues that haunt Kant's elaboration of Descartes' leaner theory. Still more disabling for Cartesians is the implication that mind is a mystery to itself. Descartes supposed that both first- and second-order consciousness are immediately accessible. Kant demurs: he says that mind's self-knowledge is a consequence of inference, not inspection. Why is second-order consciousness inaccessible from within first-order awareness? Because the transcendental ego acts "spontaneously" outside of space and time, thereby schematizing the experience that supplies content, in time, for first-order awareness.[19]

This leaves mind seriously impaired. For how can its transcendental functions exist—given Cartesian scruples—if they are not perceived? Kant isn't bothered that activities qualifying mind for its role as ontological foundation are not themselves perceived. It is sufficient for him, in the first *Critique*, that they be inferred.[20] His procedure for confirming the inference reverts to the second of Descartes' two tests of truth: namely, demonstration. For inference is an acceptable substitute for inspection if its conclusions are necessary. Kant's Transcendental Deductions infer from the character of experience to its conditions in any thinkable world. These are necessary conditions: experience could not be as it is, short of contradiction, in their absence.[21] Kant nevertheless reverts to Descartes' preferred standard of knowledge—direct inspection—when he requires that will be informed by reason's self-consistent universal maxims before it acts on particular desires.[22] For self-reflection has these three tasks: to inhibit desires, to ascertain that candidate maxims are universalizable, and to release inhibited desires while informing the will with maxims that have passed the test. Every such task is accomplished better when attention is focused. The transcendental ego turns on itself—if only for this practical reason—and says, after Descartes, "I am, I exist." Why this difference? Why is mind trusted to apply its world-making rules without contradiction—out of self-reflective sight—while the will's choice of maxims requires that it be self-attentive? Kant doesn't tell us.

His psychocentrism is baldly metaphysical, yet Kant is a principal sponsor of the idea that Western metaphysics is defunct: its traditional questions—What are we? What is the world? What is our place within it?—are unanswerable, because misconceived. Their answers would have to be dialectical, because they would specify considerations that are independent of mind for their existence and character. But *esse est percipi* (with the exception that we can infer from the character of experience to its transcendental conditions, including mind's existence). Speculation that otherwise exceeds the bounds of experience is quashed because meaningless.

Consider some things precluded, including generalities, gravitational fields, and energy transfer—hence force, dispositions, and laws. Each of these is critical to our descriptions and explanations of material events, so that Kant, like Hume, is an inspiration for thinkers who look for surrogates on the side of perception, thought, or language. Finding devices for expressing such factors, we describe the world *as if* they were present in it. Hume's assault on causation is exemplary: "The necessary connexion betwixt causes and effects is the foundation of our inference from one to the other. The foundation of our inference is the transition arising from the accustom'd union. These are, therefore, the same."[23] Kant's dispatch of objectivity is equally familiar.[24] Yet, Kant no more than Descartes has abandoned metaphysics. His ontological foundationalism is also a metaphysical theory, one that assumes mind's sufficiency as world-maker, hence the claim that all phenomena exist in me.

Philosophy in the twentieth century was often a recapitulation of Kantian themes. Yet, Kant seems less original if his claims about finite minds—all intelligibility and being reside within them—embellish Descartes' Platonic heresy. Nothing in this diminishes his influence. Kant was used, principally, in two ways: I call them *romantic* and *analytic*.

2. Kant in Our Time

Philosophers often remark on the differences in style and emphasis that distinguish Anglo-American analytic philosophy from the hermeneutics and phenomenology of Continental thinkers. These are variations in the epistemological or ontological foundationalism learned from Descartes. Two lineages derive from him. One is the psychocentrism apparent in Kant. The other is the analytic empiricism that passed from Locke, Berkeley, and Hume to Russell and Ayer.[25]

Analysts of sixty years ago—motivated by Hume's distinction between the synthetic relations of sensory data and the analytic relations of ideas—argued that science and logic are the only reputable inquiries.[26] Descartes would have recognized his claim that knowledge derives from either the inspection of ideas or demonstration. This Humean bias distinguished analytic philosophy from the Continental thinking dominated by Kant. Now, when Kant, rather than Hume, is the principal inspiration for analytic philosophy in America,[27] its relation to Continental philosophy is complementary, not opposed. Romantic Kantians emphasize will as it responds to perplexity or competition by choosing a viable interpretation or theory, hence a viable experience. Analytic Kantians describe the syntax and semantics of the conceptual systems used to create thinkable worlds. Both emphasize pragmatics—value-driven action—though the only act stressed by either side is the use of ideas or words to create or analyze a thinkable experience. Both say that mind makes the world it experiences or knows.

A. Romantic Kantians: Nietzsche and Heidegger

Kant's first *Critique* described the transcendental conditions for experience. His third *Critique* argued that the choice of empirical schemas—the rules that give specificity to experience—is determined by our values: we will such worlds as satisfy desire. In some thinkers— William James, for example[28]—the effects of willing are typically pleasing or benign. In others, will is demonic: we will to create or destroy.

Nietzsche. Nietzsche affirms that all reality is the product of mind's will to power:

> Suppose nothing else were "given" as real except our world of desires and passions, and we could not get down, or up, to any other "reality" besides the reality of our drives—for thinking is merely a relation of these drives to each other; is it not permitted to make the experiment and to ask the question whether this "given" would not be *sufficient* for also understanding on the basis of this kind of thing the so-called mechanistic (or "material") world? . . . The question is in the end whether we really recognize the will as *efficient*, whether we believe in the causality of the will: if we do—and at bottom our faith in this is nothing less than our faith in causality itself—then we have to make the experiment of positing the causality of the will hypothetically as the only one. "Will," of course, can affect only "will"—and not "matter" (not "nerves," for example). In short, one has to risk the hypothesis whether will does not affect will wherever "effects" are recognized—and whether all mechanical occurrences are not, insofar as a force is active in them, will force, effects of

will. . . . The world viewed from inside, the world defined and determined according to its "intelligible character" —it would be "will to power" and nothing else.[29]

Several points are implicit. First are mind's allegedly complementary drives and their sponsor. Dionysus reminds us of spontaneity and freedom, Apollo of form.[30] They signify the two aspects of Kant's transcendental ego. It makes experience, freely and spontaneously, from outside space and time (the forms of intuition) by imposing difference and order—form—on sensory or conceptual data. Second is the decision that recurs every moment: go on as before or create a different experience? Third is the consideration that thinkers have no discernible identity apart from the content—the lives—schematized. They create these effects in time; but time passes, so there is always a reason—indeed a necessity—for recreating the empirical self. This is the perpetual dynamic that prevents the transcendental subject from resting on its laurels. For recall Descartes' question: how long do I exist? His answer, "Only so long as I think," is also Nietzsche's: I am if I will. I am the self-creator who sustains my transcendental self by perpetually recreating my empirical self.

Other wills—other minds—intimidate me for purposes of their own. Or they constrain me, wanting me to be as they are, so that all of us may be predictable and safe. Assenting to them is an expression of weakness and self-betrayal, because it requires that I surrender to the power of other wills. But how do I know them? How do they prevail on me? Cartesianism and Kantianism are solipsistic: they have no answers. Nietzsche avoids the question by supposing that wills are intimidated by the empirical expressions of other wills: each responds to the looks or sounds that express the other's determination. Doing this is evidence of our weakness and misunderstanding. For relinquishing one's power to other wills is both the subversion of will's autonomy and a category mistake: dominated egos surrender to the empirical egos—the peremptory bark—of others, though it is only transcendental wills that have genuine, world-making power.

The *master* (also translated *overman* or *superman*) is Nietzsche's model for the healthy ego.[31] Each is impelled by self-love and the dread of bad faith. Surpassing the herd, the master also surpasses himself. Will drives and defines him, for this is the force that distinguishes him from the herd, clarifying him to himself. There is a cost: integrity isolates us. The extra-mental world—even the social world of other egos—all but disappears. Wanting socialization but fearing it, the master retreats from a social world that is ever more incomprehensible and noumenal.

Eight of Nietzsche's allusive claims are plainer now. (i) Will to power is the Dionysian side of the transcendental subject; its Apollonian side creates an orderly experience. (ii) The power of decision recurs at every moment, so there is no time for the ego to lose itself in the experience it makes: the eternal recurrence of the same is the need, recovered at every moment, of having to create a thinkable experience.[32] Heidegger summarizes Nietzsche's view thus:

> The "Momentary" character of creation is the essence of actual, actuating eternity, which achieves its greatest breadth and keenest edge as the moment of eternity in the return of the same. The recoining of what becomes into being—will to power in its supreme configuration—is in its most profound essence something that occurs in the "glance of an eye" as eternal recurrence of the same. The will to power, as *constitution* of being, is as it is solely on the basis of the way to be which Nietzsche projects for being as a whole: *Will to power, in its essence and according to its inner possibility, is eternal recurrence of the same.*[33]

(iii) Each creative moment is the occasion for reappraising one's values, for mind must choose each moment the value that directs it.[34] This may be the same value that shaped previous decisions. Or, being different, it drastically reorders the priorities that drive will as it creates experience. (iv) Nihilism—the repudiation of absolute values or the unthinking repetition of the same values—is defeated when values willed previously are thoughtfully reaffirmed or superseded.[35] (v) Experience is perspectival, because each will creates an experience and world appropriate to itself.[36] (vi) Life is art, because every moment of every experience is the mind's own product.[37] Mind's directing values are more or less plainly exhibited in its product. (vii) Life is tragic, because there is no relief from the burden of having to make a thinkable world, and no relief within that world from the labor, frustration, conflict, and neurosis that befall empirical egos.[38] (viii) Genealogy is the succession of experiences made, and our reflection on them.[39] There are two orders to record: as empirical, we are history's product; as transcendental, we escape it. This is also the equivocation in tragedy. Empirically, we suffer our immersion in events we cannot control. Transcendentally, we liberate ourselves by recovering the posture of the artist, whose materials accept the form that he or she imposes.

Nietzsche's scorn for metaphysicians—"old metaphysical bird catchers"[40]—is more allusive than focused. We expect his more detailed criticisms to be expressly Kantian. They are:

> In the "in-itself" there is nothing of "causal connection," of "necessity," or of "psychological non- freedom"; there the effect does *not* follow the

cause, there is no rule of "law." It is *we* alone who have devised cause, science, for-each-other, relativity, constraint, number, law, freedom, motive, and purpose; and when we project and mix this symbol world into things as if it existed "in itself," we act once more as we have always acted—*mythologically*.[41]

Nietzsche did not think systematically about metaphysics, because Kant had made that unnecessary. One need only explain the different world-creating perspectives, a difference explained by their motivating values. But notice: Nietzsche can only seem to have avoided metaphysics if we believe that his will-driven version of Kantian world-making is unproblematic, good sense.

Heidegger. *Dasein* is a being—a person—located here or there, with the cares, attachments, history, and prospects appropriate to its circumstances.[42] We describe this situation in its Cartesian, Kantian terms by recalling the point of Husserl's *Cartesian Meditations*: a thinker who doubts the extra-mental reality of things represented by percepts or signified by ideas nevertheless finds him or herself immersed in the intentional attitudes that construe these signs.[43] One doesn't choose all these commitments: some fall to us willy-nilly, as obligations rather than choices. But every thought or perception is biased by an attitude, and every intention exhibits one's values. Values are commitments. They are the first of three constraints on the empirical ego. Second is ego's realization that it is bounded, from past to future, because death is annihilation. Third is the set of stories—interpretations—that everywhere obscure Dasein's perception of things as they are. We never do or can strip them from our thinking, thereby perceiving the essences that are Being. But there is a dogged struggle: mind tries to discern both these essences and its unencumbered, valorizing self.

These tasks express Heidegger's assimilation of Nietzsche (the positional, perspectival self) and Husserl (essences stripped of assumptions and seen as they are). Their antecedents—Plato, Descartes, and Kant—are only a little more remote: Platonic nous rises through the flux to a vision of the Forms; Descartes described self-consciousness discovering itself as the cynosure of its beliefs; Kant once implied that the empirical subject escapes its experiential constraints by retreating (or ascending) to the perspective of the transcendental ego.[44] Heidegger summarizes the history of mind's self-discovery:

> Leibniz defines subjectivity as a striving representing. With this insight the full inception of modern metaphysics is first reached. . . . The monad, that is, the subjectivity of the subject, is *perceptio* and *appetitus* . . . Subjectivity as the Being of beings means that outside the legislation of

self-stirring representations there may "be" and can "be" nothing that might still condition such representation. . . . Now, however, the essence of subjectivity of itself necessarily surges toward absolute subjectivity. Kant's metaphysics resists this essential thrust of Being—while at the same time laying the ground for its fulfillment. That is because Kant's metaphysics for the first time subsumes utterly the concealed essence of subjectivity, which is the essence of Being as conceived in metaphysics, under the concept of Being as beingness—in the sense of the condition for the possibility of beings.[45]

Heidegger's use of representation is more ironic than literal: "[C]omplete subjectivity resists anything outside itself. Nothing has a claim on Being that does not stand in the power radius of consummate subjectivity."[46] He quotes this fragment from Nietzsche to remind us that there are no mind-independent objects to signify: "Not 'to know' but to schematize—to impose upon chaos as much regularity and as many forms as our practical needs require"[47]

Metaphysics has completed its trajectory, because "Man . . . alone is in the midst of beings as such and as a whole as a *representational, valuative will.*"[48] Ontological foundationalism is here: everything that is exists as mind, or its qualification; reality is mind's product. The extra-mental world is "constructed" (not discovered), then re-presented for inspection to the mind that made it.[49] Nietzsche carries the argument one step further: mind is self-creating.[50] No part of this is metaphysical, because the history of Western metaphysics ended when Nietzsche overcame the two distinctions that once impelled metaphysical speculation. One is the difference between *what* and *that*, the difference between essence—character—and existence. The other is the difference between appearance and reality, meaning representations and things themselves. Nietzsche resolved these oppositions by affirming that will to power constructs an experience having no extra-mental referent: there are no states of affairs set apart from mind, but represented in it. Experience is the freestanding product of a spontaneous will; will affirms its values while making "worlds" that satisfy it.

Heidegger explains: "First, we shall try to think the essence of truth to the extreme by asking what happens to truth after the abolition of the distinction between a true and an apparent world."[51] Repudiating this distinction is the thunderclap that terminates Western metaphysics. For the difference between true and apparent worlds is the difference between existence and its representations. Aristotle and Locke built their theories of perception on this difference: existents stand apart from representations that more or less accurately imitate or signify their character.[52]

Plato didn't favor this distinction. Descartes' leaner theory rejects it. Kant showed how to reduce everything extra-mental, first, to a thing-in-itself, and then, to a noumenon to which no properties can be ascribed. Lapsing into unintelligibility, it ends life as nonbeing. But what of existence, the *that*? Where has it gone? Kant and Nietzsche answer that it is displaced: once thought to be extra-mental, it is recentered in consciousness, before the mind's eye. How is this accomplished? By saying that objectivity is the product of construction: mind schematizes a thinkable world, thereby creating all of "objectivity" so far as we can perceive or think it. Heidegger glosses Nietzsche: "With the abolition of the 'true world' the 'apparent world' also is abolished."[53] Objectivity is to have no referent "beyond" the things set before mind, and inspected. The *what* and the *that* of being are presented at once:

> Therefore, a further question at once arises from the question of what the being as such is. Among all beings as beings, which one most nearly corresponds to what is defined as the What of the being? The being that corresponds to whatness, the *essentia* of beings as such, is what truly exists. In the question "What is the being?" the truly existing is thought at the same time with respect to *essentia* and *existentia*. In that way, the being is determined as such; that is, determined as to *what* it is and as to the fact *that* it is. *Essentia* and *existentia* of the *ens qua ens* answer the question "What is the being as such?" They define the being in its Being.[54]

Metaphysics is defunct, because its problem is solved: essence and existence are joined again *within the experience that mind creates and inspects:*

> To think beings as a whole in their truth and to think *the truth in them*— that is metaphysics. "Justice" is here the metaphysical name for the essence of truth, for the way in which the *essence* of truth must be understood at the end of Western metaphysics. Fixating the essence of truth as *homoiōsis*, and interpreting the latter as justice, constitute the metaphysical thinking that produces this interpretation as the consummation of metaphysics.[55]

All objectivity is "subjective."[56]

> If justice is "the supreme representative of life itself," if the will to power reveals itself properly in human life, does not the extrapolation of justice to the fundamental power of beings in general and the thoroughgoing interpretation of beings as a whole as will to power amount to an

anthropomorphizing of all beings. Is not the world thought according to the paradigm of man? Is not such thinking pure anthropomorphism? To be sure. It is anthropomorphism in the "grand style," the style that has a sense of what is rare and long in coming.[57]

Notice that Heidegger's exposition is historically odd. The emphasis on will is ascribed to Nietzsche, though it is plausibly claimed for Kant, Fichte, or Schelling: all of them credit will with the power to choose such experience-making schemas as satisfy its desires.[58] Heidegger's "end of Western metaphysics" is, therefore, one more declaration of Kantian doctrine. Metaphysics is meaningless speculation about things-in-themselves. Mind creates the only thinkable worlds, though the transcendental world-maker somehow eludes metaphysical attention. Or its status and powers are so exceptional that disclosing them is the metaphysical task for a new era. Heidegger tells us that, "Ontology represents transcendence as the transcendental."[59] Mind has become its own lure, because Kant separated consciousness from self-consciousness, reducing the one and transforming the other into a world-maker: mind must grasp and inspect itself.

Recall that Heidegger was Husserl's student. Husserl's eidetic reflection enables mind to inspect essences and mind's structure.[60] For essence and existence, too, are close at hand, if "nothing is better known to mind than the mind itself." This is Descartes' solution to the loss of Being: a mind overlaid by confused beliefs discovers itself, its responsibility for willing false ideas, and the ideas of clarified essences that are innate within it.

B. Analytic Kantians: Carnap and Quine

Carnap. Descartes' cogito inspects one or a few ideas at a time, or it surveys the several steps of a demonstration. Kant too emphasized individual judgments, not large, formalized systems of thought or sentences. Rudolf Carnap rectifies this omission by reconstructing scientific theories. Carnap's program echoes Descartes' *Rules*. Reconstructions expose the formal—deductive—structure of theories: they make the world perspicuous: "The aim of science consists in finding and ordering the true statements about the objects of cognition. . . . In order to be able to approach this aim, that is, in order to be able to make statements about objects at all, we must be able to construct these objects (for, otherwise, their names have no meaning)."[61] All intelligibility—all science and its objects—lies within reconstructed theories, hence within the minds that make and use them.

Carnap distinguished sharply between the syntactic and semantic features of his constructed systems. Syntax is form that regulates the relations of words or sentences. It comprises rules for rearranging or joining axioms to generate theorems. They follow necessarily from the antecedent lines of a proof, given consistent applications of the rules. Synthetic propositions—observation reports—supply empirical content. They are contingently true or false. Carnap didn't say that this distinction closely parallels that of transcendental logic and synthetic content, but his Kantian allegiance is plain:

> Construction theory engages in formal (logical) and substantive (epistemological) investigations which lead to the formulation of a constructional system. A constructional system is a system which (in principle) comprises all concepts (or objects) of science, not indeed as a classificatory, but as a derivational, system (genealogy): each concept is constructed from those that precede it in the system. . . . A concept is said to be reducible to others, if all statements about it can be transformed into statements about these other concepts; the general rule for this transformation of statements for a given concept is called the *construction* of the concept. . . . Logistics, in particular its most important branch, namely the theory of relations, serves as a methodological aid. . . . Consequences of the possibility of a constructional system: all concepts are elements of one structure; hence, there is only one science of all *objects*; the only distinction between "concepts" and "objects" is a difference in modes of speech.[62]

> The constructional system is a rational construction of the entire formation of reality, which, in cognition, is carried out for the most part intuitively. In reconstructing the recognition of the plant, the botanist has to ask himself what, in the actual act of recognition, was really perceived and what was apperceptive synthesis? But these two components which are united in the result he can separate only through abstraction. Thus, in rational reconstruction, construction theory has to distinguish, by means of abstraction, between the purely given and the synthesis; this division must be made, not only for the individual case, but for the entire conscious process.[63]

The given is "autopsychological" and "*solipsistic*,"[64] though such expressions as "my experience" are introduced after the construction is accomplished.[65] "Self," too, is "constructed simultaneously on a higher level,"[66] though we can hardly avoid asking about the agent who is passive to the given but active when constructing conceptual systems.

Why construct such systems? Because *the formation of the constructional system is the first aim of science . . .* [O]bjects are taken from the store of everyday knowledge and are gradually purified and rationalized, while the intuitive components in the determination of these objects are not eliminated, but are rationally justified."[67] The Platonic and Cartesian origins of this view are plainer when we substitute *concepts* for *objects*, recalling the constructional system of Descartes' *Rules* and its demand that obscure ideas be reduced to complexes of clarified simples.

Carnap's motives are more complicated. For he, like Kant, has interests additional to that of clarifying obscure ideas or theories. Carnap distinguishes syntax, semantics, and pragmatics. Syntax concerns the formal structure of systems. Semantics describes the units—words or sentences—that convey empirical information. Carnap describes "pragmatics" as the relation of persons—in the state of belief or valuation—to sentences.[68] Two sorts of values are relevant. The more familiar values are expressed by interests or desires made perspicuous within experiences crystallized by constructed systems.[69] These are the focus of everyday concerns within the "life-world" (not Carnap's phrase): what to do, what to avoid. Values of the other sort determine our choice of conceptual systems. For there are, as Carnap consistently says, a variety of viable systems. Why choose one rather than another? The answer may be sensitive to interests that arise within a constructed world; or it may be transcendental, hence oblivious to the particularities of created worlds, but responsive to "higher" values. So, the choice may be practical (a conceptualization promotes the medical technology that saves lives, for example), or aesthetic (the determining value is conceptual simplicity). Here, as in Descartes, thinkers are the measure and final cause of other things, including reconstructed systems. They, too, are valuable only as they have utility for us.

Carnap seals his ontological psychocentrism by eliminating alternative centers of being. This is the effect of distinguishing between questions that are *internal* or *external* to a conceptual system:[70]

> Two geographers, a realist and an idealist, who are sent out in order to find out if a mountain that is supposed to be somewhere in Africa is only legendary or if it really exists, will come to the same (positive or negative) result. . . . [The] divergence between the two scientists does not occur in the empirical domain, for there is complete unanimity so far as the empirical facts are concerned. These two theses which are here in opposition to one another go beyond experience and have no factual content.[76]

Remember Kant's remark that objectivity is a function of schematization, then notice that Carnap's internal questions concern the sorts of objects a system postulates. External questions are meaningless, because they pretend to specify states of affairs whose existence and character are independent of our conceptual systems, though nothing is thinkable, hence characterizable, independently of them. Such things are, in Kant's terms, noumenal. They cannot be thought to have properties of any sort.

Accordingly, all intelligibility resides where Kant (after Descartes' leaner theory) locates it: within language, hence mind. Existence too has no other site; and here, too, Kant is the point of reference. For the existence of things known is nothing but the posit entailed by the truth of the judgments or reconstructed sentences reporting them: we say that atoms exist, because "Atoms exist" is true in atomic theory.

This use of *truth* implies a distinction between the *material* and *formal* modes of speech.[72] Using the object-language, we speak of material things; in the other—the meta-language—sentences of the object-language are set off by inverted commas. In the first, we say that atoms exist, in the second that "Atoms exist" is true. The object-language seems to signify states of affairs occurring in an extra-linguistic domain. But this effect is merely rhetorical, as we confirm when supplying a justification within the meta-language for the sentence of the object-language. We say, for example, that "Atoms exist" is entailed or implied by other sentences, given accepted rules of deductive or inductive inference. Accordingly, truth is bestowed on sentences by virtue of two kinds of relations among them. First is the naming relation between sentences: a sentence in the object-language is named by one in the meta-language. Second, the sentence in the object language is derived or confirmed, using deductive or inductive rules of inference, from other sentences of the object-language. Existence and nonexistence are hereby posited by our modes of speech: something is or is not if the network of accepted sentences justifies affirming that it is or is not. Accordingly, existence or materiality, as expressed in the object-language, is a rhetorical intention. We shouldn't construe it literally, as Kant warned when he distinguished the *transcendental object* from *noumena*.[73]

Carnap's ontological foundationalism is not explicit. He never writes of foundational, transcendental mind; he never affirms that every other thing is mind's qualification. Mind is acknowledged as the subject of a special science—psychology—and not as the agent who creates thinkable worlds by reformulating scientific theories. But this is evasive when conceptual systems are reconstructed and applied by an agent that acts and abides—somehow—in a psychic space that is prior to, and exempt from. the effects of the worlds it makes. Ignoring the transcendental conditions for thinkable worlds doesn't obviate the inference that Carnap declines to make: from world-objectifying languages to the minds that construct and apply them.[74]

Quine. W.V.O. Quine described himself as a "naturalistic philosopher:"[75] "We are after an understanding of science as an institution or process in the world."[76] He favored a "naturalized epistemology," meaning a theory of knowledge grounded in an empirical, behaviorist psychology. His *The Roots of Reference* and such essays as "Posits and Reality"[77] justify his self-description: they study "a natural phenomenon, viz., a physical human subject"[78] as it acquires a language appropriate to both the world and its interactions with other thinker-speakers. Quine's naturalism is nevertheless equivocal in the way of a C.S. Lewis novel. A child regards the painting on a wall, before jumping onto the frame. He falls into the picture, landing on the deck of a pitching ship. Quine's immersion in language comes more subtly, but the effect is equally dramatic. Two remarks plot the endpoints of his trajectory: "[T]his sense is somehow in tune with the world—a world which, unlike language, we never made."[79] And: "Carnap maintains that ontological questions, and likewise questions of logic or mathematical principle, are questions not of fact but of choosing a convenient conceptual scheme or framework for science; and with this I agree only if the same be conceded for every scientific hypothesis."[80]

The trajectory that begins in a realism justified by empirical evidence terminates in ontological relativity: questions about reality are transformed into questions about the ontological constructs and posits of a conceptual system. Claims that refer to extra-conceptual states of affairs are "metaphysical" and "meaningless."[81] Why this change? Because science would be crippled if the language used to formulate its problems and express its results were suffused with obscurity. Clarifying the language of science, purging its ontological bloat— modalities, for example—is the propaedeutic to further science. But then, language envelops us. Seeing form by way of it, we no longer see through it to the form beyond. Language, like a fog, closes in upon us: intelligibility seems to have no other locus. (That scientists often revise their language—mathematics, for example—without losing track of the external world is a point Quine ignores.)

Quine's agreement with Carnap is partial. He renounces the *more geometrico* of Descartes' *Rules* by rejecting the sharp opposition between sentences that are analytic and those that are synthetic, meaning empty tautologies and sentences that are contingently true or false.[82] Quine suggests that the "interanimating"[83] sentences of conceptual system are linked like the strands of fabric in a trampoline. Sentences in the middle of a system satisfy rules that are only syntactic, because they are remote from confirming or disconfirming empirical data. Sentences closer to the edge are more directly calibrated to sensory stimulation,[84] but sentences of both kinds are overdetermined by theory, because every sentence is embedded in networks of sentences. Slightly altering the relations among sentences has either or both of two effects. It changes the theory or interpretation the sentences express, or it alters a sentence's vulnerability to empirical data. Something is ringing. Could it be my ears or the phone? Juggle the relations of the sentences, and the same empirical effect confirms either and falsifies the other.

Most of the disputes between Quine and Carnap turn on devices for exposing or creating structures of the kind each favors: formal systems, or arrays of sentences that are related, principally, by inductive rules. Their accord is pervasive and deep. Both accept the prescription of Descartes' *Rules*: discount the obscure surface of thought on the way to clarifying its logical—grammatical—structure. They also share the general outlines of a theory that transforms Kant's transcendental psychology into a theory of language. For they agree that intelligibility is a function of language, that "objects" are posited or constructed, that truth is coherence (truth as disquotation is considered in chapter six, section 1F), and that existence has no play beyond the limits of theory. Analogues for Kant's transcendental synthesis are as plainly marked in Quine as in Carnap. Sensory data (stimulations for Quine[85]) are the events differentiated and organized by conceptual systems:

> What comes of the association of sentences with sentences is a vast verbal structure which, primarily as a whole, is multifariously linked to nonverbal stimulation. These links attach to separate sentences (for each person), but the same sentences are so bound up in turn with one another and with further sentences that the nonverbal attachments themselves may stretch or give way under strain.[86]

This remark seems neutral ontologically, until we ask about the referents of our interanimating sentences. "Bodies are the prime reality," says Quine, "the objects *par excellence*."[87] Yet, bodies have neither character nor existence independent of the conceptual systems used to think them. For objects of every sort are only the posits of language's "objectificatory apparatus" (its quantifiers and pronouns[88]). All intelligibility and existence—all of objectivity—is hereby displaced from the extra-linguistic world into language. The result is a thinkable world—experience. The rest is noumenal. Talk about it lacks sense.

Quine writes of truth and existence:

> An expression "*a*" may occur in a theory . . . with or without purporting to name an object. What clinches matters is rather the quantification

"($\exists x)(x = a)$." It is the existential quantifier, not the "a" itself, that carries existential import. This is just what existential quantification is for, of course. It is a logically regimented rendering of the "there is" idiom. The bound variable "x" ranges over the universe, and the existential quantification says that at least one of the objects in the universe satisfies the appended condition—in this case the condition of being the object a. To show that some given object is required in a theory, what we have to show is no more nor less than that that object is required, for the truth of the theory, to be among the values over which the bound variables range.[89]

Object is equivocal. We may suppose that it signifies extra-linguistic things, though here "the object required" is a linguistic entity, the value of a bound variable. A theory having appropriate values for its bound variables is true, because the relations of its sentences satisfy rules of inductive inference.[90] ("It's raining" is true if this sentence has implications that cohere with those of others within a conceptual network.)

Of what things—what objects—is the theory true? Quine would have us answer carefully:

[W]e have no reason to suppose that man's surface irritations even unto eternity admit of any one systematization that is scientifically better or simpler than all possible others. It seems likelier, if only on account of symmetries or dualities, that countless alternative theories would be tied for first place.[91]

Thing and *existence* are misleading. These apparently ontological words derive their sense from the grammatical role of the existential quantifier ($\exists x$), bound variables (for example, For any x, x is a cat); and the pronouns signifying such things as are signified by bound variables (*it*). The "objects" ascribed to an extra-mental, extra-linguistic space are merely the posits of these grammatical forms. We have Quine's dictum: to be is to be the value of a bound variable.[92]

The realists among us are naive. We misconstrue the apparent implications of everyday speech—that there are objects whose existence and character are independent of the ways we think of them—until Carnap and Quine advise us that truth is a finding made within a metlanguage about sentences in an object-language. What are the "things" of which we speak; what is their "existence"? Retreating from the material into the formal mode (from *Snow is white* to "*Snow is white*" is true) we discover that *thinghood* and *existence* are functions of grammar, not features of the extra-linguistic world. Quine's naturalism reaches no further than quantifiers and pronouns.

Its apriorism is the ineliminable bias of Descartes' leaner theory: it requires that mind create a thinkable world and experience out of itself.

Kant's transcendental logic is one solution to this task: sensory data are given to mind (their extra-mental origin left unexplained), while all their character and relations are introduced by mind's schematization. There is also this collateral effect: the transcendental ego cannot escape the web of its schematizations in order to check its objectifications against the extra-mental world. Quine's psychogenetic alternative is equally constricting:

> Learning language, learning gradually to quantify over bodies and eventually over abstract objects is one phase of a continuing process that goes on to embrace also the learning and even the further developing of high scientific theory. We are working up our science from infancy onward. Each of the leaps of language learning that I have pictured is a private little scientific revolution, another step in the development of a system of the world.[93]

Notice the ambiguity in Quine's pragmatism: is language a device for engaging the world, or the network within which the world is constructed and presented? Quine, like Carnap and Kant, immerses us in language as Descartes' cogito is immersed in thought and itself. Where intelligibility derives only from language, there is nothing to which we might refer beyond the world we conceive. There is no recourse from the objectificatory mechanisms of language, and no way to check its posits against the extra-linguistic world.

The effect on science is confounding. Does science discover, or prescribe, the world's character? Quine, the naturalist, implies his approval of Peirce's hypothetical—abductive—method.[94] But his support is suspect, because abduction promotes inferences from sensory evidence—using telescopes, microscopes, or ordinary eyeglasses—to the character, constituents, causes, or conditions of extra-perceptual states of affairs.[95] The questions provoking us may be practical, scientific or metaphysical, but typically, abductions explain a phenomenon (smoke, motion, or regularity, for example) by signifying conditions that are extra-mental and extra-linguistic. Quine, the idealist, precludes abduction by restricting intelligibility to the languages used for thinking about the world. The world he describes is trapped inside the conceptual framework that makes it thinkable, though abduction presupposes a world that is intelligible—has character—in itself.

The extra-mental, extra-linguistic world doesn't always yield to thought or action. But error is a critical directive: we learn from our mistakes. Our next intervention is more effective than the last, because a rejected hypothesis is corrected or replaced. Quine ignores this advantage when he argues that disconfirming evidence is deflected by the myriad connections among a theory's sentences. For sentences other than the ones tested can be made to bear responsibility for error[96] (it was the slick floor or my new shoes, not my clumsiness, that made me fall). This turns a commonplace into a mystery. For we often exceed the web of theory on the way to testing claims about alleged states of affairs: no sign of phlogiston or the ether, much evidence of causality and the Moon. How do we make these tests? By carefully organizing our experiments so that one sentence or a few, not an entire theory or language, is at issue.

This clash of instincts—naturalistic on one side, apriorist on the other—helps explain Quine's reluctance to emphasize the special role he ascribes to mind. He refers several times to "persons," though their status is uncertain if human bodies are constructs—posits—of the conceptual system that signifies them. The issue is pressing. For how shall we characterize the subject who uses language to create thinkable worlds? Or should we suppose that conceptual systems are free-floating, with no agent to assemble, inspect, or apply them? Quine doesn't tell us. We are reminded of Plato's view that nous fails to audit or comment on itself. But nous is passive to the Forms. The agent assumed by Kant, Carnap, and Quine is active. Ignoring itself (hence Descartes' claim that nothing is better known to mind than mind itself), it creates and inspects its system of interanimating sentences.

This network—language and the conceptual systems expressed within it—exhausts the domain of intelligibility. "The relativistic thesis to which we have come is this, to repeat: it makes no sense to say what the objects of a theory are, beyond saying how to interpret or reinterpret that theory in another."[97] Every theory is subject to this stricture, so that naturalistic talk—of retinas and their patterns of irradiation, of "the three-dimensional external world and its history"[98]—is only apparently referential. For there are other thinkable worlds, each the product of the conceptual system used to differentiate and organize it. Language has become our seamless trap—we can only move from theory to theory, never from true theories to the world they represent. And all the while, we are strangely silent, never risking a word to describe the agent—the transcendental subject—who uses language to create thinkable worlds.

3. What is Philosophy?

What is philosophy after Descartes and Kant? There are four options: (i) Philosophers describe matters set before the mind's eye, including mind's acts, structure and content (in the style of phenomenalists, phenomenologists and moral intuitionists). (ii) We discern or create levels within mind or language in order to analyze concepts. Kant's empirical and transcendental orders, and the relation of object- and meta-language are two expressions of the classic dyad, consciousness and its scrutinizing self-awareness. These hierarchies are exploited in either of two ways. (a) Locke, Hume, Russell, and ordinary-language analysts replace obscure ideas (such as *cause* or *capacity*) with clearer substitutes, one at a time. Or (b) forms that are immanent within or projected onto lower-order content are rendered explicit at the higher order. One analyses the "logic" of science or morality, for example. (iii) We tell how mind constructs a thinkable experience or world while describing the powers required for doing it (Kant, Fichte, and Schelling); or (iv) we deconstruct such experiences or worlds by exposing the disguised values that drive their makers (Derrida after the example of Thrasymachus in Plato's *Republic*).

There are variations within each emphasis, for reasons of content or method. Let conceptual analyses be our example (options iia and b). Some are piecemeal (Wittgenstein in the *Philosophical Investigations*). Others are holistic because of having deductive form (Carnap), or because they emphasize the network of more or less loosely related sentences or ideas (Quine). Some are historical, as when ideas generate social systems and the experiences they organize (Hegel and Foucault), others are synchronic (Frege). Some restrict themselves to conceptual structures (Whitehead's and Russell's *Principia*); others analyze one or another conceptually founded practice (Nagel and Kuhn describe theory formation, Habermas and Rawls write of morality). Analysis identifies problematic notions, then constructs clarified substitutes; or it discerns the forms that organize a system.

We are to believe that philosophy speaks with authority whenever mind has direct access to its subject matters: namely, mind's acts, structure, or content. But there is this off-setting price: philosophy has nothing to say of extra-mental states of affairs. Why? Because philosophy requires that mind confirm the truth of its claims, by direct inspection or inference. Access to nature requires speculative, fallible inferences (abductions) that move from perceived effects to their hypothesized conditions (from the look of a face to the face itself, from motions perceived to their constraining laws). Science accepts these inferior goods; philosophy abjures them. Wanting truths it can guarantee—let mind attend to the things it knows best—Descartes' leaner theory allows nature to slip away. Descartes' heirs build walls around conceptual systems. Nature is noumenal—out of bounds to inference—because there is no intelligibility apart from the glow of articulate thought or language.

4. Response

Kant, Nietzsche, Heidegger, Carnap, and Quine tell a fabulous story. Intelligibility lies altogether within systems of ideas, thoughts, or sentences. The *what* and *that* of the world—hence character, truth, and existence—are the products of thought, value, and will. Do these authors avert speculations about the inferred conditions for experience? Is metaphysics defunct? Not when mind is everywhere implied, though unmentioned in books that exploit it.

Is mind self-sufficient? Is there nothing to reality but mind or minds and the experiences they construct? Heidegger directs us:

> If we speak pointedly that the new freedom consists in the fact that man himself legislates, chooses what is binding, and binds himself to it, then we are speaking Kant's language; and yet we hit upon what is essential for the beginning of the modern age. In its unique historical form, this essence is wrought into a fundamental metaphysical position for which freedom becomes essential in a peculiar way (see Descartes, *Meditations de prima philosophia*, Med. IV).[99]

And:

> The new world of the modern age has its own historical ground in the place where every history seeks its essential ground, namely, in metaphysics; that is, in a new determination of the truth of beings as a whole and of the essence of such truth. Descartes' metaphysics is the decisive beginning of the foundation of metaphysics in the modern age. It was his task to *ground the metaphysical ground of man's liberation in the new freedom of self-assured self-legislation.*[100]

Hegel is the apotheosis of the Cartesian project:

> "Phenomenology" in Hegel's sense is Being's bringing-itself-to-concept as absolute self-appearing. Here phenomenology does not mean a particular thinker's way of thinking, but the manner in which absolute subjectivity as absolute self-appearing representation (thinking) is itself the Being of all beings. Hegel's *Logic* belongs within the *Phenomenology* because in it absolute subjectivity's appearing to itself becomes absolute only when the conditions of all appearance, the "categories," are in their most proper self-representation and disclosure, as "logos," brought into the visibility of the absolute idea.[101]

We expect this style of expression from those who write in the tradition of German romanticism. We don't expect it from thinkers who describe themselves as *empiricists* or *positivists*. But consider: what is *reality* or *nature*? Here are the answers of three twentieth-century philosophers of science, all averse to metaphysics.

First is Ernest Nagel:

> Proponents of the instrumentalist position may, of course, reserve judgment about whether other theoretical entities postulated by the theory really do exist, since the requirements for their physical reality as set by the criterion adopted may not be clearly satisfied. But on such particular issues proponents of the view that theories are true or false statements may have similar hesitations. It is therefore difficult to escape the conclusion that when the two apparently opposing views on the cognitive status of theories are each stated with some circumspection, each can assimilate into its formulations not only the facts concerning the primary subject matter explored by experimental inquiry but also all the relevant facts concerning the logic and procedure of science. In brief, the opposition between these views is a conflict over preferred modes of speech.[102]

Now Thomas Kuhn: "[A]s a result of discovering oxygen, Lavoisier saw nature differently. And in the absence of some recourse to that hypothetical fixed nature that he 'saw differently,' the principle of economy will urge us to say that after discovering oxygen Lavoisier worked in a different world."[103] And again:

> We are all deeply accustomed to seeing science as the one enterprise that draws constantly nearer to some goal set by nature in advance. But need there be any such goal? Can we not account for both science's existence and its success in terms of evolution from the community's state of knowledge at any given time? Does it really help to imagine that there is some one full, objective, true account of nature and that the proper measure of scientific achievement is the extent to which it brings us closer to that ultimate goal?[104]

Kuhn argues that one theory may solve conceptual puzzles better than others, but not that one is "a better representation of what nature is really like." He writes: "There is, I think, no theory-independent way to reconstruct phrases like 'really there'; the notion of a match between the ontology of a theory and its 'real' counterpart in nature now seems to me little use in principle."[105]
Carnap agrees:

> To accept the thing world means nothing more than to accept a certain form of language, in other words, to accept rules for forming statements and for testing, accepting, or rejecting them. Thus the acceptance of the thing language leads, on the basis of observations made, also to the acceptance, belief, and assertion of certain statements. But the thesis of the reality of the thing world cannot be among these statements, because it cannot be formulated in the thing language or, it seems, in any other theoretical language.[106]

Where is nature? Nature—as a conceptual framework—resides in the only place appropriate to a skein of concepts: within minds that use ideas to create thinkable worlds. Nature, no less than theories that "express" it, is mind's qualification. Mind is Being; nature is Becoming: first, because the phenomena schematized by our theories are transitory; second, because we can use different concepts to schematize a different nature. Minds driven by their values choose and deploy the concepts, interpretations, or theories that create amenable worlds. "No longer will to preservation, but to power; no longer the meek expression 'Everything is *merely* subjective,' but 'It is also *our* work!—Let us be proud of it!'"[107] This, too, is metaphysics.

Chapter Five

The *Cogito's* Demise

1. Mind's Reduction to Body

Descartes established the cogito as the foundation for all Being, but then told us how to subvert it. The means lie directly above the divided line in figure 2.1. Aristotle and medieval physics reconceived Plato's Forms as myriad qualitative essences (of dog, cat, sheep, and goat, for example). Descartes reduced these differences to three modes of space—magnitude, figure, and motion—by extending the mathematicals to include all the lesser Forms (all but the Good). Kinematics (sometimes with dynamics) was to supply exhaustive explanations for all physical properties and their alterations.

Is there a limit to this program for showing that phenomena are explicable in exclusively physical (geometric) terms? Descartes usually insisted that consciousness, self-consciousness, thought, and will (the power of judgment) are mental, never bodily. His critics were less sure that matter cannot think.[1] Even Descartes conceded that some mental activities—perception and memory, for example—have bodily origins. And all the while, he encouraged research in micro-physiology: "Now I shall not pause to describe the bones, nerves, muscles, veins, arteries, stomach, liver, spleen, heart, brain, or any of the various other parts. . . . As for the parts which are too small to be seen, I can inform you about them more easily and clearly by speaking of the movements which depend on them."[2]

Descartes once remarked that there may be *no* activities that cannot be performed by bodies: the human machine can "imitate all the movements of real men,"[3] including, presumably, the internal movements of the nervous system. This physicalist hypothesis (qualified in

81

Descartes' other writings) is all but comprehensively confirmed. Mind is a natural and organic phenomenon, though activities such as thought are realizable in various ways (the figure–ground, *gestalt* thinking of human problem-solving differs, for example, from the exhaustive computer searches of logical trees). Consciousness, too, may have alternative physical expressions and conditions (hierarchically arranged neurons, or silicon chips). Either way, mind is not an extra-natural domain or standpoint. Mental states that are prior in knowledge—as consciousness is better known than brain—are not prior in being. Descartes' foundationalism loses its base when his psychocentric ontology is empirically refuted by physiologists and engineers who confirm that mind is only material. Physiological techniques—using brain imaging, for example—augment the evidence that machines represent and remember their inputs, calculate, and alter their behaviors in ways appropriate to plans that are revised when frustrated. Refutation is not fully accomplished, because the luminous sense of awareness and the qualitative diversity of its contents (colors and sounds, for example) are not yet explained in physical terms. The understanding and physical reproduction of some principal activities—representation, calculation, and memory—have, nevertheless, altered the question at hand. Descartes supposed that consciousness with self-awareness is the necessary condition and crucible for these activities. (Having ideas requires that awareness be passive and active, if ideas are presented, then inspected. Calculation implies self-awareness, if mind performs an inference by applying a logical rule while scrutinizing its application to guarantee that no mistake has been made.) Now, when thought is reconceptualized as the rule-governed sequencing of thoughts or words, consciousness seems incidental: we think without inspecting every thought or word, and sometimes without being aware that we think. These developments have this odd effect: some Cartesians distinguish consciousness from activities that were once thought impossible to perform without it. They concede that cognition has necessary and sufficient physical conditions, so that consciousness—especially the awareness of sensory data or feelings—is the residual, epiphenomenal, but irreducible, justification for their dualism.[4] This is the shrinking perimeter around a collapsing defense. Aristotle's dictum—that mind is the activity of a body having a certain complexity[5]—is still a trajectory, not yet a finished achievement. But most of the principal questions are settled: it is not a contradiction that bodies think.

Dualists sometimes hope to save their position with semantical arguments about the ostensive meaning of *mind, thought, feeling,* or *awareness*; but these are gestures, reminiscent of equally desperate vitalist arguments about the meaning of *life*. Neither saves the phenomena signified by the words from a comprehensive explication in physical terms, because the words have been reconceived: each signifies a complex of three factors: the function performed by the relevant activity (thought or metabolism, for example), its material character and conditions, and, sometimes, our experience of the activity (pleasure or pain, for example). Some functions are explained entirely by neural activity. It is little satisfaction for dualists that we don't yet know the sufficient physical conditions for awareness.

2. Diagnosis: A Philosophical Theory Empirically Refuted

There may be several reasons for objecting to the subjectivist side of one or another of the fourteen topics discussed in chapter Six, but subjectivism is always vulnerable if the arguments for it depend on the ontological claim that mind—the cogito—is self-sufficient. For this claim is falsified empirically. Subjectivity doesn't disappear, but it does lose the special status claimed for it by Descartes and his heirs.

There are five points to consider: What is the hypothesis refuted? What conceptual features make the hypothesis suspect? What empirical evidence falsifies it? Is the alleged refutation a methodological error: that of holding a philosophic theory to criteria that have no application within it? What are the consequences of the refutation?

A. What is the Hypothesis Refuted?

We distinguish Descartes' many claims about mind's powers and foundational role from the hypothesis tested. Here is one, then the other.

Descartes located the cogito at the top of Plato's line, incorporating all lower items within it. Becoming—below the dividing line—is reinterpreted as the flux of empirical data. Geometricals, above the division, are mind's clear and distinct ideas. The essences expressed by these ideas are unalterable Forms. Yet, the being of ideas is conditional. They implicate the thinking that grounds and embodies all of Being. This, the cogito, is, like the Sun,[6] self-illuminating. It is the measure for every other thing, because all intelligibility lies within it. Mind is also the one, final cause, other things being good or bad because of their effects on it. The *I think* is a substance, one whose being is its act. It exists merely by thinking, though its thinking is complex: aware of its content—whether percepts or ideas—it is also aware of itself. Percepts appear adventitiously, before thought uses its innate ideas to clarify them. Obscure ideas are reduced to their clear and distinct simples, then reconstructed. Clear and distinct ideas are the only ones affirmed. Examining its contents—whether percepts or ideas—mind also discerns its acts and structure. Surveying itself, mind affirms that *esse est percipi*: everything that is—everything thinkable—is mind or its qualification.

Here is the hypothesis falsified: none of mind's distinguishing properties—consciousness, self-consciousness, thought, or will—is or could be an activity of body.

Appraising Descartes' claim is complicated by the economy of his leaner theory. It acknowledges no existent but the cogito, so falsifying it leaves no alternative: we cannot refute and replace the leaner theory by saying that mind reduces to matter if matter is nothing but an idea. We avert this impasse by reintroducing Descartes' richer alternative, which says that mind and body, whether parallel or interactive, are categorially different. Dualism is falsified if bodies can do the things ascribed to minds. Notice that refutation of the richer theory entails that the leaner theory, too, is refuted: mind is not the self-sufficient measure of all that is or is not if mentality is the state or activity of human bodies.

B. What Conceptual Features Make Dualism Suspect?

Dualism justifies itself by remarking the difference of mind and body, and by emphasizing our inability to reduce any feature of one to a feature of the other. Descartes' characterization of mind is nevertheless obscure to the point of incoherence. Spinning implies the wheel that spins. But Cartesian mind is specified by way of its activities only: inference moves from thinking to a thinker—from consciousness to one who is conscious—with nothing but grammar to support the inference. Supposing that activity presupposes an agent, we look for the passages where Descartes describes the structural properties that bind and ground mind's attitudes and actions. He disappoints us. Only consciousness is suggested for the role of unifier, though many things credited to mind—memories and habits, for example—are not conscious, currently or ever. We also want a plausible intermediary between mind and body. Descartes proposed the pineal gland as the likely site of interaction,[7] though nothing on either side of the categorial difference between mind and body can explain their reciprocal effects.

Other problematic features—elaborated by Kant from suggestions by Descartes—are more arcane. They are focused by mind's alleged self-sufficiency. What is meant, for example, by the *"spontaneity* of knowledge?"[8] Bodies alter course in space, over time, because of being acted on or because they are propelled by internal changes. This cannot describe mind's circumstances, because bodies are objects created within mind's forms of intuition—space and time—when schemas differentiate and organize sensory data. Mind is transcendental—the condition for experience—not one of the things experienced. This is its spontaneity: mind is not in space or time.[9] Spontaneity, transcendence, freedom: these ascriptions are implied by the self-sufficiency claimed for mind in Descartes' leaner theory. What justifies them, apart from the claim that everything other than mind is mind's qualification?

C. What Empirical Evidence Refutes Descartes' Claim?

The testing process has been slow. It started, because dualism entails the mystery of mind-body interaction.[10] It was pursued because saying that matter thinks is not a contradiction, and because our incomplete knowledge of body disqualifies us from saying that thinking exceeds its capacity. Testing proceeded as mind's activities were specified more carefully. Kant's surmise, that ideas are rules, was especially helpful. Later, mechanical models performed tasks for which mind had been thought incapable: they represented, calculated, and remembered. Current machines analyze and solve mathematical theorems, or generate, sequence, and edit images. Some investigate their circumstances, before acting in ways appropriate to aims that evolve with experience. Machines deliberate, in the respect that they scrutinize data before directing an action appropriate to an aim.

Machine modeling of human life is surely primitive and incomplete. Probably no machines are conscious or self-conscious in ways that mimic human consciousness; probably none has a qualitatively rich perceptual or emotional experience. We nevertheless draw some conclusions. Dualism fails in several ways. It never explains the alleged self-sufficiency of action without an agent, or mind's relation to body. It misdescribes some mental activities. Thought, for example, is not the intuition of ideas: nothing is presented to consciousness, then "grasped" as mind inspects it. Dualism fails because its account of mind is inadequate in itself, and because activities once credited to mind are better understood as the actions of physical systems, whether animal brains or machines. Dualism's failure also brings down the psychocentric monism of Descartes' leaner theory: mind's alleged self-sufficiency is a mistake or delusion, if mental activity is only bodily activity.

Brain's role may seem speculative. We are only beginning to identify the neural pathways of mental activity. Our leading principle—that mental states are the activities of bodies having nervous systems—is reminiscent of the hypothesis that circulation, metabolism, and fertility are exclusively bodily functions. Vitalism was a plausible alternative when these processes were imperfectly understood. Yet, it was perceived as a failed hypothesis, when successive discoveries in chemistry and physiology confirmed that bodily activities have constituents and conditions that are solely mechanical. Was there a single experiment that finally destroyed its credibility? No, vitalism was strangled incrementally by each new bit of evidence for the sufficiency of bodily processes. And finally, still short of the time when metabolism or the electrochemical properties of the nervous system were fully understood, it was irrelevant.

The cogito's alleged self-sufficiency and immateriality are equally implausible. They are conceptual moves in a game that is all but lost: the score is lopsided, and players on the losing side slink rather than stride. Their fans concede, and leave. The game isn't over, but the final moment is everywhere anticipated. It might come with a discovery in biochemistry or physiology, but that would be abstract and contentious. Engineers are the likely source of innovations that are practical, palpable, and hard to dispute. Imagine the machine, however crude, that passes a Turing test—it converses responsively—*because* it deliberates and feels, wanting what we want. This may not happen for a while, but how much credence shall we give in the meantime to one who insists that "I am, I exist is true each time I think or perceive it," though perhaps nothing else exists?

Which hypothesis is empirically refuted: the affirmative one—that mind is distinguished by consciousness and self-sufficiency—or the negative one—that mind is not material? Disproving a consistent negation (prove that you couldn't have committed the crime) is famously problematic. But this is less an obstacle if we expand the negative claim— mind is immaterial—by enumerating the mental activities which no body could allegedly perform. We say that mind is distinguished by its states and activities, including consciousness, self-consciousness, thought, will, attitudes, and perception; and that no body could do these things. We also encourage experiments that would prove otherwise.

This is the challenge engineers have met: their machines do some of the things said to distinguish minds, including perception, calculation, and memory. Mind has been systematically misdescribed. Its alleged self-sufficiency and spontaneity were phantom properties posited by the fallacious ontology that extruded mind from nature. For no material agent is exempt from the causal effects of other things; gravitational effects, random interactions, and layered reciprocities are pervasive. Thought, consciousness, and self-consciousness are all but undeniable. But these are activities—functions—to explain, not the states substantialized by Descartes and Kant. No material agent has unmediated access to matters intuited; none shelters the luminous space experienced as self-consciousness. Intuitionism promised knowledge of matters set before the mind and inspected. Mind was to know itself in this way. Yet, knowledge of mind's own nature was irreparably incomplete, until we formulated and tested the hypothesis that all mental activity, hypothetical thinking included, has exclusively material conditions.

Dualists may respond that these conclusions are premature. Physicalism is not a necessary truth: it is not a contradiction that mind may be distinguishable and separable from body. This is true, but no evidence for dualism. It lingers because neurological accounts of mental activity—perceptual states, especially—are incomplete, not because dualism has its own explanations for them. Cartesians persist. They concede that the cogito, Descartes' fortress, may be shaped somewhat by social inputs such as language. They agree that there are physical explanations for thought and learning. But awareness and its contents are irreducible: there is no physical explanation for them.[11]

Dualists would have inquiry end where it starts: mind and matter are different if they *look* different. So, Thomas Nagel emphasizes the elusiveness of experience:

> The fact that mental states are not physical states because they can't be objectively described in the way that physical states can doesn't mean that they must be states of something different. The falsity of physicalism does not require nonphysical substances. It requires only that things be true of conscious beings that cannot, because of their subjective character, be reduced to physical terms.[12]

Nagel has argued that descriptions of physical things (neural processes, especially) are deficient in either of two ways: they abstract from the character of subjective experience when citing the relations of physical variables, or they acknowledge subjective experience but fail to tell how it could emerge from exclusively physical processes. Therefore, subjectivity cannot be the internal state of physical systems. Nagel's argument owes its rhetorical power to its dramatic examples: what is it like to be a roach or a bat? The argument fails, because it elides two significant differences: knowledge by acquaintance versus knowledge by description, and knowledge versus being. I am acquainted with my aches and pains, though I can't describe their neural sites and conditions.

Physiologists can image these sites, describe the relevant processes, measure the intensity of my neural impulses, and prescribe effective medication. But knowing someone's pains—by way of representation and description—is not the same as having them. (Knowing the Moon's history and materials is not the same as being the Moon. Does it follow that there is an irreducible subjective perspective, one that no lunar geologist can violate or understand?) This difference would hold were a physiologist to have comprehensive understanding of his or her own experience. The information would be communicable to others in pictures and words; the experiences would be states or processes internal to him or her. Wiring people to one another, thereby giving each access to the other's experience, would illustrate the difference between these two kinds of knowledge, because matters previously known only by description would come to have the immediacy of acquaintance. But this would not fudge the difference between the two kinds of knowledge, or the difference between knowledge and being.

Self-acquaintance—some neural sites reading the states of others—is a remarkable feature of hierarchical neural structures. The emergence of phenomenal states within complex neural networks—the sound of voices, the look of red—is equally remarkable. But nothing in the distinctiveness of subjectivity establishes that any of its features are not altogether physical. The look of things—a kind of knowledge—is no proof of what they are—their being.

Nagel's remark can be rephrased as an empirical research project: acknowledge that mental states cannot be described in the way that physical states are described, then establish that one is, nevertheless, an expression of the other by finding the sufficient physiological bases for awareness. Successful completion of this project would have two effects. It would establish that this last recalcitrant domain of mental phenomena—awareness, hence subjectivity—is exclusively physical. And it would undermine Nagel's persuasion that the abstract language of physiology or physics cannot specify sufficient conditions for complex, emergent phenomena. Emphasizing descriptive language—calling it "objective"—gives the language an ontological finality that sabotages inquiry. "Objective" physical language signifies physical variables; but they cannot be the sufficient basis for subjectivity, because the language of awareness is different. We find ourselves thinking, after Bishop Butler, that everything is what it is—or is as it is described—and nothing else. These are brittle assumptions, assumptions we confound when the "distinctive," "essential" qualities of subjectivity are reproduced using only transistors or neurons.

Is this too quick? There is nothing of calculation or memory in a computer's transistors (ignoring the promise of quantum computing), and nothing of life in the molecules of a cell. Nineteenth-century vitalists—dualists of a different sort—affirmed these truths as evidence that life must have a principle and source different from materiality. But there is a different explanation for it. Life emerges with the formation of organic compounds which are not, themselves, alive. The consciousness of biological organisms, like metabolism and reproduction, is an emergent expression of life.[13] One line-segment isn't a triangle. The tongue alone can't speak. We need the missing parts, properly arranged, to get either effect. Vitalist artguments were similar to Nagel's. But vitalists eventually ceded the points he ignores or denies: knowledge by description is different from knowlege by acquaintance; knowledge of either sort is different from being. Neither the physical explanation of life nor the awareness of being alive is identical with the complex physical processes that are costitutive of life. Progress to date—progress in the understanding and machine modeling of perception, thought, memory, searching, and self-correction—justifies the hypothesis that mind too (hence subjectivity) is an exclusively physical process.

Descartes wasn't always sure that matter doesn't think. He might not be surprised to learn that machines perceive, calculate, remember, and deliberate. Would he renounce our engineers, and deny the prospect of mechanical—physiological—explanations of sensory awareness? Emphasizing the second *Meditation* justifies saying that he would. But sometimes Descartes' experimentalism was the nerve that directed his thinking. There is, for example, this passage in his *Description of the Human Body*: "[A]lthough all these movements cease in a corpse, once the soul has quit the body, we must not infer that it is the soul which produces them; the only inference we may make is that it is one and the same cause which both makes the body unfitted to produce these movements and makes the soul leave the body."[14] This passage is deliciously ambiguous. Does the soul leave a body because the environment is no longer salubrious? Or is "soul" the activity of a properly functioning body? Clocks don't work for mechanical reasons. Consciousness, too, leaves the body, but only when and because pertinent mechanical conditions have failed.

This discovery has many implications, but one takes precedence. Dualism has been scorned for years, usually without our realizing that mind's independence of body is a cornerstone of our intellectual and moral traditions. Platonism celebrates thought, feeling, morals, and human dignity, insisting that each of them derives from mind's exalted status. Descartes gathered these powers and virtues, locating them all them within the cogito. Ontological foundationalists of the twentieth century—Husserl, Heidegger, Carnap, and Quine—are his heirs. But the cogito is defunct. We humans move and live in the midst of nature as natural creatures. Mind is a set of complex bodily activities. Hence these questions: What shall philosophy be, now that its sanctuary and foundation have dissolved? How shall we resolve the churning described in chapter Six?

D. Is the Alleged Refutation a Methodological Error?

Descartes doubted all judgments about empirical contingencies; each could be mistaken. Mind's alleged identity with neural activity is a judgment of this sort. How is it possible to refute any claim of his by adducing evidence he discounted? Generalizing this view implies that no thinker can be appraised in any terms but his own. It excuses astrologers and cultists of all sorts from scrutiny. Should we concede that their views are true merely because they satisfy their owners' criteria for meaning and truth?

We proceed by using empirical evidence in a way that is neutral as regards the issue in question: we look for the empirical differences that would obtain if a hypothesis were true, always acknowledging possible failures and abuses. Evidence may be misreported or misconstrued. Conflicting hypotheses—physicalism and phenomenalism, for example—may appeal to the same evidence. There may be states of affairs for which there is no empirical evidence. We consider these objections, dealing with each in its turn, allowing that some cases are ambiguous or unresolvable. Still, we continue to use this criterion—all of practical life and science invoke it—because it eliminates false claims while confirming others.

We satisfy Descartes by holding him to a test he endorsed. He supposed that the categorial difference between mind and body precludes bodies from thinking, being aware, or willing. It is a contradiction—a violation of each one's categorial identity—to affirm that either could do what is reserved to the other: minds do not move; bodies do not think. This dictum affirms the most extreme prohibition possible, hence the most dramatic test: can we show that human bodies do think, or that machines we design and build think as we do? Like the magician who makes his subject levitate, can we do the impossible? Granting that mind seems different from body, we ask for confirming evidence that it is. Uncertain, we analyze mind's character using two questions to focus our inquiry: What does mind do? And how is it done? Introspection discovers some of mind's acts, but little or nothing of how they are performed.

Wanting more information, we detour. Human nervous systems are complicated: we know too little about them, though we do better with recent technology. Imaging that uses tomography transforms our ability to observe the brains of living humans: we no longer wait for experiments performed on people in medical care after suffering brain damage. But brains are stubbornly complex. We sometimes learn more about neural processes if we bypass human subjects, experimenting instead on snails or other species having simpler nervous systems.[15] Animals thought to have few mental powers are irritable, hence aware. What is more, their irritability is differential: they move towards some stimuli, but away from others. Here is evidence of material systems that perceive, differentiate, and pursue things that satisfy their needs. Descartes agreed that animals are mechanical systems able to do many things without minds. But we go further than he did, by finding elementary forms of cognition in other animals. Or we mimic physiology, learning to understand the functions that need to be performed if a system is to think, by building machines that think.

Formal inference is one of the functions Descartes ascribed to mind, though machines that apply it are commonplace. Some machines that differentiate their inputs also make inductive inferences—they generalize about kinds on the basis of several or many of their instances. Abductive inference—explanation—is mostly beyond the capability of our machines, because their "imaginations" aren't rich enough to generate salient hypotheses. Still, some current machines respond to unanticipated circumstances by searching for alternative, viable procedures.

Will is another of the faculties or actions that Descartes ascribed to mind, though it, too, yields to machine design when we construe it as inhibition or activation. Even self-awareness is less opaque than before. It occurs in hierarchically structured nerve networks when one level registers a lower one. Only the sufficient conditions for the phosphorescence of self-awareness and the presentation of feelings and sensory data currently elude us. We don't know how these phenomena emerge in an electrochemical system.

These are some current results when mind's alleged irreducibility to body is tested empirically. Descartes alleged that bodies cannot think or will. He was mistaken. Mind's activities are, as Aristotle said, the states, powers, and acts of a physical system having a certain complexity.[16] We don't need a categorially different agent—the cogito—to do such things as bodies do. Nor do we agree that the incompleteness of our explanations is evidence that some aspects of mind are not bodily. For now, as before, dualism describes mental phenomena without explaining them. Having no explanatory power of its own, it survives on the hope that awareness and it contents will forever resist the engineers and physiologists.

3. Consequences of the Refutation

One epoch-defining idea—psychocentrism—is replaced by another—physicalism. Descartes' leaner theory acknowledges only mind and its qualifications. The physiology he inspired has different implications: it locates humans within nature as natural creatures. Our fate and values have no other context.

Refutation is best understood in two ways: logically and psychologically. Poll-takers predict elections before ballots are cast; candidates who lose in the polls are properly demoralized. Mind's special status is comparably devalued in technologically informed cultures. We are sometimes exhorted by authors who allege that consciousness is immaterial; but conviction wanes. No one knows how to reestablish either dualism or psychocentric foundationalism. Their demise would be complete but for the absence of a mechanical model for conscious perceptual states (the look of colors, for example), or a concept or metaphor that would explain the generation of such effects within mechanical systems.

Some materialists can't wait. Believing that mind–body identity is true, though awareness and its contents are still unexplained, they suppose that introspectable phenomena—looks and feelings, for example—are a myth inspired by dualist theory.[17] This is poor strategy: phenomenal states don't disappear just because we haven't identified their sufficient material conditions. These materialists may fear that awareness and phenomena can't be explained physically. But this conclusion is premature, and reminiscent of Descartes' mistaken guess that calculation and will are not the activities of a physical system. The cure for these doubts is a better theory of physiology. Their solution—there are no data of awareness—has the contrary effect: denying phenomena apparent to everyone discredits the belief that all of mind is the activity of body and brain. Physicalism is an empirical hypothesis, one confirmed by the success of its explanations. Clearing the deck—denying the existence of phenomena that test the theory's explanatory power—converts hypothesis to dogma.

Our leading principle—mind's exhaustively material nature—is nevertheless highly confirmed: most mental activities—including some that Descartes ascribed only to mind—are known to have material conditions only. The implications of this discovery are vastly consequential for those aspects of culture that make dualism their fulcrum. Mind is not the crucible of intelligibility, but only one of its expressions. Things in the extra-mental world—human bodies included—have intrinsic differentiations and relations that are knowable and often known. Humans are valuable, if only to one another, but not because some aspect or part of us is immaterial and immortal. This is a rare moment in philosophic history. *The* dominant philosophic idea—the mentalist ontology founded by Plato, privatized by Descartes, then embellished by Kant—is empirically falsified.

Philosophy is disrupted, because its claims about the world are not privileged: nothing is set before the mind, inspected, and seen, hence known. There is no exemption from this forced choice: thought creates domains it controls—sentential logic, for example—by stipulating rules, or it hypothesizes about the character of things. Rules are neither true nor false; though they are apt or not. Hypotheses—including the maps embodied in plans of action—are true or false of matters whose character and existence are independent of our speculations about them. We determine that they are one or the other by deriving predictions about the empirical differences that would obtain if our hypotheses were true, then by looking for the evidence. Most hypotheses are testable in this way. It happens only rarely that a hypothesis cites an alleged factual difference—the existence of worlds parallel to, but decoupled from our own, for example—without there being an empirical difference that would confirm it. Such hypotheses may be true, though we lack the data required to validate them. This is a limit on testability, not on material truth.[18]

Rediscovering our place within the material world requires that we take our bearings. What is our context? What resistance incites our hypotheses and experiments? Descartes and Kant disoriented thought by reducing this world to shadows. Giving it a name—"the thing-in-itself"—Kant made it mysterious and remote. Peirce wrote, more accurately, of "secondness" and "struggle."[19] Truth, he said, is "the ideal limit towards which endless investigation would tend to bring scientific belief."[20] Quine objects that there is no single, ideal limit: there may be several competing theories that satisfy all our observations.[21] But it is truth, not the limit, that is ideal. Nature is everywhere within and about us. Living in the middle of things as one of them is consistent with having a partial conception of it. Struggle, with its successes and failures, is evidence of our circumstances. Forever revising our theories expresses their partiality and our irresolution. The two are different: the first—the limit—isn't compromised by the second—partial or failed truths.

How did the Cartesian-Kantian tradition convince us that nature is remote and unthinkable, beyond our reach? It conflated two things that turn on the human desire to locate ourselves within the world. One way of locating us is unproblematic: I am here or there, in these circumstances and this body. The other is noetic: how do I know what and where I am? Wanting knowledge (and certainty) rather than belief (and possible error), I begin by doubting my circumstances, doubting even that I have a body. For there is always a gap between opinion and the matters believed. How do I close the gap? The tradition that moves through Plato, Descartes, and Kant endorses mind's incorporation of the divided line. For the gap dissolves if things to be known are in me. I know what and where I am by turning awareness on myself and my innate ideas. But this sabotages the lessons of practical life. The mentalist tradition entails that the material world, my body included, has no reality apart from data I entertain. Or materiality is noumenal: I think, but cannot know it; or it has no reality apart from my stubborn inclination to believe that sensory data are the effects of extra-mental causes. The physical location confirmed by practical life is delusory if all materiality is sucked into mind or repudiated as unthinkable.

This is the result nullified when mind proves to be the activity of body. For then our physical location is again the point of reference for empirical inquiries that describe us and our circumstances. Yet, the old myths persist. It is dogma to philosophers that nature is a thing-in-itself. Locked within the hierarchy of awareness and self-awareness, or object- and meta-language, we discount the practical successes of daily life and science. Nature is the "transcendental object," a vanishing horizon that forever retreats as we reach to touch it. Do we ever touch it? Perhaps we never do, given that hypotheses are fallible. Reliance on them provokes defensiveness in thinkers who make a fortress of the cogito. Mind was to be the domain where reflection is master of all it inspects: principally, logic, experience, and itself. But that hope is past. Mind's materiality entails that every knowledge claim is mediated by signs, including percepts and words. The questions that occupy us— What are we? What is the world? What is our place here?—have answers that are always hypothetical and fallible. This should discourage pictures of philosophers distinguished by their penetrating eyes.

Thinking hypothetically—inferring abductively from effects to their conditions, from smoke to fire—should be easy, given that we do it throughout our practical lives. The task for materialists is harder, because of the centuries old belief that philosophy has little to say about nature. Even philosophic realists sometimes stop after saying that the existence and character of things are independent of the ways we think about them. No wonder that glossing scientific claims is our way of speaking earnestly about some feature of the world. For there is no respected tradition of philosophic inquiry that is empirical and abductive, and no respectable metaphysics of nature since Aristotle. Contemporary materialists are obliged to invent a cogent metaphysics, all the while establishing that their speculative—hypothetical—method is used responsibly. This is difficult, though the cogito's demise leaves many topics that require naturalization. Some were exploited because of their apparent accessibility to thought: values and mind's structure, for example. Others were ignored, either because physics dominates them (matter and motion) or because claims about them seem to exceed empirical testability (natural necessity and normativity). And there is categorial form, meaning the integrated system of nature's most general features, including spacetime, motion, matter and energy, cause, dispositions, laws, modalities, and nature's hierarchical organization.[22] Scientists are usually too preoccupied with issues of a smaller scale to care about this scheme or its details. But this task is all but obligatory, granting the danger that fragmentary information about the parts promotes distortion of the whole. We risk it, because understanding categorial form is, since Aristotle, philosophy's *telos*.

Philosophers who vaunt their special methods and access to Being often scorn the hypothetical method. Like Plato, they claim direct intuitive access to Forms or essences.[23] But this way to truth is a fantasy, if mind is the activity of body. For brains do not have unmediated access to anything. Percepts—immediately grasped and inspected—seem to be a counterexample, but they require four or more distinct acts: receptivity to an input, constructing, then noticing and construing—classifying—the perceptual content. The fourth is a fallible reading of the second. We reduce the likelihood of error by staring at the source of the input, confirming beyond doubt that something looking red at first sight still looks red. But the stability of the percept is not surprising if the thing perceived—a stoplight—does look red in natural light. Nor is it safe to assume that the datum construed is rightly classified. We could be mistaken, though now, after repeated observation, this possibility is reduced.

Some thinkers use this admission—error is possible in the case of perception, and all the more likely when hypotheses are theoretical—as an excuse for doubting that mental activity is the typically unconscious, uninspectable activity of body. Why identify mind with surmised physical activity when mind is known directly and unproblematically to itself? The threat of error together with mind's paradoxical self-alienation—having to hypothesize about itself—makes physicalism seem speculative and circumlocutious. Yet, that which is first in knowledge—feelings and percepts, for example—may not be first in being, meaning prior in the order of generating conditions. One knows one's pain better than any dentist; but it is dentists whose hypotheses direct the actions that relieve it.

Philosophers' ideas shape other peoples' thinking for hundreds of years. But here, in the rubble of Descartes' mentalism, philosophy's reputation suffers. Tenured professors find little good to say of it. Many would have philosophy die. Others retool as commentators on the arts or the sciences. But this is loss of nerve, not the demise of philosophy. There are deep, general truths to be told about the world. Finding and integrating them is always philosophy's task, whether or not it succeeds.

Chapter Six

Churning

1. Disputed Questions

The dialectic of contending ideas has distinguished philosophy from its beginning. Ideas fall to one side or the other of two or more organizing themes. And sometimes, because one side of the debate is all but undisputed, we concede its truth. The conflation of intelligibility with thought, and being with knowledge, has been a truth of this sort throughout its elaboration from Parmenides and Plato through Descartes, Leibniz, Berkeley, Hume, Kant, Fichte, Schelling, Hegel, Nietzsche, Husserl, Heidegger, Russell, Carnap, and Quine. Many beliefs about mind's special status—ontologically, epistemologically, and morally—make this assumption. Yet, these beliefs are indefensible if mind is a physical process explicable in terms that are common to material processes everywhere.

Descartes' reformulation of Plato's line loses its footing when mind falls headlong into nature. For dualism was more than an isolated, but stubborn, problem: this was the basis for the intuitive powers and moral entitlements claimed for mind. Where is the firm ground for intelligibility, selfhood, and the good if the cogito is defunct? Debate churns. The Cartesian side emphasizes raw feels, or the conceptual systems that mind constructs and inspects. It objects that physicalist alternatives (reports of brain imaging or the effects of drugs on thought) seem oddly unphilosophical. Cartesians temporize, exaggerating skeptical doubts about the external world's accessibility to thought. Physicalists counter by emphasizing the reliability of empirical inquiry and practice—engineering, for example—and the implausibility of the dualist ontology: a subjective perspective, awareness, and reflexivity are not evidence that mind is not the activity of body.

Descartes' two opinions—his psychocentrism and his physical-ism—are contraries that organize the fourteen disputes that follow. Psychocentrism alleges that all reality, intelligibility, and value are lodged in mind, be it of one thinker or many. (I ignore the view—affirmed by Descartes' richer theory, Leibniz, Hegel, and Whitehead—that God is the infinite mind in which finite thinkers dwell, or from which they derive.) The mind so described is self-sufficient and every-where self-transparent, but opaque to other thinkers, save for the ratio-nality or language that thinkers share. Physicalism locates every mind in a body, and every body within the dynamic milieu of matter and motion in spacetime. One of its two versions affirms that physical real-ity is the shifting aggregate of quarks, atoms, or molecules as they col-lect or divide.[1] The alternative avers that the causal reciprocities of mutually affecting bodies generate modular systems: atoms, molecules, cells, and animal bodies, then families, tribes, cities, and states. Reality, it argues, is an array of systems, some that are mutually independent, others that are reciprocally related, nested, or overlapping.[2] Both ver-sions agree that we humans perpetually engage the things about us, either responding in innate, programmed ways, or inventing the maps and plans that direct us as we achieve our aims. We go from practical engagements with people and things we need to abstract, theoretical questions, from watching a building fall, to explaining the fact that everything falls. Bodies locate us definitively in this place or that; thought struggles—provisionally and fallibly—to discover what place this is.

Physicalism requires that ontology and epistemology be natural-ized.[3] But Cartesians are not defenseless. Ordinary language and estab-lished theories are suffused with the mentalism now contested. Why suppose that one of mind's own products—the physicalist hypothesis—trumps mind's authority? Isn't mind the measure of all that is or is not? This is the issue disputed. Does mind prescribe what other things are or may be; or does it find and locate itself in the midst of nature, engag-ing, adapting to them? This stark alternation emphasizes the contrari-ety of the two sides: both cannot be true. But sometimes, there is a third term that integrates the contraries, reconciling them.

The sequence of these fourteen issues is (roughly) the trajectory of Hegel's *Phenomenology of Mind*: from mind's preoccupation with itself to the more ample self-understanding achieved when we locate our-selves within the physical, social world. My characterizations of the fourteen contraries are schematic rather than detailed. I emphasize the alternatives, not the details or refinements that distinguish formulations of a single contrary

A. Mind's Knowledge of Itself:
Introspection, Behaviorism, or Inference?

Others sometimes predict my behavior more accurately than I. "You always do that," they say, though I am unaware of some patterns that make me predictable. I resist, for what do they know of me apart from behaviors reduced to habit? The habits liberate me to reflect and dream as I like. Others see the husk and imagine they know me. They never guess what I think and feel, unless I deign to tell them, as usually I do not. Are these feelings and reflections the whole story about me, or even a vital part of it? I observe my observers, knowing their sensibility and style, gait and speech, vulnerabilities and virtues. Surely, others know as much of me. Their responses—welcome or recoil—are often informative in ways that self-perception is not. One may spend years trying to perceive oneself with the clarity of those who observe him or her briefly, but closely.

These perspectives are not so much contrary as different. For there is an alternative that reconciles them: infer to the condition that expresses itself in these two ways. Someone habitually generous or angry is likely to have had formative experiences that were observed by the person him or herself, and by others. Both may know the consequences, and both may correctly identify the cause. Individuals sometimes speculate about their motives. Parents and psychologists do it often, and correctly. Their successes reconcile the two perspectives by inferring that the two kinds of evidence—introspection and behavior—have a common cause: namely, an intrapsychic, usually unconscious, state.

Behaviorists decline to speculate about processes occurring within the mind, though inferences that correctly predict behavior (speech, for example) are welcome to them. Introspectionists object that inferences to uninspectable mental states (the neural formations expressed in awareness and behavior) are empty, because they introduce theoretical terms that have no empirical content apart from the introspectable data they predict. This objection is misplaced if an adequate physiology identifies the relevant neural state. But often, this state is unknown, so the objection seems better founded. Why speculate about the conditions for well articulated experiences. Don't I hear the music distinctly? How would I know it better if there were a neural state that conditions my hearing it?

Each perspective works to exclude the other by alleging that the other's concerns are incidental to the matter at issue. Where is mind: in bodily behavior or the phenomena inspected? The mediating solution proposes that these two are expressions of a third. It cites the intra-psychic, uninspectable neural state.

B. Experience: Schematization and Inspection, or Interaction?

What is experience: mind's solitary inspection of contents it differentiates and organizes, or the perpetual weave of initiatives and responses, intrusions and reactions? A thinker may be described as active either way, though the ambit and character of action differ radically if experience is one or the other. Schematizing a thinkable experience—manipulating, reporting, or observing the contents of one order from another—is an action internal to mind. Interactions with other people and things require that thought test itself in the social or natural world. This difference is exaggerated if conceptual puzzles (the Liar Paradox or Prisoners' Dilemma, for example) are contrasted with stubborn kinks in the maps and plans that persistently misdirect our engagements with other things. Fixing paradoxes is not the same as repairing flawed maps and plans, though the difference is invisible if we suppose that reality is nothing apart from the intelligibility of our theories. For then it follows that puzzles express the complexity or confusion of our conceptualizations, not the failure of theories that misrepresent extra-mental states of affairs.

This, too, is a contrariety that invites mediation. One side describes experience by emphasizing our passivity to empirical data and the reflections that discover or impose their differentiations and relations. The other side sees thought as the antennae of action: thought anticipates the direction and aim, then turns back on itself, reconnoitering when a plan hasn't worked as it should. Both stories are partial, because each is subordinate to a third: we alternately engage other things, perceiving and responding to them, then withdraw to revise our maps and plans. Having spent the day at work, we retire to think about it. What did we do? How well? What shall we do tomorrow? Reflection joins current experience to memory and anticipation. Subjecting facts to attitudes and values, it expresses the desire for order and significance in the details of life.

Both science and literature are expressions of this mental activity: one locates the particular in the universal, the other finds universal significance or values in the particular. This similarity is easily misconstrued. For it may seem that both interests are achieved as mind withdraws into reflection, averting encounters with other things. Turned in upon ourselves, reflecting on complexities that mind discerns or constructs—expressing our findings in the language of fiction, history, mathematics, or science—we are self-sufficient because self-intelligible. We forget that this is one of two, constantly recurring steps in the formation of experience, not both steps at once.

All our thinking requires the engagements that test its hypotheses, and supply its information. We are perpetually challenged by encounters that check the accuracy of our responses and the degree of our control. Turn a key, and the car goes; the light turns red, and we stop. Mentalism proposes that mind is a theater where data are presented or rendered intelligible. The alternative affirms that thought maps our circumstances, then expresses its aims in plans that organize our engagements with other things. It says that plans are hypotheses used as directives, and that data are the evidence of success or failure: success is fulfilling, failure requires that we alter course. Technology focuses the difference, because designing isn't doodling. It exploits a hypothesis that effectively directs our interaction with the states of affairs represented.

We don't need scientific theories to address many things used or encountered—forks and spoons, for example. Still, technology owes its power to a few applicable theories, not to the many conceivable theories that might be used to differentiate and organize sensory data. Error, frustration, and death remind us that nature has a character of its own, one that resists us if our engagements are not directed by appropriate theories. This resistance mystifies anyone who believes that intelligibility lies only within ideas, theories, or language. Let him shave with a dull razor.

Idealism obscures such contacts by citing the incommensurability of scientific theories, or the evolution wherein "true" theories are falsified or replaced. Duhem contrasted the succession of opposed ideas (Kuhn's "paradigms"[4]) with the incremental advance of theories that incorporate their antecedents. Is there a true story about heat to support the technology of things that make or resist it—from matches to boilers and nose cones? Or is heat one more datum created by the theory used to think it? Thermodynamics was Duhem's example of theories that are successively refined as we learn more of phenomena we experience, but do not make.[5]

Effective science and practice rely on three things as individual inquirers make, test, and correlate their readings of the world. First is the hard edge of a world having a form of its own, a form that resists each of us in many of the same ways. Second are testable hypotheses. Third are plans that coordinate behavior. For nature yields to cooperative, plan-directed activity: a boat at sea moves on its charted course when tiller and sails are calibrated to wind and current. This is the effect when crew members, motivated by shared or complementary aims, coordinate their actions. Cartesians (of the lean theory) and Kantians should find this hard to understand: what explains coordinated activity, if every person makes his or her experience, "objects," and "world," with no common reality to constrain them?

C. Ideas: Innate or Acquired?

Innateness speaks to mind's self-sufficiency. But is anything innate? It is usually agreed that percepts are created within us when extra-mental causes affect sensory organs, or when bodily processes affect body's proprioceptors. There is little support for saying that the productive imagination generates percepts by applying innate combination rules to a stock of elementary, innate prototypes. Innate ideas have more support, because they sometimes convey information that exceeds empirical data. There is, for example, no apparent empirical content for the distinction between first cousins and first cousins once removed (ignoring DNA, because the terms signified a relevant factual difference before its discovery). We may infer that such ideas are innate, though to assume this is premature if we can extrapolate from relations that do make an empirical difference—parent and child, for example—to those that do not. Innateness is also sometimes favored because it promises to guarantee cogency: we suppose that innate ideas would be true of important matters (Forms or essences, for example).

Other implications cut the other way. Innate ideas may differ from mind to mind. With no external source as referent, we may be unintelligible to one another, each of us isolated from others by ideas that are untranslatable. This may happen even if we suppose that each one's ideas cover the same range of phenomena. For we may carve a subject differently: you divide it with a grid of horizontal and vertical lines; I use diagonals. There may be no way to coordinate our ideas, because neither of us has access to these domains in ways that discount our differences. Acquired ideas avert these pitfalls, because each of us can test his ideas against their extra-mental source or referent by considering the sensory difference that would obtain if the referent were tested in specific ways. Each may repeat the test, so a procedure for correcting and coordinating ideas is available to everyone having faculties of similar acuity. Add the homogenizing effects of speech and cooperation, and we generate uniformity without assuming that all of us have the same innate ideas. This externalist argument has an evolutionary justification: viable reproducers accommodate effectively to their circumstances, because they accurately represent them, and because they use other means—language and teamwork—to coordinate their responses.

Externalism is sometimes construed too narrowly as the claim that every thought or utterance is caused by an external stimulus. Saying this leaves no room for the many occasions when imagination embroiders our percepts. Seeing a straight stick as bent is caused by the different velocities of light in air and water; but it is context and my state of mind that explain the figures I see in shadows. Thoughts and words are all the more liberated from the control of our surroundings, as when we analogize, generalize, and extrapolate—in science and in fiction—from information directly acquired. Much of what distinguishes human thought from the mental states of flies or mosquitos—also affected causally by their circumstances—is the extended network of thoughts and meanings supplied by these embellishments. How should we control the inclination to pursue vivid but mistaken fantasies? By requiring that imagination's products be tested against states of affairs that affect us causally: which empirical differences would obtain if embellished ideas were true?

Which is the greater good: a priori knowledge with the possibility that each thinker's ideas are incommensurable with those of every other, or beliefs and behaviors coordinated under the control of the complex physical and social environment that affects and informs us similarly? There is a middle ground: perceptual and conceptual powers may be an acquired evolutionary response—now innate—to our circumstances.[6] Perhaps color vision was selected because the hues and shades perceived enhance human survival (as things edible or dangerous stand out visually from their circumstances). Or the planes and angles of Euclidean geometry are prominent in human perception because seeing them has survival value for creatures that move as we do. Fish and birds may have a different visual geometry, because their medium and perspective require that they analyze sensory inputs in other ways.

Evolutionary, externalist arguments are well known, but unevenly received, because apriorism retains its dialectical force. What do we know of things in themselves if the very differentiae and relations of the data used to confirm our claims are prescribed by the theories tested? What is the "external" world of which science informs us? Just the projection of our favored theories, say these apriorists. Mind's alleged self-sufficiency is slow to yield.

D. Meaning

How do ideas, words, sentences, and rules acquire meaning? Is it derived from resources within the mind, or by way of our encounters with things we engage and perceive? There are three bases to touch: first are several versions of the apriorist thesis, then the pragmatic counter-argument, finally a synthesis that incorporates the two.

Instuitionists sometimes argue that meanings are apprehended as they stand before the mind. This claim is most plausible when ideas or words signify sensory data. So, *red* signifies—means—the quality I currently perceive or imagine. Innate ideas would be inspectable, if their contents were geometrical figures or the representations of familiar things (triangles, tables, or chairs). This project isn't irreparably flawed, until the ideas to be inspected are more arcane: God and the square root of minus one, for example. Sentences, too, may have inspectable meanings if, like geometricals, they have the required syntactic form, and if the terms substituted for their variables create an inspectable complex: "See the rising moon."

The difference between rules and ideas complicates the task of explicating meaning in terms of presentation and inspection. Ideas of circle, square, and triangle may stand before the mind as distinct shapes, but the meaning of a rule is either the action it prescribes, or the effect achieved when the rule is applied. A rule may be easily discerned, because the domain of its applications is clear-cut (as $2 + 2 = 4$ expresses a rule). But it often happens that a domain is not easily specified. For we can't fully discern a rule in its applications if we can't foresee all of them. Semantic rules that control the use of words in ordinary language are a familiar example. We want to create a map—the "logical grammar" of its uses—by using the word in varying contexts; but the map is always incomplete—meaning is elusive—because of the inexhaustible diversity of the sentences in which the word could appear.

The account of intrapsychic meaning is radically different, if we emphasize the flow of meaningful thought or speech. *Meaning*, on these occasions, is neither the intention that construes successive thoughts or words as signs, nor the senses thereby signified.[7] For we don't stop to consider the meaning of each word or sentence: doing that would impede thought or communication. Instead, thoughts or sentences are meaningful, if a sequence of thoughts or sentences is consistent (not contradictory), well formed (it satisfies relevant rules of inference), and coherent. Coherence is problematic: what rules does it satisfy? Having no well-formulated answer, we invoke the protean gestalt familiar to authors who write and edit for integration-with-cogency-and-clarity. Meaning flows as the story builds, but writers or speakers don't know the rules that make their discourse coherent.

Still, there is an explanation for coherence: thoughts or sentences expressed sequentially are, more fundamentally, synchronic, because related deductively or located within networks of interanimating—inductively related—sentences. Either way, we can regard the relations of sentences as uninterpreted or interpreted. Uninterpreted sentences are a syntactic system: they satisfy the rules of deductive or inductive inference. Their relations are necessary in one case, probabilistic in the other. These are rules for joining sentences; but equally, there are grammatical rules that order words within sentences. Sentences satisfy a first condition for meaning, even when uninterpreted, if they fulfill the requirements of grammatical form: s is p, or a, b, and c stand in some relation.

Neither speakers nor auditors stop to construe individual words, because we rely on these guarantors of meaning—deductive or inductive rules of inference, and the grammar of sentential form—when discourse flows. The speed of neural sequencing, and the need to communicate information makes stopping the flow inefficient. The possibility that we can stop, then start again, expresses the two sides of mental activity: engagement alternates with the deliberation that tests for empirical meaning. For grammatical sentences require interpretation. They acquire empirical meaning when their terms are correlated ostensively with sensory data, with reports of the data, or with words that are themselves defined in either of the two previous ways. We can stop the flow to consider—by perceiving or imagining—the differences signified by the words.

These are the principal considerations when theory locates meanings within the mind, saying either that they are inspectable contents or that the relations of thoughts, words, or sentences are meaningful because rule-governed. *Meaning* has contrary implications, if reality is not reducible to mind and its qualifications. Kant, Fichte, and Schelling supposed that percepts are created by the productive imagination. This other view explains them as evidence—effects—of our encounters with extra-mental things. We learn the signification of many nouns, adjectives, verbs, and adverbs by engaging and perceiving the differences they signify. Remarking that things have properties and are multiply related, we infer that sentences having subject–predicate or relational form represent features of the extra-mental world: their form is evidence of something more than syntactic convention.

Externalist accounts—from Aristotle to the present—found the meanings of thoughts, words, or sentences, and the significance of feelings, norms, and intentions in trajectories that reach from external states of affairs to perception and thought, and the reverse.[8] Engaging other things, we learn their character and represent it in thought and words. The latter are a viable record of these encounters, but not their perfect mirror. For externalism errs if it supposes that the trajectory of meaning always goes from things encountered to the mind in which they are registered. We often endow thoughts, words, and rules with meanings that are not derived from things encountered. Thinking and language are replete with conventions that facilitate speech and thought: variant conceptual styles and the notations of written languages are examples. So, too, ideals are meaningful though never instantiated: we know what *justice* signifies without a trajectory that anchors its meaning in something perceived.

This is a clue to the synthesis that resolves the opposition of internalist and externalist accounts. Let *great aunt* be our example. It signifies a class of people that mind has not created. Yet, nothing perceived is sufficient to supply its meaning. That sense has two origins. First are the empirical data supplied by the perception of parents' relations to their children. Second is the network of relations that mind generates as it represents kinship relations. This network functions as a hypothesis, one that is partially confirmed by data that include the evidence of DNA. (The hypothesis is only partially confirmed, because the network is usually not articulated in ways that would make it comprehensively testable. It may be full of stipulations and special cases: for example, the neighbors called "aunt" or "uncle.") Accordingly, *great aunt* and the idea it signifies do have extra-mental reference, though the idea originates in the network of relations mind constructs, not in the perception of something that is empirically recognizable as a great aunt.

What explains our ability to extend a system of thoughts and words beyond its empirical base? We do it by using generalization, extrapolation, and analogy to organize and embroider the thoughts or words that signify perceptual data. Laws of nature are generalizations; *great aunt* extrapolates; religious claims analogize from the relations of parents and children to God's authority. None of these ideas originates directly from our encounter with things perceived, but each is warranted when empirical information is construed and extended within a network of concepts. No one may have perceived or counted the legs of a millipede, but we can extrapolate from ants or spiders, using ideas or words sanctioned by our conceptual framework, to look for confirming evidence. Where is the engine that facilitates these elaborations? In the syntax and semantical rules of language. Words can be joined up to the point of solecism—"It's raining hard," but not "It's raining numbers—thereby articulating possibilities that would be otherwise unimagined.

The relation of syntax and semantics is also notable for the way that word-order modulates empirical meaning. Dictionaries define words out of context, only sometimes indicating the difference made to meaning when words are used in sentences. This semantic core is often nuanced by a word's relations to the other words of a sentence. Poets know these effects better than the rest of us, but everyone can hear the semantic shift from "great hall" to "great victory." Empirical meaning is determinable. It waits on grammar—use within sentences—to make it determinate.

Syntactic and semantical rules are likely to be innate products of body's evolutionary adaptation to its circumstances: they survived because of making us more efficient when we respond to extra-mental stimuli. Fictions of all sorts are evidence that many of the meaningful thoughts or words generated within conceptual networks exceed our practical needs.

E. Thought

Descartes believed that thought combines representation—ideas that exhibit essences—with analysis and synthesis. Analysis divides complex but obscure ideas into their clarified, simple parts. Synthesis combines the simples—"pure and simple nature[s]"[9]—to produce clear and distinct, complex ideas. His favored construction rules were the syntactic—logical—rules used when conclusions are proved deductively. (The rules of inference in Euclid's *Elements* were his likely point of reference.) Kant also emphasized rules that organize and unify simple elements, though his simples were sensory data, each unrelated to others until organized as rules prescribe. The schemas he emphasized are rules of association, not rules of inference: their product is an object perceived, not a theorem. Kant would say that thought is generically the association of data under rules. Deduction is one sort of association; the association of data under rubrics that create the apparent unity of dogs or cats is another. Other coherence-making rubrics include narrative, utterance and response (in conversation), and the plans that direct action in pursuit of an aim. Such rules organize words, thoughts, images, or actions (always ignoring questions about body's extra-mental reality), so that periods of random association or dreamless sleep are interspersed with articulate, coherent sequences of thought.

Kant's hypothesis—that mind is a faculty of rules—is widely believed to be true. Speech, writing, hypothesis, planning, and calculation are evidence for it. Descartes supposed that mind is always aware of itself when attending to content, or applying its rules. Yet, rules are typically applied without our being aware that they are applied, and often without awareness of their content. Gilbert Harman describes such a rule:

> Important aspects of language are not learned in any explicit way, as in the following somewhat oversimplified example. In dialects of English, questions can be formed by moving a question word to the beginning of the sentence and following it with the first auxiliary verb, as in `Who is Alfred asking Bob to talk to?' which comes from `Alfred is asking Bob to talk to *who*?' But this rule cannot apply if the question word occurs in grammatical conjunction with another noun phrase, as in `Alfred is asking Bob to talk to *who* and Mary?' because the result, `Who is Alfred asking Bob to talk to and Mary?' is not a well-formed question. Now it is very difficult to see how a child might learn such a constraint (the `coordinate structure constraint') given the available evidence. Indeed, the coordinate structure constraint was unknown to linguists before 1950. But if children do not learn the constraint, that can only be because it is somehow built into language acquisition ahead of time. So it should apply no matter what language is learned, which is to say it must be a universal constraint, one that holds in every language that is acquired as a first language in the normal way.[10]

Many—perhaps most—of the rules acquired innately or learned as habits, and applied in thought or language are never brought to consciousness. Such rules are comprehensible, though sometimes difficult to analyze because they are deeply nested, or vastly qualified. Consciousness of them is not a condition for either their use or their intelligibility.

The emphasis on confirming awareness is, nevertheless, prominent in John Searle's claim that "an unconscious rule has to have the kind of content which could be consciously understood interpreted, followed, or violated."[11] Though "For a number of reasons rules may be unconscious and in some cases, such as brain damage or repression, a person may be unable to bring the rule to consciousness."[12] This is a strong version of the dualist claim that nothing is intelligible if we cannot perceive that it is. Yet Searle's requirement—that mind give its imprimatur to rules already applied—is moot. For we apply numerous rules without requiring conscious mind to certify them. Who but a careful student of language would have noticed the rule that Harman describes?

Searle agrees that "there are innate mechanisms in the human brain for acquiring and using language;"[13] but he invokes Descartes' view that nothing is reliably done, or said to exist if it is not consciously scrutinized and validated:

In order to make an explanation of behavior as following rules work, we need to be able to distinguish cases which are guided by a rule from cases which are merely described by a rule. One condition of rule-guided explanation is that the rules have to be the sorts of things that one could actually *follow*. If you spell out those conditions, you find that unconscious rules have to be the sort of things that at least could be conscious.[14]

Why is this so? Is it that unconscious thinking is virtual or mechanical, so that following—inspecting—each operation performed is the condition for certifying a rule and its applications? This requirement—emphasized throughout Descartes' *Rules for the Direction of the Mind*—is challenged by Harman's example. Conscious reflection is incidental to the application of many rules, grammatical rules especially.

A different consideration requires that we alter perspective: rather than describe thought from the standpoint of consciousness, we try to identify the conditions for unconscious thought, or the unconscious conditions for conscious thought. Several are critical. They include formation rules and sensory content when an artist or composer thinks about his work; percepts, maps, and plans when the thinking is practical and the time for action has come; grammatical rules (syntactic and semantical) for sequencing thoughts or words, with or without sensory content; syntax when issues are mathematical; and pertinent attitudes, hence feelings and values, in all contexts.[15] Any of these factors may be conscious; but they also function when unconscious. What does consciousness contribute to thought? It often enhances focus and efficiency, though other times, it confounds us: thinking is sometimes deepest when one turns away from a problem, letting it stew—out of conscious light.

How will this dispute be resolved: which perspective—Cartesianism or physicalism—supplies a more accurate account of thought? Engineers answer this question definitively when they build machines that invent, modify, and use rules without bringing a rule to consciousness. Some machines make and test plans or hypotheses, doing complicated chores. Some converse. These thinkers, like us humans, are *natural* in every relevant sense: they are physical objects by virtue of their materials, the causal relationships in which they participate, and the laws satisfied by their actions. Using linguistic rules is one of their natural activities.

Imagine that Searle's views about rules were extended to natural laws: the laws might be applicable without having been inspected, but they could not be intelligible (hence followable), unless inspectable by a conscious mind. Should we infer that the laws of motion are not applicable without a God to inspect them? Descartes' richer theory makes God responsible for certifying—indeed for establishing—the intelligibility of natural laws and logic. Is Searle's criterion for rule-following a first step on the way to theologizing everything thinkable?

F. Truth: Identity, Coherence, or Correspondence?

Truth is identity when mind inspects things set within and before it, seeing them as they are. Plato's Forms were early candidates for inspection: they were intuited as inscribed in thought. Identity was still the implicit idea of truth when Kant argued that mind creates its experience by using rules and sensory data to create a thinkable experience: we perceive differences and relations that mind has projected onto the data. The product of this activity—experience—stands within and before the mind: truth is achieved as mind perceives its own states. World-making stories, hence the experiences they schematize, are a modern substitute. A self-sufficient thinker establishes the conditions for intelligibility by guaranteeing the meaning and truth of the stories it tells. Such thinkers satisfy several imperatives: Discover an array of innate ideas including relations, or invent a grammar and vocabulary. Formulate thoughts or sentences, then take care that their assembly satisfies semantic and syntactic rules (consistency, for example). If the story is fragmentary, fill in the gaps. Now survey the objects hereby "re-presented" or "expressed": see things as they are in the luminous space where thought creates them.[16]

Truth as correspondence proposes that we represent or signify things known. It attenuates mind's relation to them with mediating percepts, thoughts or sentences. Signs are always less informative than intuition, because they pick out one or a few of their objects' many properties. Worse, there is the chance that we misrepresent a state of affairs, because information is scanty or flawed, because properties of the sign mislead us, or because we misconstrue them, Truth as correspondence risks error at every turn, hence its disfavor.

Construing truth as coherence averts the difficulties of correspondence while preserving the advantages of truth as identity. The factors cohering may be ideas, thoughts, sentences, or theories, though the emphasis has evolved from psychological phenomena to items that are linguistic or logical. The ideas emphasized by Plato and Descartes are superseded by words or sentences: they stand before the mind when thought, seen, or heard. There are two tasks to complete if coherence is to be a plausible theory of truth: establish what truth could be if it is not correspondence, and explain—discount—the mistaken impression that sentences are true because they represent extra-linguistic states of affairs.

We satisfy the first demand by saying that sentences are true because their relations to other sentences satisfy deductive or inductive rules of inference. There are, for example, stipulated, entailment relations, such as "Strike three! You're out." This is a deduction, given the rules of baseball. Empirical examples—"I'm shaking your hand with mine," "You see and feel my hand," "I see and feel yours"—are only somewhat less convincing. Each sentence is more likely to be true if the others are true; but truth is conditional—probabilistic, not categorical—when the support of observation sentences may be reduced or withdrawn because a revised theory integrates sentences differently.

Coherence is the theory that dissolves the difference between science and literature. For if the truth of a scientific theory is established by its coherence, so is every novel true because its sentences cohere. Each system of cohering sentences—be it science, fiction, or ideology—is, by this criterion, a viable interpretation of our circumstances. Though there is one saving disanalogy. Coherence is vulnerable to a surprising qualification: we cannot say that whole networks of mutually supporting sentences are true—though our confidence in them is all but unshakable—because the coherence theory defines truth as a relation between or among sentences. Networks of truths may be counted true only if they relate to one or more other networks—one array of sentences to another. Scientific theories are mutually confirming in this respect. Novels and ideologies are not.

Think again of individual sentences said to be true, and notice that the coherence theory precludes our naive assumption that a sentence is true if it accurately represents an extra-linguistic state of affairs—a hand, for example. Two considerations direct us. Negatively, we shun the correspondence theory because it makes us susceptible to error. Positively, we want to preserve the confirming immediacy required by the identity theory: let the matters judged true stand before the mind *without mediation.* We hope to satisfy this aspect of the identity theory while finding a substitute for Plato's Forms and Descartes' clear and distinct ideas. Forms and ideas are generic. Informing us about possible states of affairs, without committing themselves to particulars, they answer better to contemporary ideas of meaning, not to the requirements for truth. Sentences do both: they are meaningful if we can specify the difference that would obtain if they were true; they are true if they rightly ascribe (or deny) properties or existence to a thing or things. Neither meaning nor truth requires that we exceed the network of thoughts or sentences if confirmation too is a relation among thoughts or sentences. For we may say with Carnap and Quine that the truth of theoretical sentences is confirmed by observation sentences. "All of us are genetically disposed to red hair" is more likely to be true if "All of us have it" is also true.

Coherentists try to avert questions about extra-mental, extra-linguistic realities—hands, for example. Yet, truth as they describe it—explicitly as coherence, implicitly as identity—does too much work at too little cost. We have thoughts or sentences spread before the mind's eye, so that the states of affairs signified snap into being. But these alleged matters of fact are described, not seen. They are "expressed," "represented," or posited, not inspected. They exist by virtue of a beneficent inference: from thoughts or sentences judged true because they satisfy rules of inference to the states of affairs they signify. Coherentists encourage the inference from sentences to things while carefully limiting its interpretation. Having used quantifiers (*there is* or *are*, for example) to posit the things signified, they say that thoughts or sentences are true because their relations satisfy inductive or deductive rules, *not* because they represent things distinct from themselves.

Don't we reasonably believe that sentences are *about* something, hence true *of* something? This question is the opening toward truth as correspondence. Wanting to avert the inference to extra-mental or extra-linguistic entities, coherentists say that sentences are *expressive*: they express truths about the world without signifying anything beyond themselves. Or this deflating strategy is phrased in the vernacular of the *formal* and *material* modes. Speaking in the material mode—the style of ordinary, naive speech—we seem to be speaking of extra-mental states of affairs, though there are none, or none that can be known. Philosophically savvy speech is conducted in the formal mode. We rise to a meta-language, and comment on the logical relations of sentences in the object-language. We say, as above, that my report of shaking your hand is confirmed by your report, and by my report of feeling your hand in mine. Inductive logic confirms that the relations of these sentences satisfy its coherentist standard for truth. It is, however, truth as identity that carries the day. Mind never loses sight or control of its mutually implicative sentences: exhibiting their formal relations, these sentences satisfy the intuitionist standard for truth.

You protest that truth as coherence and identity doesn't translate a belief we share: that your hand makes sentences true without being their product. Coherentist solutions are unconvincing, because they contrive hands out of thoughts or sentences about them. Distrusting this creation story, we infer that the truth of sentences, massed or otherwise, derives from something additional to their coherence and immediacy.

Correspondence is the only truth theory left standing when coherence fails to provide for extra-linguistic truth conditions. Knowledge of every state of affairs is mediated by representations. Percepts are natural signs. Thoughts and words are conventional signs. Truth is the relation of propositional signs—thoughts or sentences—to states of affairs that satisfy them. We who live in the middle of nature as natural creatures have sensory evidence for many thoughts and sentences because many things affect us.[17]

There is also this bridge to coherence. For many truths for which evidence is scanty or absent are inferred from thoughts or sentences that are better confirmed. Using networks of sentences, some or many that are well confirmed, we successfully make predictions that would evade us were we to rely on one thought or sentence at a time. Imagine having only a single sentence to direct us, probing our circumstances as we would use a single crutch. Because networks of thoughts or sentences cover the ground more efficiently, it often happens that a dense fabric of sentences mediates our contact with the world. No wonder that coherence supersedes correspondence in our thinking about truth. But we do, or should, resist this temptation. Thoughts and sentences are signs, not the things they represent. Coherence tests correspondence, without replacing it. We expect that truths about the same state of affairs will be mutually reinforcing: evidence for one should also confirm, to some degree, an other. Yet, coherence is not sufficient evidence of truth. *Huckleberry Finn* isn't true for being coherent.[18]

It may seem that the dialectic of correspondence and coherence has been superseded now that a different theory—*redundancy*—dominates many discussions of truth. Discount the novel word, and consider Kant's formulation. He provides for redundancy in the first *Critique* when arguing that the transcendental ego has complementary effects. First are schematized phenomena, meaning experiences of distinct states of affairs. Second are the empirical judgments that report them. The one act—transcendental judgment—has two effects: experience and the empirical judgment acknowledging it. Neither occurs without the other. Or, as we may formulate the same point, transcendental judgment expresses itself both materially and formally: as one, it is an objectified state of affairs; as the other, it is the thought or sentence that this state of affairs obtains. Calling the thought or sentence true is redundant, because the judgment that creates it also creates the state of affairs. Notice that we don't need—and aren't offered—a redundancy theory of error. Why? Because transcendental judgment doesn't make errors or the nonevents they signify. It creates empirical thoughts or sentences and, simultaneously, the objects that are their truth conditions.

Why invent this theory? Because it enables Kant to provide for truth as identity.[19] Descartes aspired to clear and distinct ideas, ideas whose truth is guaranteed as they stand before the mind's eye: they are necessary because we see that altering them would generate contradictions. Yet, mind as Descartes describes it is a *witness* to truth, not its *guarantor*, for mind does not create the essences it thinks. Kant's solution confirms the self-sufficiency that he and Descartes claim for mind: there is no shadow in Kant of the prototypic ideas or essences to which thinking must conform. Instead, productive imagination creates objects of whatever sort are required to satisfy mind's reports of them.[20]4 The identity theory is satisfied on both counts: mind inspects both its thoughts or sentences and the empirical objects of which they are true. We have the appearance of a correspondence theory without its extra-mental referents. Kant also takes this further step: he supports the truth claims of individual sentences by embedding them within networks of truths.[21] Coherence, not correspondence, braces the truth claims of single sentences.

Contemporary redundancy theories dispense with Kant's transcendental mechanics. Their purport is, nevertheless, his: true sentences don't need extra-mental referents or the qualification "true." They supply all the intelligibility we do or can have merely by standing before the mind in logical relations that meet the standards of deductive or inductive logic.[22] Here, as above, we have coherence in the service of truth as identity.

G. Knowledge: Intuition and Demonstration, or a Network of Hypotheses?

Descartes described intuition and demonstration as the two modes of knowledge.[22] Intuition—the presentation of inspectable content—is passive. Demonstration is active. It generates necessary conclusions in a skein of logical steps. Proofs sometimes satisfy both demands: necessities are demonstrated (their negations are contradictions), but then all their steps are surveyed and grasped at once.

Intuitionism is proposed as a cure for the belief that thoughts and percepts are signs signifying states of affairs that obtain, principally, in the extra-mental world. Yet, the clarity and distinctness of ideas or percepts are no guarantee that we have identified salient features of their referents. Thoughts that are clear may misrepresent things signified. Clear percepts may misrepresent their causes. There is a gap between representations and their objects, a gap where error breeds. Accordingly, knowledge is not achieved unless two considerations are satisfied: the gap between signs and their objects is eliminated, so that things themselves (not their representations) stand clearly before an inspecting mind. We are to see things as they are, be they Forms, ideas, percepts, sentences, theories, or mind itself.

This objective is critical for Descartes and his idealist successors. Refusing to concede that minds are separated from the objects of knowledge, they say that *esse est percipi*: nothing is known if it is not inscribed in mind, then inspected and seen.[24] Berkeley applied this rule narrowly when he supposed that cherry trees are congeries of sense-data. The implications are all the more dramatic if we apply his principle to conceptual systems. For then the objects of knowledge are constructed by using a theory or interpretation to create an inspectable experience. Kant tells us that a mind armed with a priori categories and empirical schemas differentiates and orders empirical data to create the experience of "objects." This implies both that all the things about us, our bodies included, are mind's own constructions, and that nothing else can be thought or known. For there is no thinkable world apart from experiences that mind synthesizes and objectifies.

This inference is dangerous. It obliterates the difference between literature and science by implying that physics and science fiction are alike: both make certain possibilities thinkable and immediate; neither can say that its "world" extends beyond the experience that mind renders thinkable. Theology, too, contrives a thinkable experience, for even God is inspectable if our experience of him derives from the doctrines used to think about him. Should we believe that truth and fantasy are indistinguishable? This would be true if immediate access to compelling experiences—whether conceptual or empirical—were the measure of truth. But there is a prior question: is anything set before the mind or created, then inspected? Is intuition a power properly claimed for mind?

Plato said that mind intuits the Forms, but this is an extrapolation from things seen or heard. Descartes' leaner theory supposes that nothing is or can be real if it is not inspectable. Kant decried rational intuition, but exploited the sensible intuition of "objects" (including empirical particulars and a priori, geometrical constructions) that mind schematizes and sets before itself. Do any of these thinkers confirm that mind has unmediated—intuitive—access to the matters allegedly inspected? Or is each of them riding a metaphor, extrapolating from the immediacy of things seen or heard to the claim that knowledge is achieved when intelligible phenomena—ideas, sentences, or theories—are set before the mind's eye?

The houses and trees beyond my window stand vividly before me. I seem to see them—without mediation—as they are. But nothing is set before me and inspected if my brain creates perceptual arrays from its sensory inputs. For then, every "intuited" content is evidence of the brain's hierarchical organization: one set of neurons constructs a pattern, another reads it. Like good tailoring, the work is disguised. We notice the apparent stability of the arrays constructed, but not the orders of activity or the ongoing construction. The reading may be slower than the constructing, so that we always seem to inspect a finished array. But all of this is physical and mechanical. Intuition—unmediated inspection of content thought or perceived—never occurs.

Descartes believed that demonstration is less desirable than intuition, because mind risks error if its assumptions are not known intuitively, or if the sequence of steps is not grasped at once. Demonstration nevertheless survives as an autonomous method for insuring truth and knowledge when philosophers lose conviction that we may inspect the Forms, essences, or whatever contents or objects are deemed appropriate to knowledge. Aristotle argued that syllogisms are the appropriate form of expression for the sciences.[25] Descartes agreed. His *Rules* were a principal inspiration for the belief—common from the 1930s to the 1960s—that sciences should be reformulated as deductive systems. Theoretical statements were to serve as axioms; observation sentences would be lowest-order, deductive consequences.[26] There is a reasonable motive for favoring this simplifying, canonical form: we want to digest our knowledge claims, determining their relations, eliminating repetitions and inconsistencies. Confirming what we have, we know better what more to seek. Does it follow that thought's format—the order and paraphernalia of demonstration—is relevant to the structure of the extra-mental world? The cautious answer is that we don't assume it if we believe that thoughts and sentences represent states of affairs whose existence and character are independent of the ways we think of them. We organize thoughts and sentences deductively in order to diagnose the state of our knowledge, not because deductive form is essential to the things represented.

Suppose, however, that we deny the existence of anything apart from our minds: we say that intelligibility lies only within mind, especially in the logical order of its thoughts or sentences. Form, not content, is the principal object of knowledge: formal truth is prior to the empirical interpretation of a theory's sentences. Such truths apply to the "world" only as we establish that their empirical interpretations are satisfied by—apply to—actual states of affairs. But this is no concession to an extra-mental reality if we believe, with Descartes and Kant, that empirical data acquire their character and relations from mind's ways of construing them. This implies that a formalized theory can be made applicable to the "world" merely by prescribing the character and relations of its empirical data. Mind's self-sufficiency empowers it to construe empirical data in ways that confirm its theories.

Here, as above, we risk conflating fantasy with empirical testability, reality, and truth. Not every theory is viable: some theories—those embodying contradictions—are not. Kantians persist: an attentive mind should prove its self-sufficiency by defending every consistent theory against disconfirming evidence. For interpretations test the ingenuity of productive imagination. Revise a theory confounded by evidence. Differentiate and organize the data in ways more congenial to it. Imagination (and rhetoric)—not an alien, extra-mental reality—is the measure of all that is or can be. This bias remains when deductive systems are replaced by Quine's fields of interanimating sentences. They erode the sharp distinction between logical form and empirical meaning, but this is secondary to the claim that intelligibility lies altogether within conceptual systems, with none left over for an extra-linguistic world. Indeed, Quine's "ontological relativity" is justified by the diversity of ways in which sentences may be organized. Different arrangements exhibit alternate forms of intelligibility. Each posits—by way of existential quantifiers—a different complex of existents.

The contrary persuasion is experimental. It emphasizes that a theory's logical form has pragmatic value only. Concision and order make perspicuous what we know or believe, but we don't construe a theory's grammatical form as the deep structure of Being: the structure of the physical world is spatiotemporal and causal, not inductive or deductive. Equally, we emphasize that material truth claims are hypotheses, not axioms or theorems. The first hypotheses are perceptual judgments: we say that a datum is red, or we elide the datum with its cause, saying that this is an apple. Both inferences are hypotheses, and both may be mistaken. The second inference—from the look of things to apples—is especially critical for claims about the material world. We surmise that the constituents, causes, or conditions of sensory data have the character specified by our hypothesis. There should be evidence of these factors if our surmise is right. We confirm or falsify it by testing—looking—for the empirical difference that would obtain if the hypothesis were true. The array of confirmed hypotheses represents the world as we know it, sometimes with depth, often superficially. It is heterogeneous and unevenly integrated—some hypotheses-from practical life, some from science—and much less disciplined than Quine suggests.[27]

Confirmation implies that there is significant convergence between hypotheses and the character and order of things they represent. Either may be richer than the other, but there is a margin of useful overlap when the organized differences signified in thought correlate with a matrix of organized differences in the extra-linguistic world. This inference is supported by the success of our repeated forays: actions directed by maps and plans are often effective. Still, this "merely" pragmatic criterion is scorned by thinkers who disdain hypotheses as merely likely. Only the certainty guaranteed by direct inspection or demonstration appeases them.

Would their point be made were we to formulate a comprehensive scientific theory unified by its deductive form, a theory so powerful that one could use it to predict every detail of nature, including its experiential effects in us? This, no more than less successful formalizations, proves that deductive form is essential to either the intelligibility of the world or to the truth of our hypotheses about it. Why? Because a unified theory would be evidence that our conceptual practices are effective (they produce accurate representations), not that nature itself has a structure isomorphic with, or similar to, the form of the theory. Accountants accurately register a company's assets and liabilities. No one confuses double-entry bookkeeping with the productive relations of workers, suppliers, and clients.

Cartesians, like accountants, are conservative. They would have the cogito control the thinkable world merely by ordering or analyzing its thoughts and percepts, or by constructing its experience. This is a story challenged, especially, by philosophers of biology. They emphasize that thought is critical for survival where stability is laced with chance and change: "The hazardous quality of the world can be inferred from the existence of thought, because dealing with hazard is thought's *raison d'être.*"[28] The cogito's demise leaves us riding the waves, with thought as rudder and compass. Making and testing hypotheses, not intuition or deduction, is thought's principal activity.[29]

H. Does Mind Prescribe or Investigate the Features of Things?

Two sections above—B. Experience, and G. Knowledge—illustrate the difference between two styles of thought: prescription and investigation. Prescription lays down the conceptual network within which the world and questions about it are experienced, formulated, and answered. Every feature of the world would look triangular, never oblong or round, if mind were to project a grid of triangles on everything seen. Investigation is less imperious: we inquire, rather than prescribe, by using empirical evidence to test hypotheses. Plato, Descartes, and Kant argued that mind imposes conditions for the intelligibility of all that is thinkable or experienced, hence for all that is or can be thought to exist. Aristotle, Locke, and Peirce reverse the order of priority: the extra-mental world is intelligible in itself; we struggle to know it. Some of the world's features may exceed our understanding: we don't know how to extrapolate to them, given our linguistic and conceptual resources. But this is a variable limit to understanding, not a permanent logical barrier. We exceed the limit when musicians invent new scales, or mathematicians invent procedures or notations that open new domains of intelligibility. The contrary belief—that thought prescribes the limits of all that is or can be—puts stipulation where only hypothesis should go.

Prescriptivist claims are a fixture in contemporary philosophy. Could there be a private language, meaning a language that is understood by no one but the person using it? No, said Wittgenstein: I can only speak meaningfully to myself if my speech satisfies grammatical rules. (Speech is nonsense if it satisfies no grammar.) But I don't invent and apply these rules for my private use, because (among other reasons) I can't trust my fallible memory to interpret the rules consistently each time I apply them. I avert inconsistency by using the grammatical rules that others use, allowing them to correct my grammatical lapses. But this defeats my project: a language using a public grammar isn't private. Others, too, can learn and use it.[30]

This is an odd defense of prescriptivist thinking. It invokes a contingency—speakers' memories may fail—to disqualify the possibility of private languages, though Wittgenstein makes a strong, a priori claim about the conditions for meaningful linguistic usage: it is contradictory to suppose that a language is intelligible in the absence of a public grammar, because there is no reliable way to distinguish within a private language between correct and incorrect utterances. Nothing so rigorous is justified by Wittgenstein's argument: private languages fail, he says, because their inventors defer to speakers whose memory of grammar is better than their own. Speakers who know themselves to have faultless memories (they never lose things, no one corrects their public speech) survive the objection. Their memories are accurate here as elsewhere.

Descartes and Kant are better examples of prescriptivist practice, because their justifications for it do not invoke contingencies. Descartes sides with Plato: experience presupposes mind's apprehension of innate ideas that differentiate and organize sensory data; mind knows by inspecting the matters set clearly and distinctly before it. Citing its ideas, it prescribes the limits of all that is or can be. These regulative claims are embellished by Kant: experience presupposes the forms of intuition—space and time—so every event must have antecedents and successors. Knowledge is an "objective perception." A phenomenon is grasped intuitively when thought under a "pure" concept—the image of a geometrical figure constructed a priori—or an empirical schema gives determinate expression to the Categories when an empirical object (this dog, that cat) is schematized. Thought is prescriptive in both cases, for nothing can be thought or known unless our conception of it exhibits the form imposed by mind's a priori determinations.[31]

Prescriptivism thrives wherever conceptual analysts consider the conditions for a phenomenon: could it be as it is in the absence of this or that condition? Analysis advances as necessary conditions are identified, though this procedure risks circularity. Is freedom every person's inalienable right? Only if we stipulate that personhood is inconceivable in the absence of liberty. Or we say, as above, that private languages are impossible, because their grammars would necessarily be public. Is this so? Imagine that a cryptographer's machine generates the syntax and symbols of a code. The inventor memorizes the symbols, adding translation rules that join coded expressions to the phenomena they signify. Delighted by his new language, he uses it to write numerous books and poems, but then dies before translating them into English. This outcome is on all fours with the untranslated languages of extinct tribes, except that this one was invented and used by a single speaker-writer. What precludes it? Prescriptivists may object that the language is solitary, rather than irremediably private: it could have been taught to other speaker-writers. This is true but incidental, for the cryptographer has learned and used the language without needing public rules or other speakers to testify that his memory is accurate. It is also incidental that the inventor of this language was already fluent in a natural language. For we can extend this thought experiment. Let the cryptography machine do all the work. It spins a code, adds semantic rules, then writes books in its new language. Suppose, too, that the code is unbreakable, implying that the new language is irreparably private. Notice that this example is suggested by empirical inquiry, not by a priori prescription: machines do invent codes.

What is valid in the philosophic analyses that identify conditions for the phenomena discussed? Conceptual analysts often tell us that an activity or phenomenon must, or cannot, be as described, on pain of contradiction or incoherence. Only three of these logical gates are legitimate:

(i) Contradictions cannot obtain.

(ii) (a) Violations of natural laws cannot obtain in our world, though they may occur in possible worlds where natural laws are different: the inverse square law—force declines in proportion to the square of the distance between bodies—is one factor constraining motion in our world; but there may be worlds where the analogous constraint is an inverse cube law. (b) Natural laws lay down necessary material conditions for the phenomena occurring here. Alleged phenomena may have no place in our world, because our characterizations of them ignore these conditions. There is, for example, no thinking without brains or machines that think, so dualism is incoherent for two reasons. It describes mind as activity, never providing for the material character of the agent who thinks. And it postulates mind-body interaction without specifying the mediating link or ground between mind and body (discounting the pineal gland). These objections to dualism are benignly prescriptive. Practical experience and scientific experiment have taught us that there is no activity without an agent, and no interaction without mutual accessibility.

(iii) We sometimes discover natural features that are categorial and inviolable. So, motion is a trajectory through space and over time: it presupposes space and time, or spacetime. This is a discovery, not a prescription.

Compare the "inscrutability of reference."[32] Reference, using words or gestures, is a commonplace of daily life. Each of us refers successfully dozens of times a day. "Allez à la maison," he says to you; "Go home," he tells me; and we go our separate ways. How should we respond when a theory of language affirms that reference is opaque across languages, because each differentiates and organizes its "world" comprehensively but differently. Ignoring the empirical and practical bases for meaning and reference common to many or all natural languages (context and ostensive meaning, for example), Quine affirms that reference is fixed by considerations internal to each language, including quantifiers (*there is*, *some*, and *every*, for example), and semantic rules for combining words. So, rules for using *home* or *maison* with other words differ from English to French. One can't select a sentence in each, saying that they signify the same state of affairs, because quantifiers in the sentences create—"objectify"—distinct ontological domains. Suppose we test this claim by altering the example: we live together. Hearing the words in our respective languages, we go to our shared home. Should we infer that apparently successful, cross-linguistic references have failed, or that reference is misrepresented for two reasons: first, because the context and aim of speech are ignored; second, because Quine cannot acknowledge or explain the common references regularly made by people speaking different languages? Inscrutability of reference is prescribed, given that languages objectify different worlds. Are these assumptions sound? Isn't it likely that meaning and reference have considerable overlap among languages, given that people of every culture solve common problems in similar ways?

What is the proper standpoint from which to adjudicate these questions? Do we retreat from the natural language where life is transacted into a higher-order interpretive language, the better to emphasize the indeterminacy of translation? Or do we settle questions about reference by looking to see what people do?

I. Space and Time: Forms of Intuition or Spacetime?

Are space and time the forms of sensibility—"forms of intuition"[33]—or the media within which nature, mind included, is arrayed?

Should we speak of space and time, or of spacetime? We often say that space and time are separable, because sight and sound are different: we see complexity spread before us, but hear it sequentially. Kant, after hints from Descartes and Leibniz, converted this distinction into an ontological doctrine: time was described as the form of internal intuition, space as the form of external sense. Time has priority, because the river of consciousness includes sequenced words or ideas, feelings, and spatialized percepts. This is the stream whose contents or direction are altered by thought or desire.

The experience of time is incidental to the static form of buildings; space is incidental to melody. We nevertheless deny the separability of space and time, because motion—change of spatial position over time—presupposes both. Clumsy technology once precluded experiments to test the hypothesis that our perception of space and time has an exhaustively physical—neural—basis; but techniques are less intrusive now, so drugs and electrical probes are safely used to locates the brain centers and circuitry engaged by particular mental activities. Are the experiences of space and time—the spread of the sky, the string of words heard as speech—effects of one neural network, or of separate networks, one or more for each effect? Neither answer is an argument for the separability of space and time: the movement of electrical signals through neural systems—one or many— requires both.

Mind's physical character alters the agenda for discussions of space and time. Before, we supposed that they exhibit their character as we experience them. Now, things of every sort are distinguished from their phenomenal representations, so information about each requires inferences from sensory data to their conditions. This is a familiar pattern. Having realized that color and sound are effects in us, not the actual properties of things perceived, we infer from the data to causes that are within or outside us. The difference between spacetime and our experience of space and time requires equivalent inferences. Can we explain the phenomenal character of space and time by citing the body's design and materials? Can we test hypotheses about the extramental character of spacetime by citing stable features of experience? Given the likelihood of competing hypotheses (that spacetime is continuous or discrete, for example), what considerations—conceptual or empirical—dispose us to one or the other?

*J. Freestanding Mind, or an Array of
Causally-related Bodies or Systems?*

Doubts about the status of space and time express our uncertainty about the context of self-knowledge, perception, practical life, and inquiry. Are space and time the forms of sensibility for a reality presented wihin awareness? Or is mind the activity of bodies that engage other things, be they aggregated atoms (other bodies) or nested and overlapping systems? Decide the status of space and time, and context is implied: mind is self-sufficient, capable only of thinking itself and its qualifications; or we humans are social animals living among other things in spacetime. Our views about prudence and ethics—is morality egoistic or socially constrained?—follow appropriately.

It may seem that no one would elect self-sufficient mind as the entire context of life and awareness. Yet, this is the more or less explicit choice of the many Cartesians trapped within one or another pair of mutually-conditioning orders (consciousness and self-consciousness or object-language and meta-language, for example). The quotation from Husserl closing chapter three and the thinkers discussed in chapter four affirm the project of a priori reflection: they would have us rise to the higher order of thought or language where mind discerns or stipulates the ideas or rules used to clarify or schematize the materials of the lower order. Ideas and rules are the only intelligibles. There are no domains, but the two orders—consciousness and self-consciousness— where they are applied or inspected. For like knows like: the relation of the two orders implies the complementarity of differentiation and order on the one side, the projecting and recognizing of intelligibility on the other. The extra-mental or extra-linguistic world falls away. Everything is text or commentary. Mind's only context is itself.

This posture tweaks credibility. It is harder to sustain if thinking, perceiving bodies are everywhere engaged by their social, physical circumstances.

K. Freedom or Determinism?

Cartesian minds are free, because certainty about one's existence coupled to doubt about the existence of other things implies that one is free of their constraint. They may not exist; or they do, but mind is categorially different from bodies and independent of other minds, if any there be. Mind's freedom is a touchstone for many of Descartes' successors. Kant secures it by supposing that mind is transcendental: its every act is free, because spontaneous, never caused.[34] Mill is less speculative, more phlegmatic. There are, he says, three regions of liberty: thought and conscience, tastes and pursuits, and the liberty to unite with other people for shared aims.[35] Each region is a domain wherein no choice is legitimate if it does not express mind's unforced assent. This autonomy, founded in the difference of mind and body and the mutual independence of minds, implies our exemption from any relationship we renounce. More, it implies a dose of contingency in relationships we choose. Listening to the offers and promises made us (taking care not to ask about the unthinkable material or spiritual conditions for these communications), we choose some or none, never yielding the autonomy we may reclaim at any moment. Freedom *from* is complete because intrinsic to mind's self-sufficiency; freedom *to* is limited only by our understanding and initiative, or (acknowledging other thinkers) by the costs of broken contracts.

The autonomy that Kant and Mill ascribe to us mixes Luther with Descartes, moral soul with self-sufficient mind. This is a precious inheritance, one turned problematic when mind's physical character locates us inextricably within the network of physical systems and causal relations. We swim in a sea where many things affect us, with only this to mitigate our relations: each of us is a module, a structural and functional unit established by the reciprocal causal relations of its parts.[36] A module's internal relations are a barrier to some influences and a filter for others. Information doesn't affect me until I interpret it; your memories cycle through you, not me. What are freedom from and freedom to in these circumstances? Freedom from others is sometimes the luck of having remote—richly mediated—causal relations to them. Or freedom from others derives from the modularity that attenuates their effects. Freedom to act expresses the effective organization of a system that initiates and sustains activity in the midst of its relations to other things. You make and enact a plan that suits you; but the context, strategy, and details of your plan engage you with associates, resources, and obstacles. Your exemption from them is never more than relative. Someone who fails to achieve the resolution and skill that come with a certain education, opportunity, and respect may be incapable of launching or sustaining any but the most trivial initiatives, either with others or alone. Overwhelmed and reactive, he or she is barely or never free.

Cartesians have a reciprocal fear. Prizing freedom and creativity, they worry that materialism implies the reducibility of all complex phenomena to the activity of neurons or atoms, and that technicians who manipulate these elementary processes (molecular biologists and pharmacologists, for example) will control all thought and feeling. This implies that modularity is no defense of our Enlightenment ideals, including the freedom and creativity that are the core of our self-regard. Vanquish them—as materialism threatens—and we humans are at risk of becoming captive machinery: engineers may organize us for efficiency when they have decided the work we shall do and the beneficiaries of our doing it.

We protect ourselves by resisting those who manipulate us for their purposes. And we take advantage of the modularity of body and its parts, especially the brain. Freedom is not guaranteed—there is no transcendental barrier to interference—when mind is the activity of body. But threats to freedom are reduced, because control of what I do lies principally within me (*soft* determinism), and because I have learned to differentiate myself from the several, sometimes competing systems in which I participate. This is the power to choose one's roles, the autonomy acquired as one is socialized. I express it each time I resist a demand that threatens or offends me.

L. Control or Accommodation?

Descartes cleared a space wherein thought and will have total control. For nothing can intrude on them if a mind qualified by its thoughts and perceptions is the only thing that exists. Everything set before the mind is seen. Nothing is alien or remote. Mind alone decides what to think about, and what to think of it. Descartes' truth test— clarity and distinctness—is a constraint (no idea lacking them can be true), but the cogito is otherwise master of all it inspects. Accordingly, mind is two things: the ample space that is everywhere self-transparent and the gatekeeper to existence. This last point assumes that truth is the necessary and sufficient test of existence. a state of affairs obtains if the thought or sentence affirming it is true. Some things pass this test, when mind has evidence sufficient to affirm that they exist. Others are barred, because mind doubts or denies them.[37] Kant adds that mind determines the character of everything thought: its categories and schemas differentiate and organize experience after will and desire decide the schemas to be used to create experience.

Control is easily confused with freedom. Freedom from is exemption from interference. Freedom to is liberty of choice or action. Yet, freedom to act or choose is toothless in the absence of *control*. For control is power over oneself or resources. One may be free from interference, and free to act, but unable to do so because one lacks control of other things or oneself: I may be free to use a piano, but unable to play because I don't know how to coordinate my fingers and hands.

Making music or throwing strikes are two examples of control, but they are incidental to its deeper motive: we value control in proportion to our vulnerability. Are circumstances baffling or dangerous? Descartes and Kant promise total relief, the one as he doubts the existence of everything but mind, the other as he argues that the world we experience is mind's own product. Modern ideas of democracy embody this persuasion: their emphasis on freedom is often the demand that every person have the power to control the conditions of his or her life. We sustain this Cartesian-Kantian aim even as we abjure their claims about mind's autonomy. For the technology that thought creates extends mind's power into nature. We gladly tolerate other things if we can order them as we choose.

Where is the balance between accommodation and control? We are sometimes clumsy, sick, or incompetent. Other people, things, or the weather perpetually confound us. Self-control makes us more efficient, less frustrated, but no one controls his or her circumstances in the comprehensive way implied by Descartes and Kant. Living in the middle of natural things, as one of them, we adapt to circumstances we alter but do not make. Ecology and environmentalism share this perspective with everyone living in a city or puzzled by other people. It may be too late for humans to live unobtrusively, reducing consumption to ecologically viable levels. But we can reduce the ferocity of our industrial profile. we won't flourish if every other thing is eliminated, or bent to our will.

M. *Egoism or Sociality?*

"Common" interest is sometimes read distributively as the self-interest proper to every member of an aggregate: each of us has, for example, a prudent interest in civil order. This way of construing the word is expressly egocentric. Each regards him or herself as an intrinsic good; other things are valued, instrumentally, for their good or bad effects. Robert Nozick was succinct: "There is no *social entity* with a good that undergoes some sacrifice for its own good. There are only individual people, different individual people, with their own individual lives.[38] This claim is inspired, partly, by the cogito: it exists.

Individualism is currently defended in either of two ways. one is the claim that egoism is psychologically honest. The interests of others are incidental or secondary to me; I would do as I please, but for the distorting effects of social pressure and law. The other defense is the evolutionary gloss of this idea: nature rewards self-concern if we perpetuate our kind. These claims are mutually supporting: self-sufficiency and self-love are justified if we prove our worth by surviving to reproduce.

Egoism is nevertheless flawed in a way that is obscured when its evolutionary and Cartesian biases are joined. It assumes that character is loosely joined to its circumstances, including the context of its development. But character has social, not only biological or mentalist, conditions. Distinctive information, attitudes, and skills are learned as a human body moves through increasingly complicated social roles on the way to becoming a person. The responsibilities hereby acquired may over ride personal desires. Egoism turns problematic: does it imply the steady effort to balance self-regard with regard for others? Or is it the pathology of those who are only self-concerned?

Figure, 6.1 illustrates socialization as it applies throughout nature:[40]

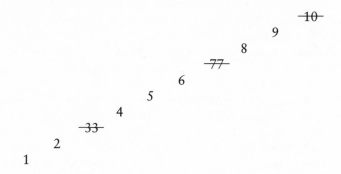

Figure 6.1. Progressions with Termination Points at 3, 7, and 10.

Quarks are not stabilizable apart from atoms, as typically atoms are not stabilized apart from molecules. Molecules are stable systems. They survive as individuals, though their descendingly proper parts (atoms and quarks) usually do not. Animal bodies are the stable final states for a succession of things which are not stabilizable in themselves: namely, cells, tissues, and organs. Each dissolves into its molecular components if the stability of plant or animal bodies is not achieved. Why are bodies stable? Because the complete animal or plant—but not its constituents—can incorporate or obtain energy sufficient to nourish it.

Individualists suppose that personhood is fully explained or anticipated when cells, tissues, and organs have achieved the integrity of bodies. Mental and moral powers develop principally or exclusively, they suppose, from internal formations. Like plants destined to flower if light and water are supplied, bodies achieve thought, a point of view, character, and selfhood when encounters with other things provoke the development of inherent structures and capacities. Socialization provides regimented ways of satisfying a body's established needs and interests, but relations with other people—the context of self-development—add nothing essential to selfhood. Or individualists describe persons as the idealized subjects of moral theories that abstract from our distinctive bodies and circumstances, saying, like Kant, that we are intrinsically free and equal moral beings.

Neither formulation should satisfy us, because persons are more than bodies, souls, or minds, though having a body is a necessary condition for participating in the systems wherein bodies becomes persons: families and friendships, for example. Socialization supplies information, attitudes, and skills appropriate to our roles. These sensitize us to the responsibilies—the duties—that bind us to a system's other members.[41] They also express each person's interests and expectations as he moves among the systems that engage him. Selfhood is the distinctive posture, having information, attitudes, and skills as its content. They, together, promote autonomy, criticism, and choice, as we appraise the systems that engage us. How shall we divide time and labor among them? Do we approve their aims and organization? Are they good for their members? Is this one good for me? Selfhood locates us among our roles, but it is equally a power for disengaging from them. Unable to separate ourselves from all our roles, we do or can decide the time and intensity of our commitment to each particular one.

Socialization is often raw and confrontational, not buffered by distance and abstraction. Psychic depth is created when these engagements waken us to other people and their aims. Individualism describes bare, needy bodies, or self-sufficient minds. Ignoring the feelings and responsibilities that bind us to other people, it is blind to the meanings and intentions that emerge in social roles. These commitments are apparent wherever desires center on the interests of others, not merely our own. Family members, friends, workers, and citizens calibrate their objectives: each person accommodates him or herself to others so that three interests are satisfied: those of the individual, those of the corporate entity—the family or business, for example—and those of the other members. Is this a dream? Not when most of us devote the greater part of every day to the interpersonal reciprocities that sustain valued systems.

Compare Locke and John Stuart Mill. They assume that one enters the social world as a fully formed adult, though socialization begins when babies are handled by doctors, nurses, and mothers. These are first moments of give-and-take, of expectation, satisfaction, or frustration. They are intimations of all that is to come for a child, who will learn to anticipate his responses to others, and theirs to him. What will the child know of him or herself? An accurate list includes the expectations, intentions, rights, and duties that relate him or her to others.

A considerable percentage of people convicted of murder in Britain commit suicide. It is guilt, not prison conditions, that drives them. Having sabotaged their attachments, commitments, and self-esteem, they destroy themselves. Egoism is nevertheless supported by pillars that include Aristotle's notion of primary substance, Luther's moral individualism, Descartes' mentalism, the individualist reading of evolution, and the reactions we feel when thwarted. Frustration enhances the belief that all good sense and intentions lie within me, all else being stupid or perverse.

The once dominant, mentalist tradition neglects social reciprocity, thereby confirming our grievance and rage. For there is no place on Plato's line for social relations. There is no provision within the cogito for the intentions or shared meanings that relate us with other people: Descartes ignored them throughout the *Meditations*. I am, perceive, and understand myself without regard for my relations with others. How could I think of them when mooting their existence is preliminary to discovering my own?

Socialization is a mystery to Cartesians, but a practical necessity for the rest of us. A priori thinking gives us very little leverage as we manage it. Let Kant be our example. No other apriorist has done as much as he to ease social conflict. Yet, the very conditions for a priori reflection thwart its resolution. Suppose that each of us confirms that his or her preferred moral maxim satisfies the categorical imperative: each is universalizable without contradiction. (Every rational agent could apply his or her maxim without creating conditions that would prevent acting in the way it prescribes. Belief is sabotaged, for example, when no one believes, because everyone lies.) Yet, universalizability is not a sufficient test of moral rules, if each person occupying a shared social space wills a maxim that is different from and contrary to the maxim (or maxims) of one or more others. You would have all of us drive on the right; I propose that every one drive on the left. Each maxim satisfies the categorical imperative, though chaos would result if both were applied in the same space.

There is no solution for this conflict in Kant's transcendental psychology or moral theory, because each thinker tests his or her moral maxims without consulting others. Their conflict is not resolvable, unless an authority intervenes to choose one of the otherwise universalizable maxims. The authority might be a prince, though Kant's preferred solution is the well-informed, deliberating public. Its members are autonomous thinkers, each now liberated from its transcendental isolation, but not from its transcendental status: the many transcendental egos must collaborate to make laws for the civil society in which all will acquire their empirical selves.

Social theory would have few modern options if Descartes' egoism and Kant's apriorism were the only foil to Hobbes. All three might agree that sociality requires nothing more than chance encounters stabilized by coercive laws, whether transcendental or conventional.[42] Cartesian-Kantian moral theorists have an alternative, because Hegel—like Leibniz—construed the cogito in neo-Platonic terms. Our finite minds are shards of World-soul and more remotely of God, the Absolute, the One. Far from being atomized, the human social world is the schematized manifold of God's thought. Its rules affiliate or coordinate us, in families, at work, or in states. We identify the conditions for sociality—the rules used to establish or justify social institutions—by rising to the perspective of the Absolute. Inquiries in this mode are a priori interpretations or inferences. Foucault, like Hegel, argues that particular ideas are construction rules for whole epochs.[43] Rawls and Habermas tell us the regulative (Kant would say "transcendental") conditions for morality, sociality, or politics.[44] But two things are confused: are these thinkers describing the practical deliberations of people making hard choices, or is this the a priori reflection that makes social and moral relations abstractly thinkable—rational—and edifying?

Compare their Hegelian view to a different way of investigating sociality. We describe the reciprocal causal relations that create systems, the personal identities thereby generated, and the relations among systems. Systems are simple or complex, stable or ephemeral. Personal identities point in two directions: to an individual's understandings, attitudes, and choices, and to the social contexts where these powers are formed and nuanced. Possible relations among systems include mutual independence, reciprocity, overlap, and nesting.[45] The anomie of a city encourages independence, but some people—friends, for example—are mutually engaged. Coming from different families they exhibit overlap: each is a member of a system in which the other doesn't participate. There is also nesting: the friendship started in a club or a church of which both are members.

Life is conflicted because of the diversity of our circumstances and motives, and because the systems in which we participate often make contrary demands. Self-regulation goes in several directions at once: to self-control as we determine how much time and energy to give to each of the systems that engage us, to the system in which we are reciprocally—skillfully—joined to other members, and to the nested set of publics in which we participate. Each public comprises people who come together to deliberate about the policies, laws, and priorities of their respective system or systems. They may be family members discussing their conflicts or plans, neighbors worried about public safety, or citizens formulating public policy for their state.

Empirical inquiry describes this process of self-regulation. It identifies relevant constraints without prescribing solutions. But practical life requires solutions. Is there a single, comprehensive plan, one that would solve all conflicts once and for all if enacted? This is most unlikely when competing interests and limited resources assure that fairness and mutual respect are ideals, not the institutionalized standards guaranteed by our social arrangements. Compare traffic laws to the hope for peace on Earth. We legislate effectively to achieve the first; we struggle fitfully to sustain the other. Why this difference? Because the complexity of systems—their competition for members and resources—guarantees inequity and conflict. We achieve partial, local successes, not the structural transformation prefigured by universalizing a priori designs. Balancing the contrary interests of conflict resolution, social cohesion, and individual freedom is a perpetual surd. Fairness and mutual esteem are achieved over time, if at all. We sometimes right yesterday's inequity with today's indulgence, but scarce resources, conflict, and complexity extinguish the hope that we may install a system of norms that will institutionalize fairness, forbearance, and mutual esteem.

Individualism buffers our disappointments by arming us with rights. It repeats, for example, that all men are endowed with the rights of life, liberty, and the pursuit of happiness. Someone mistreated is to fight for the recognition of his rights, not for the rights themselves. This is useful rhetoric grounded in practice and law, but not an accurate rendering of the process wherein rights are negotiated, legislated, and acknowledged. Each of us has interests; each of us makes claims. These are pleas for recognition, not inalienable entitlements. Claims become rights when others acquiesce. This may happen informally: I win the right to cross your fields, because I and others have been doing it for years. Other times, there is no right—to property or a passport, for example—unless the acknowledgement is legislated.

It isn't odd that rights—the core of one's moral autonomy and prerogatives—are products of social practice, given that personal autonomy, too, is the effect of our experience in systems. First discovering oneself as an infant amidst a family, each of us separates him or herself from that system in order make friends or go to school: we learn to rank the demands of the systems in which we participate. Autonomy is principally this power to choose our roles in systems, and the time or energy given to each. Why is it paradoxical that we also acquire rights in the systems that engage us—marriages or states, for example?

The rights we acquire are not unencumbered. Elections are sometimes cancelled or delayed; free speech doesn't license seditious speech. These are some limiting effects of complexity and conflict. Deliberation and social regulation are, fortunately, two antidotes for them. Controlling ourselves while investigating the obstacles to our plans, we also regulate the systems that engage us. Individualists—"libertarians," especially—don't like regulation: or they accept the need for self-regulation, but fear coercive, governmental control. The possible expressions of state authority, and the occasions for exercising it are problematic. But there are no apparent alternatives to organization and authority when self-control fails. Traffic laws facilitate movement, partly because they are well-formulated and learned, partly because they are punitive: break the laws, and one is fined or jailed. How could we manage social complexity and conflict without the organizing authority and discipline of systems that include families, schools, and the state? Anarchic alternatives—every man an island, houses in the woods—only beg the question.

Why not surrender the mythology of innate rights and transcendental autonomy to the reality of our social circumstances? They include the systems created by the causal reciprocity of their members, and the social deliberation that makes policy and law. We work to reduce conflict or facilitate cooperation, because we are afflicted or inefficient, not because we observe these failures from the aesthetic distance of the transcendental ego. A priori reflection emphasizes the "logic" of social processes, or the virtues that would crown them. It has little to say about the systems created or abandoned, or the struggles where rights are negotiated. Practical life always seems incidental if thinking is dominated by universal categories, innate entitlements, or clear and distinct ideas.

We humans are unique for being able to think and talk about self-regulation, but not for being self–and socially regulated. Mutual accommodation is common to all or most animals. Ethologists study simpler versions, both to distance themselves from the human systems wherein familiarity distorts understanding, and to identify their essential features. Our similarity to chimpanzees is not surprising. Affinities to chickens are more surprising, but not always less helpful.

N. Human Significance

Descartes' leaner theory makes gods of thinkers. It affirms that I exist each time I think, though nothing else may exist except such things as qualify me, including my activities or states and the ideas or percepts inspected when they stand before me. What is more, I am the Good, for everything else is good or bad only as it affects me. This view of things turns contentious if there are other thinkers who, somehow, challenge me. How they could do that is never explained. For each thinker should be isolated from every other when each exists within the ambit of its own awareness. Being and self-importance should go hand in hand.

Locating mental activity within the body and brain transforms our self-perception. We are natural creatures, complex systems whose internal parts and rhythms are constrained by the same physical laws that operate everywhere in spacetime. Having short life spans, but a distinctive evolutionary history, we are recent additions to the efflux of living systems on Earth. Are we important? Nietzsche didn't always think so:

> Once upon a time, in some out of the way corner of that universe which is dispersed into numberless twinkling solar systems, there was a star upon which clever beasts invented knowing. That was the most arrogant and mendacious minute of "world history, " but nevertheless, it was only a minute. After nature had drawn a few breaths, the star cooled and congealed, and the clever beasts had to die. . . .There were eternities during which it did not exist. And when it is all over with the human intellect, nothing will have happened. For this intellect has no additional mission which would lead it beyond human life. Rather, it is human, and only its possessor and begetter takes it so solemnly—as though the world's axis turned within it. But if we could communicate with the gnat, we would learn that he likewise flies through the air with the same solemnity, that he feels the flying center of the universe within himself. There is nothing so reprehensible and unimportant in nature that it would not immediately swell up like a balloon at the slightest puff of this power of knowing. And

just as every porter wants to have an admirer, so even the proudest of
men, the philosopher, supposes that he sees on all sides the eyes of the
universe telescopically focused upon his action and thought.[46]

This passage needs balance. We are vain and ephemeral; but we do
value one another and ourselves,[47] and we are exalted by some things
we do—in music, law, science, sport, and art.

Are we significant for others? Only as we fill a niche in an ecosys-
tem that supports them, or as we alter or destroy the conditions for
their well-being. Believing that all the Earth is our capital to use as we
please is the fantasy encouraged as much by Descartes as by the Bible—
though we are slower to believe that we can safely multiply without
limit. We know that destabilizing our ecological niche—killing off its
other species—sabotages us. This new humility, however slight its effect
on industrial production or daily life, is testimony that self-perception
has altered. The realism that makes us pragmatic modulates the fantasy
that made us careless.

2. An Altered Focus

What can reflection achieve in the breach where we engage other
things? What part of belief is the effect of action, perception, thought,
or feeling; what part represents the extra-mental things that affect us?
There may not be conclusive answers for every question.

Several of the fourteen topics above are equivocal: they express
the vantage point of self-observing, interpreting mind, prior to being
reformulated to describe how we engage other things. One side emphasizes the world-as-it-looks-to-me; the other infers that all our behaviors
are accommodations to, or products of, our physical context. I have
described these perspectives as contraries, though several are more
complementary than opposed. There is a difference between things as
they look and things as they are; but one is evidence of the other.

Joining the two sides implies many questions. How accurately
does sensory content represent things perceived? What part is remade
to satisfy mind's requirements? Granting the use of language to report
and communicate about extra-mental states of affairs, which of its syntactic or semantic aspects are sensitive, and which are incidental to the
character of the things reported? What part of well-being is the effect of
one's relations with other people and things? How much endures when
relations to them are disrupted? Discovering our materiality doesn't
settle these issues, because mind's bodily origins are consistent with its

being a functional module, one that engages other things on its own terms. We aren't altogether clear about these terms, because *engage* is richly ambiguous. What do other things contribute to our interactions with them? What do we contribute? What part of itself does either communicate to the other?[48]

Abduction supplies good, but tentative, answers. Inferring from sensory data to their causes or constraining laws, we specify possible conditions for the data. These are inferences from smoke to fire, from diminishing gravitational attraction to the inverse square law. We want principled ways of inferring from perceptual data to their causes, ways that save thought from isolation. For Berkeley's dictum—nothing is like an idea but another idea[49]—is unpersuasive: a triangle is like the image of a triangle without itself being an image. We pursue this opportunity by exploiting invariances like those of projective geometry: they abide when a form in three dimensions is projected into two. Searching for structure in the data perceived, we infer to isomorphisms in their causes, however much the look of things differs from the things themselves (the look of a face from the face). Hypotheses are tested when engaging other things generates predicted effects: what looks to be a friend responds to his or her name. Regulative principles are confirmed when, for example, the condition for a coherent narrative is isomorphic with the condition for successive events in nature: every difference is conditioned by a difference in both cases. Not every principle of inquiry or practice has this double role—alphabetizing one's files does not. But significant others do have it: blueprints are spatial, because of the ease with which carpenters and engineers can interpret them when constructing the buildings they prefigure.

We use the leverage supplied by hypotheses, leading principles, maps, and plans, while conceding that engagements with other things are perpetually equivocal. For there is no way to eliminate the gap between them and our perceptions of, or inferences about, them. What is credibly said of the thing perceived? So much to perceptual content, so much to glare and astigmatism. Uncertainty is not reduced by appraising information acquired from one perspective with a standard that expresses the perspective of several or many others: absolute pitch may be construed as evidence of uniformity in a class of perceivers, not as evidence of the pitch perceived. Equally, the ambiguity is not eliminated by the inferences encouraged by projective geometry. Which percepts are to count as accurate before we infer from them to the structure of their causes—sticks looking bent or sticks looking straight?

We nevertheless accept our materiality without becoming solipsists, isolated and skeptical in our skulls. For we map our circumstances, proving the accuracy of our maps by the success of our interventions (making a reservation, then boarding the plane). Nothing eliminates the gap between natural or conventional signs (percepts or words) and the things represented. Error is always possible, though the efficacy of our maps and plans is sound evidence that many of them are good (if partial) representations of things we engage.

This last inference—from hypotheses to things they represent—is sometimes confounded by an anomaly. Some hypotheses are ontologically opaque, though the predictions they make are very accurate. Quantum theory is the principal example.[50] Its characterizations of quanta—electrons and photons, for example—seem paradoxical against the backdrop of classical assumptions about particles. Every particle was thought to be separable from every other, and each was said to have a trajectory that evolves deterministically as it reacts to collisions with others. These are reasonable inferences from observations of middle-sized things, but quantum theory precludes the first, and is sometimes construed in ways that question the second.

The experiment most often cited to illustrate its implications requires that an electron or photon pass through either or both of two holes in an opaque screen. Passing through one when the other is closed, it registers on the screen behind as a dot. Passing many electrons through either hole leaves the pattern of dots appropriate to a particle: the screen behind resembles the bull's-eye of a target, with dots scattered about the center. Repeat the experiment, leaving both holes open, and the pattern of dots is the interference pattern typical of waves.

Quantum theory violates classical assumptions, because wave-particle duality entails that electrons and photons are neither classical waves nor classical particles. This would not be so confusing if we had a well-articulated alternative, one that neatly integrates these apparently contrary features. But this formulation eludes us: we have an effective theory rife with implications that seem anomalous to sensibilities trained by classical theories. Quantum theory is also disruptive, because it implies that a thing's character is a function of its relations to other things: an electron behaves as a particle or wave according as we open one hole or two. We have usually assumed that the existence and character of things are independent of their relations to others. Should we now infer that its character and existence are sometimes (usually?, always?) a consequence of an electron's relations to observers?

These issues justify the impression that we don't understand something fundamental about quanta, despite the predictive power of quantum theory. But this is not my principal concern. For ontological confusion is also apparent in a respect more relevant to the dialectic that opposes experimental and a priori thinking: namely, the role of principles that direct inquiry. Are they procedural only (like the four principles of Descartes' *Discourse on Method*)? Or do such principles direct inquiry effectively, because of being generic truths about natural processes?

One reason for the agitation provoked by quantum theory is its subversion of regulative principles that have long justified inferences from sensory effects to their extra-mental conditions. Nature doesn't make leaps; no action at a distance; every event has a cause; something can't come from nothing: each of these maxims is sometimes disputed, but all are used in practical life and science because they facilitate inquiry in three respects. First, the principles are tacit hypotheses about the character of things. Seeing fire, we infer to smoke because of invoking the hypothesis that every difference is the effect of another, its cause. Second, a principle is regulative, because procedural. Regulative principles are directives: infer the likely cause, given its effect. Third, these are leading principles. They express an orientation and intention: let thought leverage itself in the extra-mental world by identifying possible conditions (whether causes, constituents, or laws) for sensory effects. Inquiry would be paralyzed—we could not escape the isolation of minds turned on themselves—if we could not infer from mental content and activity to the character of the extra-mental things that affect us.

Some physicists report the experimental evidence for quantum theory with a minimum of speculative interpretation.[51] Others construe the theory in ways that sabotage the regulative principles on which inquiry relies:

> Dr. Wheeler refers sometimes to one of the supreme mysteries of nature. That is the ability, according to the quantum mechanic laws that govern subatomic affairs, of a particle like an electron to exist in a murky state of possibility—to be anywhere, everywhere or nowhere at all—until clicked into substantiality by a laboratory detector or an eyeball. Dr. Wheeler suspects that this quantum uncertainty, as it is more commonly known, is the key to understanding why anything exists at all, how something, the universe with its laws, can come from nothing.[52]

This passage is useful for the points it exaggerates. The desire to update our regulative principles is always reasonable. But should we agree— does quantum theory entail—that something comes from nothing, and, by implication, that *esse est percipi*, to be is to be perceived?

Consider the difference between something and nothing. A thing qualifies for existence because of its properties: mass with shape and size, for example. Strip away every property, and nothing remains, nothing exists. Nonbeing is propertyless: hence, it does not—cannot—exist. The trajectory from non-being to being—coming to be—is puzzling, because nonbeing supplies no properties or powers from which the emerging state could derive, hence no properties it inherits or transforms. *Coming-to-be-from-nothing* is, therefore, shorthand for self-creation. A thing that was not (one having no origin in other things) comes to be, because of endowing itself with properties that give it character and existence. Yet no one has supplied a satisfactory explication of self-creation, or a way of averting the implication that self-creation would introduce energy into a world where the quantity of energy is constant because energy is conserved. (We could assume that the accounts balance, because a quantity of energy is annihilated whenever something comes to be; but this reasoning is ad hoc, with nothing in the phenomena to justify it.)

These issues are unresolved, because no one comprehends the slogan that provokes them: we don't understand how the universe can "come from nothing." Indeed, where nothing can come from nonbeing, and one or more things exist, we infer that there was always something. There was never a time when there was nothing, because anything that is or was had an antecedent qualified by its properties as its ground or cause. Some of us resist this vertiginous result by asking and answering a simple question: Why is there something rather than nothing? Because something has come from nothing. Imagination need not reel as we go backwards through the infinitely extended chain of antecedents, for the chain isn't infinite: it stops somewhere, with only nonbeing behind it. This is consequential, as much for quantum theory as for theology. For suppose that we shrink the series of changes as being emerges and evolves. Grant that being once ensued from nonbeing, and we concede that this could happen everywhere and always. Why couldn't electrons pass in and out of being, like cell phones passing in and out of tunnels. Is it merely that contact is lost when you don't hear your caller? No, he or she has, momentarily, ceased to be.

Self-creation is a possible regulative principle, but one that makes inquiry unnecessary. Seeing a friend, I move toward him or her. But should I? Couldn't this be a self-generated memory or delusion? Why act on any datum or explain it with a hypothesis, if explanation is obviated because data are self-creating: they aren't construed as evidence of their conditions, because they have no conditions. Spontaneous creation might be an odd effect occurring only among very small things, but for the exception that the universe, too, is alleged to have come from nothing. Inquirers might discount phenomena at the extremes when explaining middle-sized effects—rain on a window, for example.

But why look for antecedents at any scale? Why not suspect with Hume that there is no reason in nature or metaphysics why any phenomenon need have a cause? We are back in the world of Kant's or Fichte's transcendental ego. It never infers from data to their extra-mental conditions. It doesn't need to, because all experience is created, spontaneously, from itself.

How do we defend so fundamental a principle as sufficient reason when theorists speak blithely of quanta that come in and out of being, like flickering lights? We shift in our seats, not knowing what to say. Afraid of the dogmatism that distinguishes a priori thinking, we don't say what we believe: that sufficient reason seems unexceptionable, because its alternatives—something from nothing or self-creation (two versions of the same principle)—are rhetorical phrases without a plausible logic to explicate and justify them.

Hume replies that the principle of sufficient reason is a habit—or "custom"—without foundation in things perceived: "The true state of the question is, whether every object, which begins to exist, must owe its existence to a cause; and this I assert neither to be intuitively nor demonstratively certain."[53] And again: "We can never demonstrate the necessity of a cause to every new existence, or new modification of existence, without showing the impossibility there is, that any thing can ever begin to exist without some productive principle."[54] Hume comes to this conclusion after supposing that reality reduces to the flux of distinguishable and separable impressions and ideas. He adds that existence is only the vivacity of our impressions, and that there is no contradiction in thinking that an effect (vividly conceived) may exist—because imagined—without its cause.

It isn't unreasonable to say that any two ideas may be coupled, short of contradiction. It doesn't follow that any two moments from disparate physical processes may also be joined. There is no superconductivity at room temperature, not because joining the two notions is contradictory, but rather because the energy transfer appropriate to one is absent in the other. The principle of noncontradiction applies in our world as in every other, but this logical principle is not—contrary to the implication of Hume's argument—the single physical law in our world. The rules of a game are definitive within it, though they don't apply to other games. Equally, laws that apply without exception in our world—the law or laws of motion, for example—don't obtain in other possible worlds. These additional laws preclude the many combinations that satisfy Hume's single principle.

Notice that our world's laws of motion, $E = mc^2$ or $F = ma$, satisfy the principle of sufficient reason: the values of force and energy (F and E) are functions of the values of the other variables. Notice, too, that the energy powering change in our world is known by its effects, not in itself. There are no impressions of energy, obliging Hume to say that it doesn't exist. But physics says it does exist, implying that Hume's theory of causality is mistaken. Existence swells beyond the realm of associated or distinguished ideas to the limits of spacetime. Humeans don't believe that these considerations diminish their notion of cause and effect. It shouldn't matter to Hume's arguments that impressions are presented for inspection, or construed as the effects of external causes: either way, we may distinguish and separate them. But there is a significant difference. The contiguities that Hume would have us perceive and analyze are relations between or among impressions or ideas, not the correlations of intrapsychic effects with extra-mental causes. We often perceive the effects of things in the absence of the things themselves: we dream or remember them. But could we do either if no percept were ever the effect of an extra-mental cause? Yes, we could: every percept might be self-caused, coming from nothing. Or, as we could describe it, each is imagined.

The implications for practical life would be momentous, were this true. Abductive inferences from effects to inferred causes—the face that causes the look of that face—would be discouraged, because they promote the delusion that self-caused percepts have causes distinct from themselves. Communication and cooperation—all efficacy—should stop. It doesn't, because the terms of discussion have changed. Hume is a Cartesian who ignores mind's structure and context in favor of its content. His argument against universal causality is, among other things, a question-begging defense of the isolation and self-sufficiency that Descartes claimed for mind. We are to believe that mind is not the effect of other things: it would exist even if they did not. This, the myth of mind's self-sufficiency, dies with confirmation that mind is the activity of body.

Hume applied his principle to ideas and impressions, not to processes powered by energy transfer. Yet, separable if distinguishable remains the decisive assumption when unobserved particles are said to be "anywhere, everywhere, or nowhere." It would have us distinguish particles observed from their status when unobserved, thereby implying that phenomena observed are decoupled from their dynamic conditions. But nothing in physics justifies saying that an arbitrarily chosen moment in a dynamic trajectory is separable (not merely distinguishable) from the others. The Schrödinger equation doesn't sanction this inference: it represents the evolving probabilities that a particle has one or another position or momentum, never implying special status for the moment when a particle is observed. Imagine converging trajectories before cars or particles collide. Are they incidental to the result?

The status of unobserved particles is uncertain in two respects. Uncontroversially, they may have any of the positions to which the Schrödinger equation assigns a probability. More problematically, there are several philosophic views about a particle's status prior to the observation that records its position at an instant (as when it leaves a dot on the screen behind a hole). One view is that there are as many worlds as there are probabilities constitutive of the wave function.[55] A complementary suggestion avers that each of these possible worlds is given life by the mind that perceives it. (Whether each mind thinks the probability function, or perceives the particle, is obscure.[56]) Or we discount these "realistic" views, saying that particles are only virtual until their effects are perceived. The second and third of these claims imply the same regulative principle. Both affirm that particles exist only when perceived. One postulates an array of minds, each observing a world in which a particle has one of the positions or momenta prefigured in the wave function; the other denies that particles exist until perceived by an observer in this world.

Both proposals invoke Berkeley's *esse est percipi*. This, too, is a regulative principle, and it—like the principle that something comes from nothing—devastates abductive explanations by entailing that there are no extra-mental objects for mental intentions, and no extra-mental conditions for sensory data. Mind reclaims its place at the center of things; awareness is the measure of all that is or can be. Abduction is the rational delusion of Kant's transcendental dialectic.[57]

It would be odd and inexplicable if practical life were to require leading principles that violate the principles of our best science. We expect to intervene in the world around us, doing such things as create effects we favor. But we are deceived if something can come from nothing, or if *esse est percipi*. For these principles entail that there is nothing to engage, nothing to do. All the apparent evidence of our successes and failures is a conceit: we only imagine that we affect or are affected by things in the extra-mental world. Passive to the stream of impressions and ideas—a lifetime at the movies—we can only remark similarities and differences in data that appear, self-created, before us. We do make mistakes—error and frustration are commonplace—but these interruptions are better described as the surprise we feel when the conscious flow deviates unexpectedly.

Are we obliged to misdescribe practical life in order to defend the regulative principles commended by some interpreters of quantum theory? There are alternatives. One avers that practical life effectively exploits the principle of sufficient reason, though deep science has no use for it. This too is problematic. How could practical life deviate from experimental science in this schizoid way, when both the plans of one and the hypotheses of the other are tested by engaging other things? Hence, this third option: wanting to avert having to say that practical life and science use different regulative principles, we look for sobriety in the interpretations of quantum theory. Does the theory require that we dispense with the principle of sufficient reason? Or is this is an exaggerated reaction to the anomalies generated when this theory's claims jar our classical sensibilities?

We expect that practice will defer to science. How could petty human interests dictate to inquiries that have all of nature for their domain? Accept that something may come from nothing, and that things exist only as perceived, then recast practical life in Humean terms. But this alternative isn't viable, because practical life is inflexible. We can't live without engaging other people and things. Perceptual data are the effects of these interactions, and the stable ground for inferences that our hypotheses and plans are accurate and effective, or not. Science, too, is more than the catalogue of sensory data organized by its theories: we discover the duality of particles and waves by opening and closing holes in a screen. The sharp point of our third alterative is here. The two-hole experiment is puzzling, because we suppose that the difference between the patterns created when an electron passes through two holes or one is caused, respectively, by a particle and a wave. Is quantum theory committed to saying, additionally, that something comes from nothing, and that *esse est percipi*? Or are these the careless glosses of interpreters who don't realize the implications of abandoning sufficient reason for their slogans?

Perhaps this use of Berkeley's dictum expresses our anxious recognition that our understanding of photons and electrons depends on the mathematically formulated theories that represent them. Wanting empirical evidence for such theories, we don't trust their factual import beyond the data perceived. Hence these questions: How should theorists distinguish a theory's factual import from the implications of its mathematical formalism? How are they to avoid the temptation to draw paradoxical inferences about the character of particles, because of supposing that an empirically confirmed theory represents them comprehensively? Should we believe, for example, that particles are only virtual, with neither a specific character nor a position, until they are observed? Behaviorists describe the brain as a black box: it could be empty. Physicists sometimes regard individual particles similarly when they are yet to be observed. Concluding that an electron is "anywhere, everywhere, or nowhere" expresses this point of view. But this is a methodological, not an ontological, posture, one we may describe as *operational nonbeing*: caring only that particles (or the universe) be seen when observed, we are casual or careless about things that are unobserved: they may lapse between observations. The status of unobserved particles is nevertheless equivalent, in principle, to that of larger things that are unobserved, including the back of the Moon or one's own head.

Which is more likely: paradoxes in nature, or those created when we think about it (Zeno's paradoxes, for example)? One suspects that nature is rather simple, though successively layered combinations of things create a mosaic that seems deeply complex. Clarity comes in three steps.

(i) We formulate and compare alternative ways of describing the same states of affairs, thereby distinguishing theories from things they represent. This is helpful, for example, when we undo the tangle of complexities that a theory introduces. So, quantum theory is statistical, though the indeterminacies this introduces have nothing to do with the indeterminacy that Heisenberg described (the inability to determine the position and momentum of a particle concurrently). Does the theory's statistical character entail that information is lost when the theory cannot specify the state of individual particles? Does the theory cover its traces, insisting that nature is inherently statistical merely because quantum theory has this structure? The history of science makes us suspicious of theories defended this way. Action at a distance was decreed by Newtonian theory, however paradoxical it seemed, until Maxwell's and Einstein's field theories established that this structural feature of Newton's theory need not be ascribed to nature. It is premature to insist that there can never be a theory that describes individual particles, one that is not inherently statistical.

(ii) We clarify the features and assumptions of the mathematical theory used to represent the phenomena at issue. Do we construe some term of the notation, for example, as the sign of a corresponding feature in nature? Is the wave function a natural phenomenon merely because the Schrodinger equation contains the psi-function?[58]

(iii) We fold apparently disparate theories into a single one.

There are comparable steps when we hear witnesses report an accident. We listen to their testimony, trying to distinguish the events themselves from the perspectives that color each report. An expert witness distinguishes his procedures from the claims they justify. One side or the other supplies the context that eliminates ambiguity and conflict. This result is harder to achieve when phenomena are not directly observable, or when hypotheses about them express complex mathematical notions. Still, the task is the same: infer from hypotheses to the states of affairs signified. Some crimes aren't solved, because we can't decide among competing explanations. Good theories may also confound us: successful at predicting effects, they remain ontologically opaque.[59]

Someone baffled by theory may prefer the direct inspection—the rational intuition—of things conceived. Why not inspect and describe the nature of particles? This is the fantasy punctured forever, if mind is the activity of body. Natural and conventional signs—perception and thought or language—are the only access we have to other things. They aren't always accurate or adequate. They are never transparent.

Chapter Seven

Ideas to Reformulate and Save

Descartes' reading of Plato is vastly influential in culture at large, not only in philosophy. He encouraged mathematical physics when Aristotle's qualitative science of substantial forms was still dominant. He helped launch the individualism that reshaped political and social life. He explored the self-reflection that eventuated in Freudian practice. Descartes' characterization of mind—emphasizing thought and will—was the point of reference for subsequent descriptions of God. His *Meditations* was a paradigm for confessional, autobiographical literature. Some of Descartes' predecessors—Augustine, especially—anticipated his style. But he, more than they, focused our self-understanding and cultural practices in ways that are sure to be affected by the cogito's demise. Purging the excesses, we should defend the benefits: refuting Cartesian mentalism shouldn't be the excuse for annulling his every effect. Here are four rubrics considered above, all of them restated in ways appropriate to the discovery that mind is the activity of body.

1. Intelligibility: Are Thought and Language Autonomous?

Descartes' leaner theory and Kant's first Critique argue that the intelligibility of thought and experience is founded in mind's ideas or rules: they exhibit or create mind's thinkable content. The order of priority is reversed if mind is the activity of vulnerable, active bodies, for then hypotheses of all sorts—including theories, maps, and plans—are useless if they don't signify differences and relations in the extramental world.

How are natural signs (percepts) and conventional signs (words) used to represent differences and relations in other things? We resist this question if we believe that intelligibility is restricted to mind and its products. For mind's role as creator of order is everywhere familiar: in thought, language, music, science, and law. Carry on listing achievements like these, and we convince ourselves that every difference in things is the effect of rules used to organize experience or practice. We say that the world of common experience is created by the steady application of the rules that make it conceivable.[1] We add that everything extra-mental is noumenal and unthinkable.

This attitude cannot stand if humans are material agents living in the midst of nature. For now, mind is obliged to represent differences and relations it has not made or discovered within itself. Survival requires, and practical life confirms, that nature is intelligible, because of its properties, relations, and immanent constraints—its laws—and not because mind has made it thinkable. Are its differences and relations nevertheless inaccessible to understanding, because independent of it? No, mind tracks them in itself and other things, because of having two critical powers. The natural structure of eye and brain maps differences and order in things perceived; the conventional signs of language represent matters perceived or thought. Things perceived are likely the first ones described; but thought vastly extends the array of properties and relations signified—kinship relations, for example. Still, the two orders—perception and thought or language, and things perceived or thought—are not isomorphic. Nothing in the extra-mental world corresponds to many differences in our representations: font, for example. Nor do things labeled capriciously—your star, my star—acquire the relations implied by the labels. Conversely, many differences and relations in the world escape notice, some because of their scale and remoteness, others because mapping them requires styles of representation or notation that are currently beyone us. Successful accommodations to the world—behaviors directed by maps and plans—are evidence that some of the rest is well represented and known.

Engineering isn't fiction: we know where we are, and prove it by the interventions we make. Theory and analysis are its complement. Properties that differentiate things from one another turn out to be variants of common properties; or some properties emerge when others, more elementary, are variously organized. Triangles have properties different from their isolated line-segments; pyramids have properties additional to thoes of triangles: both emerge with successive orders of complexity. A small set of geometrical rules is sufficient to construct every such figure by manipulating line-segments. Equally, a small number of physical laws operate in nature, generating everything from atoms and simple protozoa to galaxies and complex brains. Here too, properties emerge with complexity—life and mind, for example.

These assumptions are a revised statement of Plato's. He affirmed that Being is comprehensively intelligible, and that knowledge is achievable because nous is inscribed with the Forms. Knowledge is harder for us who know the extra-mental world by making and testing hypotheses. Plato's surmise is, nevertheless, our leading principle: reality is intelligible because of its intrinsic differentiations and relations. We press this speculative idea in every accessible domain, though testing is easier with things we make, because plans may be interpreted in either of two ways: they are directives for creating effects, or hypotheses confirmed by the sensory effects of things made.

How did we come to misconstrue the vehicles signifying differences in the world—percepts, thoughts, words, or sentences—as the basis for all intelligibility? Descartes made this error, because he believed that mind intuits ideas standing clearly and distinctly before it, but not the extra-mental differences they prefigure. Kant argued to the same effect when he substituted Categories abetted by empirical schemas for innate ideas. Extramental reality becomes a surd, the unthinkable thing-in-itself. Twentieth-century thinking reformulates this claim by making language the source of intelligibility. Wittgenstein's remark, "*The limits of my language* mean the limits of my world."[2] is paradigmatic. He construed this sentence realistically: possibilities in logical space are the world, while sentences represent possibles, instantiated or not, because of having the same form.[3] Idealists prefer a Cartesian, Kantian reading. They suppose that the boundaries of possibility are fixed by meaningful discourse. Intelligibility in the world is derivative: it results from the projection of differences and relations expressed in language. Anything else—everything extra-linguistic—is noumenal and unthinkable.

The plausibility and danger of this claim derive from the apparent autonomy of natural languages. Each has a vocabulary of interdefinable words, and a grammar that secures the coherence of sentences thought or said. We have the example of novelists who use the familiar words and forms of language to create their fictions. It doesn't matter that events they describe could not happen in our world. They are plausible enough in their context, because language enables us to spin coherent, detailed yarns. Plato described the pleasure of rational intuition as it dwells among the Forms. We are equally pleased by the rounded isolation of these world-making stories. Like an articulate dream, they swathe us in a make-believe universe, no exception taken to any claim they make.

Suppose that every such novel begins as a private reverie, then consider reasons for denying the possibility of private languages. These reasons are as interesting for what they suppress as for what they say. Their persistence is recognition that the intelligibilities which language supplies are oddly monadic: each of us may use this public resource to create the impenetrably private worlds of novels or delusions. We don't avert this result by emphasizing that principal words are keyed to common observables—colors, for example—or that the rules of speech are standardized in the give-and-take where each speaker corrects, and is corrected by, others. Intelligibility is nuanced and specific, but also global: it is present in large-scale, integrated stories or theories, as well as in the fine discriminations of words and grammar. Always remembering the latter while ignoring the former doesn't save us from personal isolation. For we are mutually unintelligible if your world-construing story is different from mine, whatever our agreement about colors and shapes.

This threat is reduced (though never eliminated) because we coordinate our actions for shared or complementary aims. Communication is vital to these reciprocities, and language is its principal instrument. We use it to make ourselves mutually accessible, to locate relevant features of our circumstances, to coordinate our work, and to explain and justify our projects. We can use language to do each of these things, because it is shaped by the demand that vocabulary and grammar be pertinent to differences and relations in the extra-linguistic world. Saying "This is red and square" creates an expectation that others may test and confirm. Saying "I promise" creates an obligation in circumstances where shared needs promote reciprocal duties. Stability in semantics or syntax is instrumental to stability in cooperative arrangements. The contrary—idiopathic variation in meanings or grammar—is discouraged, because it disrupts or precludes effective coordination.

Acknowledging that we respond effectively to extra-linguistic circumstances mitigates the assumption that intelligibility has only my mind and experience as its domain. An ambiguity nevertheless persists. What is the extra-mental world to which I accommodate? Is it nature, including other people and social systems? Or is it the community of minds, especially the members of a culture or linguistic community? This second alternative implies that the relevant unit is us, rather than me: you with your linguistic expectations are joined to me with my complementary expectations. It avers that each respondent is a language user, and that all adaptations are linguistic: we speak to one another. The autonomy ascribed to language is therefore uncompromised, though it is better ascribed to a community than to individual thinker-speakers. A single speaker resembles one hand clapping: intelligibility in him awaits its complement in one or more others.

This is consequential for mind's alleged self-sufficiency, because it implies that societies or cultures, not individual minds, are self-sufficient. Religious sects endure when each member believes an orienting story because, in part, the other members believe it; communities endure because of their common language. Perhaps no one learns the ideas or rules that create intelligibility within him if he doesn't participate in social reciprocities wherein partners test and affirm one another's perceptions, beliefs, and roles. It is no matter, therefore, if the stories exchanged among a community's members have no application beyond their system. The story is "true for them": their habits and expectations are confirmed when each ratifies the other's story or role. Multiculturalism reminds us that the range of possible experiences is broad, and that conflict is frequent among peoples who are offended by the "worlds" and practices—the intelligibles—of their neighbors. Should we concede that all of intelligibility has its necessary and sufficient conditions in the mutual exchanges and confirmations of social life?

This proposal seems to eliminate the isolation of individual minds without liberating intelligibility from the control of minds. But socialization is moot when we remember the argument of Polemarchus: that justice is helping friends and harming enemies.[4] Atomizing self-interest elides with Cartesian self-sufficiency, if each of us has only one friend, himself. This reduces community to an aggregate, and rouses our solipsist fears. How can we be sure that public meanings are more than ceremonial cover for private interpretations? This fractured result coheres nicely with the individualism of our time. Insisting on the diversity of thinkers and their interests, we inherit the problem of coordinating individuals who have opposed values and differing criteria of meaning and truth. Producing a common world is as much a political, practical, and moral problem as it is a metaphysical puzzle. The "language" of civility is our social glue, though each of the speakers may construe it in a way that suits him. The risk of idiopathy subverts the confidence in a public language.

Socialization hasn't saved intelligibility from subjectivism and idealism; but it does go halfway to the suggestion proposed several paragraphs above: social practices are never routinized without the participants' accommodation to circumstances that include one another, roles, and rules. Monologues, reveries, or novels that respond to nothing extra-mental are wheels turning idly: they are limiting expressions of a practice, not the standard examples from which to generalize about intelligibility. For there is more to acknowledge: linguistic usage is a set of practices calibrated to circumstances that include the terrain and natural laws, as well as partners and their intentions. Sentences that are appropriate, because of their role in social rituals (saying "Thank you," for example) are not the best or only expressions of order. The conversations of workmen—even the primitive talk of the first pages of Wittgenstein's *Philosophical Investigations*—have a different vector. They locate linguistic usage within contexts where words and sentences signify the lay of the land, including obstacles to our projects. Language is the principal instrument of communication, because it is exquisitely sensitive to differences and relations in situations where people speak accurately or cooperate effectively. But language is not the only practice adapted to the context of its use. Many practices—including teaching, medicine, and mining—are intelligible in this respect: they are differentiated and sequenced in ways appropriate to the circumstances in which they apply.

Some mathematicians and logicians persist in believing that intelligibility is founded principally or only in the syntax or notation of language. Here, as before, language is considered autonomous, so that none of its differences or relations is conditional on its applicability to extra-linguistic states of affairs. This conviction is hard to share. Material particulars are numbered and counted. The intensity and magnitude of a thing's properties—temperature, for example—are fixed by its causal relations to other things.[5] Spacetime has an intrinsic topology, geometry, and metric.[6] We sometimes ignore the material basis for abstracted, mathematical properties, elaborating mathematical ideas in ways that are facilitated by their formal syntax. But neglect becomes amnesia when we suppose that it is only these abstractions (most of them incidental to the actual world) that make nature thinkable in mathematical terms.[7] There is also the risk of paradox. We infer from the relation of a circle's circumference and diameter to the mystery that the numerical value of their quotient has no finite value. Should we suppose that nature is incomplete? Not when we have the simpler explanation that our mathematical procedure converts a specific proportion into an infinitely expandable decimal ($\pi = 3.141 \ldots$). Or we find that the square root of -1 is critical for the formalism of quantum theory, and then suppose that this irrational number must itself be a factor in the extra-mathematical world, not merely evidence of the complex relationship obtaining there. Intimidated by mathematicians, we may fail to ask if their constructs are literally projectable onto reality itself. But we hold our ground, remembering other domains where similar mistakes are avoided. Musical notation is a concise representation of some values and relations, but the notation is misconstrued if we suppose that notes represent discrete values, with nothing in the intervals between them. This is the point to emphasize: intelligibilities in thought and language map differences and relations in the extramental world. But the fit is imperfect: some differences and relations prefigured or present in one are absent in the other.

These considerations deter us from interpreting syntax and notation as the basis of whatever intelligibility is discerned in the extra-linguistic world. Yet this isn't the end of the matter, because of the special role claimed for demonstration. Descartes and Carnap believed that deduction exposes the deep structure of intelligibility. Hence this question: what do demonstrations prove? Considered in formal terms only, a proof establishes that relations among least units of thought or language (sentences, for example) are coupled or transformed—with no change in truth-values—in ways prescribed by rules of inference. This is validity: the sentence created by joining all the sentences in a proof is necessary because its negation is a contradiction.

What do demonstrations prove about the material world, given that proofs are a priori contrivances? Proofs display elementary limits on relations, limits that satisfy the principles of identity, noncontradiction, and excluded middle. Limits on inference are a vital constraint on representation, because these principles apply everywhere, in the extramental world and in language.[8] Conversely, a demonstration having true premises is a directive to observation: we are likely to observe what we predict.

Grammar and logic are useful—calculation apart—to the degree that they facilitate our representations of actual or possible differences and relations in nature. For the pairing of nature and language resembles a dance for two. Each partner does steps while accommodating him or herself to the other. Each one's understanding of difference and relation is a function of these two things: recognition of the partner's moves, and some plan for one's own. Intelligibility requires both sides if we are to respond effectively to our circumstances: difference and order in nature are tracked by difference and order in thought.

Think of the excitement aroused by seeing the apparent contradictions in Escher's drawings. The layered negations of complex sentences also give the (often) mistaken impression that they generate contradictions. For our limited interpretive abilities set practical limits to the representational uses of language and two dimensional spaces.

Solecisms are also an obstacle to representation. Grammar forbids them, because they violate semantic identity: a solecism's two predicates ("raining numbers," for example) cannot be joined, unless we suppose that the identity of one or the other is altered to permit the combination. This logical constraint applies as much to things as to thoughts: nothing that is, or is said to be green all over can be, or be said to be, red all over. Grammar forbids solecisms, as it purges all contradictions, because their incomprehensibility and material error impede the communication and cooperation that are required as we engage one another and our circumstances.

Yet, nothing in the practical uses of thought and language precludes individual perspectives, interpretations, or intentions. Imagination coupled to language and personal values gives each of us the power to contrive a rich set of personal meanings, one that reduces the "public space" to an aggregate of distinctive privacies. They guarantee different perspectives in the midst of agreed meanings, behaviors, and aims. Still, these privacies are no basis for the relativist world-spinning promoted by post-modernists: "Different values, different worlds" might be their slogan. John Findlay once spoke of "the rumor on the square," the variations on a theme or value that circulate through many thinkers as they elaborate and inflect the views they share. There is a continuous span of meanings—private at one end, communal at the other—and a constant tide that surges back and forth along this span: each of us is socialized, but irretrievably private. Findlay's metaphor expressed his reading of Hegel's *Phenomenology of Mind*, a book that elaborates this theme on every page.[9] Hegel implied that idiopathy is intelligible, only obscurely, even to its subjects: it locates them too far back in the cave. They become self-intelligible by learning public meanings while merging private aims in shared objectives. But Hegel was excessive: he misconstrued this difference as a contrariety. Extremities that he described as oppositional and mutually exclusive persist in everyone. People who are socialized but reflective regularly challenge the received wisdom of public meanings and commands. Nietzsche observed that freethinkers suffer isolation and self-doubt; but he was sure that the combination of failure and success makes them resolute, and ever plainer to themselves. Why insist—as Wittgenstein did in the *Philosophical Investigations*—that such people must be opaque to themselves until fully socialized?[10] Philosophers who ignored idiosyncrasy in Wittgenstein averred that there are no private languages,[11] though Wittgenstein himself once argued the other side: "The world of the happy man is a different one from that of the unhappy man."[12]

Attitudes and values (hence the significance of facts) differ among us, thereby creating all that is required for a matrix of privacy. Usually, idiosyncrasy flourishes in a common world (autism apart), one whose characters and relations erode our differences.

This is a world of actual states of affairs. Its public character, its exemption from particular perspectives and values, is nevertheless founded elsewhere. I mean that the senses—the meanings—of thoughts and words are the properties or complexes of properties that exist in the first instance as eternal possibilities.[13] Thoughts and words acquire sense by virtue of our contact with actual states of affairs—possibles instantiated. Because every actual difference is prefigured by a possible difference, we quickly establish mediated contact—using words generated by analogy, generalization, or extrapolation—with some of the infinitely many eternal possibles, most of them uninstantiated. Possibles are the senses, the meanings, of our thoughts and words, so that everyone constructs an interpretation of the world using thoughts or words whose meanngs do not depend for their existence or character on his or her use of them. Accordingly, the order of our learning—from actuality to fantasy—expresses reality's control on perception, thought, and imagination. Every consistent fantasy relies for its intelligibility on differences and relations that are represented, not made.

How do we confirm that this objective pole dominates meanings in disparate people? Why suppose that they use the same words to signify the same possibles? For three reasons: because the possibles at issue are usually instantiated, so that it is this actual bear, not the possibility, that concerns us; because we learn to speak and think as we cooperate with others, joining them in tasks that secure and satisfy us; and because our common physiology is the promise of similar effects in the presence of similar causes: the apple that looks red to most of us is our common point of reference for *red*. These commonalities of meaning point to the complementarity of intelligibles in thought and language, and the world: senses and uses are standardized in the thought and language of people; the senses of their words are the characters and relations instantiated in actual states of affairs. "Block" and "slab" signify to me what they signify in rocks.

Is there also this other complementarity in the intelligibilities of mind and the world? Descartes speculated that material differences are variations of magnitude, figure, and motion. This may prove to be a very canny guess. Perhaps mind too operates with a set of intelligibles that is much smaller than we would infer from the familiar array of thoughts or words, percepts, and feelings. This would be so if, for example, every perceived quality has its relative position on one of a relatively few quality scales. Color is scaled, when sensitivity to frequencies of light translates as perceived color of a particular hue.

Scales are likely to have been acquired during our evolutionary history. All or most would have survived because of their applicability to an array of differences in nature. Some animals may have a few, precisely differentiated, hard-wired scales within them: tastes are sweet or salt, for example. The scales within us humans may be differentiated at birth in some cases, determinable in others. Learning may supply specificity for the determinables, including ranges of values and intervals between values. The apparent, phenomenal differences among scales—color, sound, and touch, for example—may belie their affinities, given that neural impulses have scant resources—variations of wavelength, frequency, and duration, for example—to produce all the phenomenal differences we perceive. Phenomenality may be a single scale, varied in expression—sights or sounds—because of differences in neural structure and the variability of neural signals. This may explain the experience of people who mix phenomenal modalities—seeing colors, for example, when hearing tones.

It may seem that the diversity of thoughts or words is not scaled. Yet, both signs and their referents may be scaled. Signifiers are typically introduced by descriptions, or ostensively by way of scaled percepts. Signs—words, paradigmatically—are assembled from letters that have been combined in ways prescribed by a small set of rules, so each word is scaled by reference to the kinds and numbers of operations required to produce it.

This surmise would resolve the montage of sensible or verbal differences and relations, as Descartes eliminated Aristotle's substantial forms. The intelligibles within us—whether phenomena or words—would be generated systematically from elementary resources, while calibrated to those outside us.

2. Mind as Foundational: Culture

Psychocentrism was ambitious: it located all of being in human minds. This idea founders but doesn't perish, because culture is a domain in which every difference and relation expresses mind's intervention.

Culture's foundations are hypothesis, interpretation, stipulation, and habit. *Hypotheses* are critical, because human beings are not hard-wired to their surroundings: testable hypotheses supplement instinct.

Every culture maps its terrain, and each learns the behaviors required to survive there. Many prize routine, hence the authority of old books and habits. A few make hypothesis central to their aims. These are societies determined to control their circumstances, and willing to accept the altered values and habits promoted by science and technology. *Habits* emerge without forethought when people respond to their circumstances and needs—individually or jointly—by doing such as things as save or satisfy them. These spontaneous effects are eventually rationalized, but *stipulations*, not these justifications, are the decisive next step. They may be simple directives (skirts for women, trousers for men), or they prescribe complex behaviors, such as courting rituals, games, or the rules of political systems. Stipulations are constructive: they create social practices. Sometimes the people responsible for rules or laws are teams or committees. More often, codified practices—habits prescribed by stipulations—are the effect of many thinkers, each imitating or amending a practice in his or her own way until consensus is achieved or enforced.

People everywhere have similar interests and needs, but cultures differ. A core of interests—including nourishment, reproduction, and governance—is shared. The causes of difference are adventitious (forks or chopsticks), or they express the historically formed, situationally determined practices of the people engaged: we are fishermen or farmers. Particular formations and behaviors—gender relations, for example—exhibit the accidents of a culture's history while expressing its values. The values evolve with practices that satisfy individual and social needs. Once malleable and unstable, they crystallize, limiting change.

Interpretations are proposed as people reflect on their circumstances and practices. What and where are we? Why act as we do? Interpretation answers these questions by locating us within a conceptual framework that valorizes us and our projects: there are gods, for example, and they like us. Interpretations resemble abductive hypotheses, because both specify the conditions for things observed. But there is this difference: hypotheses are tested and revised, confirmed or discounted; whereas interpretations are merely affirmed. We excuse the difference, because valorizing stories imbue life with significance. Why believe them? Because belief is intensified when mirrored back and forth among a society's members. Others expect us to believe and value as they do. Most of us don't resist, though friction is assured when a society values hypothesis and interpretation, science and religion.

Cultures are as much constrained by physical laws as any leaf or stone. Physics may eventually describe the construction principles that carry us from simple molecules to complex cities. But this is not the look of things. For there is no apparent explanation in chemistry, physiology, or social utility for the music of Cimarosa or the design of great mosques. This doesn't imply that the inception of cultural phenomena is mysterious, only that such phenomena have complex conditions. Two are critical. First are capacities that emerge with human evolution and human societies: languages developed when the need for communication exploited an acquired physiological capacity. Second is culture's opportunism: its solutions are frequently accidents routinized by imitation. Someone likes the sounds made by tapping on stones; others experiment with strings. Their successors build harpsichords. The unpredictability of the result is evidence that stable cultures are constrained but not explained by their history, constituents, or circumstances. Skirt lengths rise and fall for reasons that have nothing to do with anatomy or climate. Fads come and go, because cultures have rhythms of their own. Like living bodies, they ground and explain themselves.

Culture's autonomy implies that Kantian world-making is the grandiose extrapolation from a core of truth. Mind has two problems: one practical, the other interpretive. Surviving—thriving if we can—is a practical interest; locating what we are and do in a reconciling, conceptual system is an intellectual need. The sense we make of food is different from having to eat; but both are critical to a culture's values, identity, and stability. For we live at once in two worlds: the natural world where nourishment is required and the interpreted world where food is symbolic. Cultures may seem oddly schizoid. None would survive without the well-confirmed hypotheses that enable us to move effectively in our surroundings. Yet, all are suffused with mythic stories that make life significant.

The diversity of interpretations guarantees mutual incomprehension among people who solve the same generic problems in different ways. Some of us look for the spaceship trailing a comet that will carry us to a higher place—no matter that no one else sees it or shares our hope. Our behavior mystifies them, but only because they don't understand our interpretation or values. Culture justifies and sustains us. Its niches and vocations, successes and failures, have no other currency. Only sickness or accidents break the surface of these concerns, recalling us to our merely animal condition. Someone in a mixed marriage describes the response of relatives on hearing of her illness: "One side prays for me; the other is looking for doctors to save me." Each of her cultures overlays the shared physical world with a tissue of meanings and aims. They are two of many possible interpretations: neither puts her in a boat and sets it adrift.

Our awareness of culture and its relative autonomy is critical when physicalism supersedes Cartesianism mentalism. For we may believe that cross-cultural variations are incidental to hard truths about us. We are hungry or fed, naked or clothed, homeless or housed; niceties of food, clothing, and shelter—feeding the hungry with *foie gras* or pumpernickel—may seem irrelevant to needs for which these are a few of the possible satisfiers. Perhaps all the human world is a contrivance and conceit. This impatience with cultural differences ignores the reciprocity of interpretation and practical interests. It forgets the determinability of human needs, hence the many occasions when mind must choose the manner of our satisfaction. For there are no generic satisfiers: food, clothing, shelter, and government come in determinate forms. Appropriate determinations differ among cultures. One who takes his satisfactions in the preferred forms of his culture may be unable to accept the goods of another—their beef, our rice. These cultural differences are a point of honor among us. We achieve personal and social identity in their terms: we don't, and wouldn't, do what others do.

Is culture also our necessary point of reference for appraising the truth-value of the many claims before us? Does culture shape our beliefs about reality? This is a question about the scope of mind's role as world-maker. Granted its power to prescribe the rituals of family life, is mind also the self-sufficient validator of its hypotheses about genes and cosmology? We can't answer without remarking that individuals and their cultures are self-valuing, and that self-valorization encourages us to regard truths in a merely instrumental way. What do they prefigure, opportunities or obstacles? Do they favor or hinder our interests? These considerations make cultures insensitive or cynical about truths. We go where interest prescribes, often careless of truths and consequences.

There is no way to avoid a culture's perspective, because there is no posture outside every culture from which to appraise the candidates for truth. But nothing in this entails that cultures must blind us to every reality inconsistent with or irrelevant to their interests. Priests sometimes agree that their piety is unsupported by empirical or logical evidence. They are pious anyway, because they value a faith that doesn't rely on hypotheses supported by empirical and conceptual evidence. Should truth override every value? This question implies the opposition of truth and value, though minds having practical concerns are obliged to find a route through states of affairs truly reported—a route through truths—as they satisfy one or another value. Are there viable routes mapped by falsehoods? Certainly there are. Many plans and behaviors merely crush the states of affairs and truths that thwart them.

Now the question is joined without the hope of additional evasions: can we forever ignore the truths that define our circumstances? There are many reminders of this limit, from bank managers to ecologists. When should value override truth? When should we limit our power to override current truths by altering circumstances in ways congenial to our values? There is a pragmatic answer: we consider the benefits and harms of the values at issue. We compare them to the costs of being thwarted by truths we cannot evade or suppress.[14] Mostly, we prefer our culture's values to frustrating truths, always allowing that cultures may be slowly transformed by useful truths. Where are the limits? Physics and biology describe limits we increasingly evade, as molecular biology enables us to alter our animal nature. Cultural imperialism is more than the opposition of weak and strong cultures: it expresses culture's will to override nature.

3. Self

Selfhood is one of the principal things to save when mental activities are understood in physical terms. But selfhood is vulnerable. We risk ignoring all our reflective powers and achievements if the cogito is passé.

Two lines of argument have this effect. One is the behaviorist disdain for introspection. Think of the anxious waiter: he concentrates on keeping his balance but drops the tray. The other is the physiologists' impatience with intrapsychic reports that reveal little or nothing about the neural character of thought, perception, or feeling. Adopting both attitudes, we say that self-reflection is an ineffective way of directing activity, and a poor source of information about the bodily activities described as *mind*.

This is excessive: self-reflection may enhance self-knowledge and spur effective action without being a necessary condition for either. Imagine machines that mimic our thinking. They calculate and remember, but most of them cannot override their programs by weighing alternatives, sometimes scrutinizing or altering themselves. We humans do such things, because of a mechanism within us that deliberates, hypothesizes, values, interprets, and prescribes. One might duplicate these functions in machines without making them self-aware, but they would seem lobotomized and subhuman. We do them, while aware that we do. What is more, we do them better when self-awareness promotes focus, discrimination, and cogency. Devaluing self-reflection—

preferring machines that are faster, cheaper, and more efficient—ignores the difference it makes.

Descartes' cogito was the site of representation, memory, analysis, calculation, value, and judgment. It was also the place of self-reflection, the act of a mind confirming that it is and what it is. This perspective has become the vital center of human purpose, understanding, and self-regard. One commands a horse or a dog; but we speak to other humans, expecting them to reverberate with the meanings and intentions we express. A legion of novelists, dramatists, and poets learned from Descartes (as others knew before) that life may be described from the inside. What will happen if we conclude that our reflective center is epiphenomenal or incidental? Isn't it likely that people will be perceived as machines, as much by themselves as by others? We use machines, then scrap them without sentiment when their useful lives are finished. Why not use and dispose of humans in the same, unsentimental way?

This point was made for me when the dead son of a prominent father was cremated without a funeral or a memorial service. He had died of AIDS after spending years in prison for selling drugs. Much embarrassed, his father eliminated the cause of his shame. The son's anguish was invisible. It could be ignored, in life and in death. This father was somewhat ahead of current sensibility; but he was not a monster or unusual. The English local council, mentioned in the Introduction, would have its retirement homes do to many what he did to one.

Dualist cultures treasure the body as the instrument and platform for the soul or mind.[15] The body reflects the glory of its pilot. The culture that acknowledges mind's reduction to body must take care that it does not treat bodies as instrumental values only. Think of used tires or sheep. Is this our future, and the measure of our worth? Are utility and efficiency the only measures of value? We needn't revive the myth of an immortal soul to justify saying they are not. We do better by acknowledging that we are self-reflective (hence self-perceiving), self-directing, and self-correcting. The evidence for these powers is as well confirmed empirically as anything can be. Why else do we read or converse with other people, before withdrawing to reflect, decide, and act? Mind loses the illusion of self-sufficiency, exhaustive transparency, and self-control when its activities are shown to have complex, exclusively physical conditions. But nothing in this diminishes what we do or entails our loss of dignity, unless we choose to treat one another differently and worse.

Do I err in supposing that self-reflection is a distinguishing expression of selfhood and a reliable source of information or efficacy? There are other ways to determine or influence the states of a brain—

electrodes or chemicals, for example. Still, I don't need a dentist to tell me that a tooth aches. Yogis are keenly discerning. They control blood pressure and metabolism by focusing on discriminable, intrapsychic states. Is it surprising that a hierarchically organized, neural network reads and controls its states? We should expect a better-developed physiology to explain how the brain is able to do what patently it does.

Notice that the question disputed here is not the one of privacy. The activities mooted—introspection and effective intervention—would be as they are if people could eavesdrop on one another by wiring their brains together. Each would perceive, in himself and the other, these seven overlapping functions: perceptual experience; the making or testing of hypotheses, rules, and plans; calculation, the play of valorizing attitudes, surges of feeling, memory, and fantasy. You would confirm these activities within me; I would do as much for you. We would praise the technology that makes the experiment possible, though it would teach us nothing that wasn't known before about these acts and states. How do we know them? We introspect.

A harder question remains. We are troubled by the array of properties inspected, properties that are nowhere anticipated in the palate of material properties. If Descartes' list of primary properties—extension qualified by figure, magnitude, and motion—is Spartan, there is no expanded list that plausibly includes the properties discerned introspectively—secondary properties or those of consciousness, for example. Mind's reduction to body is an invitation to eliminate every such property from the list of those ascribed to us. But this is mistaken and unnecessary if complexity generates emergent properties. Suppose we create a circle by bending a straight line. The closed line has many new properties, including an inside, an outside, and π, the ratio of the circumference to the diameter. Joining the parts of body or brain is equally productive. So, Descartes appealed to will when he sought to distinguish mind from body. Yet will is one of the easier features to explain in physical terms: we redescribe it as inhibition and excitation. It is not surprising that the patterns of these two are complicated and idiosyncratic within a network of many neurons. Nor should we be surprised that a hierarchically organized network is capable of self-consciousness, because of reading its own states. This does not explain the feeling of self-illumination; it does explain the accuracy of our readings. Other intrapsychic phenomena are harder to explain. We infer that the generation of colors, sounds, smells, and feelings of all sorts is an emergent result of neural complexity. This enrichment is our stunning good luck, but it is not more bizarre than other emergent properties already mimicked by machines, thought and memory, for example.

Cartesians identify selfhood with the power and contents of self-reflection: they suppose that each of us is comprehensively self-aware. But this is the wrong emphasis, because selfhood is the developmental, usually unconscious result of our engagements with other people and things. The effect of these engagements is a distinctive cognitive-affective posture.[16] Its constituents are information, attitudes, and skills. Information locates us in nature, directing us as we apply our skills. Attitudes combine good or bad feelings with intentional objects (love or hate, for example).[17]

Attitudes are acquired when feelings of vulnerability or security are excited and confirmed: something scares or assures us. Those acquired early are hard to change: we are "constitutionally" open or anxious. Attitudes acquired in later life resist change though they are alterable, given information suported by other attitudes: we enjoy smoking, but give it up because we prefer health. Attitudes fix values, values express attitudes, so that attitudes,hence values, are the psychic gyroscope that rights and stabilizes us.

We see our values expressed in the interpretations that orient us toward other people and things. For information is filtered and warped by attitudes: we may not hear or remember news that offends them. Using information to reinforce our hopes or fears, we construe our circumstances. These interpretations—one foot in information, the other in attitude—are a principal expression of psychic posture. Others know us by the words and practices that exhibit our orientation.

The real, but limited, utility of self-awareness is plainer now. Mind's access to itself is partial, probably because introspection requires the hierarchical arrangement of groups of neurons—one group reading another—and because this arrangement is not pervasive in the brain: some neurons in which information or skills are virtual—stored—are not accessible to neurons that could read them. It doesn't follow that self-perception is valueless for being limited. Let self-understanding proceed from both directions: hypotheses about physiology and development on one side, self-reflection on the other.

Freud is sometimes scorned for a faulty psychology, one that credits mind with an unconfirmable structure and powers. These complementary perspectives—introspection on the one side, physiology on the other—are his vindication. Seven of Freud's claims are apposite. (i) Mind has a tripartite structure—Id, Superego, and Ego. Ego contains impulses, learned social rules, and strategies for securing itself in ways that satisfy the other two. (ii) Mind has a developmental history. Each of us acquires a distinctive cognitive-affective posture as our maturing bodies engage other people and things. (iii) Repression—inhibition—

seals off disruptive passions or memories. Sometimes, it limits the affects of the matters excluded from awareness; other times, the things repressed become the unacknowledged focus for defenses constructed to hide them. (iv) Attitudes—hence values—are expressed by interpretations, desires, and feelings. Intrapsychic conflicts are usually conflicting attitudes. (v) Memory supplies partial access to the history of our formation, including memories of attitudes to, and feelings about, formative experiences. (vi) Some current beliefs and attitudes are conscious; more—probably most—are unconscious. (vii) Bringing unconscious beliefs and attitudes (feelings) to conscious reflection is a decisive condition for altering behavior.

Several of these claims are criticized for methodological or epistemological reasons,[18] but all the features here ascribed to mind—including impulses, bodily needs, learned rules, and the executive functions of planning and self-control—are explicable in physical terms, if only provisionally. Repression is not more complicated than inhibition, a much-discussed physiological phenomenon. Memory is reasonably well understood in brains and machines: computers have more and more of it. Attitudes are elusive, but not an enigma: they join fear or well-being to excitation or inhibition and the information which supplies their object: we favor things that don't scare us. Developmental history is a constant in living things, however much human intelligence and variable circumstances complicate it. Nothing Freud described is anomalous with the organic, material model of human life.

Where is the mystery in his descriptions of mind? Is it Freud's emphasis on sexuality that annoys us? Pardoning him for using repressive Austria as a biological standard, we concentrate on the issue that bothers us most: self-consciousness exposes mists and fumes from the distressed attitudes and feelings within us. Cultures that require self-mastery, stability, virtue, and calm discourage us from revealing our underside. Nor do we want this exposure for ourselves. Freud is the messenger who tells us that there is an underside.

But, he is not the only medicine for troubled people. We may someday have chemicals that alter information, attitudes, and skills, as drugs used currently reduce anxiety, depression, or mania. Such drugs might also have social uses. Leaders who see us as inefficient machines or recalcitrant animals could use them to make us pliable or efficient. This would be a significant breach, for it would violate the self-directed commandment that we be responsible for ourselves and respectful of this responsibility in others. Recall the slogans that shape this idea of us: Thinkers are unconditionally free, and never so much like God as when they will to affirm or deny an idea.[19] A rational will withholds assent from any maxim that cannot be willed as a universal law.[20]

Freudian psychoanalysis helps people who want to reclaim responsibility for themselves. Compare psychopharmacology: it gives doctors power over the behavior of their patients. Does the medical power to manipulate also entail the doctor's right to supersede or suppress the patient's responsibility for his choices and acts? Are the pain and difficulty of self-knowledge sufficient to convince us that others will do a better job of understanding and controlling us? Should we accept their control if confusion or conflict diminishes our ability to control ourselves? What shall we need to know of ourselves—what shall we be allowed to know—if we have no responsibility for what we are and do?

Freud makes us responsible for curing ourselves. He would have us change the attitudes that constrict us, the better to make our values consistent with one another and consistent with our talents, circumstances, and responsibilities to others. This responsibility is compromised by illnesses (including schizophrenia, manic-depression, and obsessive neuroses) that do not respond to self-understanding and altered attitudes. Taking medicine is the better solution in these cases, because reducing illness enables one to recover moral control of one's life. The rest of us don't need or want the medicine. Disciplined self-reflection is usually enough to liberate us from the disruptive parts of ourselves, sometimes with the help of a therapist.

Consider our altered circumstances. Descartes' leaner theory, then Kant, affirmed that the cogito is nous made concrete and particular, all intelligibility incorporated within it. Selfhood—cognitive-affective posture—is more fragile and less cosmic, but still the center of all we are and can be. This is our psychic core. It develops and changes, sometimes because reflection reintegrates or alters its parts, more often because we accommodate ourselves to evolving circumstances. Selfhood is one of the functions that emerge in bodies having a certain complexity.

4. The Good

Plato's Good was cosmic. Descartes' good was private: one should enjoy life while living virtuously, leaving the monarch and the Church to keep social relations on an even keel. When they fail (as during the Thirty Years' War, 1618–1648), one hunkers down and bides one's time. We don't expect more from Descartes' social philosophy, because his ideas about society were atrophied by the arguments of his leaner theory: I needn't worry about the good for others or a corporate good when my existence is the only one known with certainty.[21]

Descartes' privatized good is a distinguishing feature of modernity. Replacing the Good with the cogito signifies that I am the final cause for all the lower entries on the line. Recall his distinction between the two kinds of value: "[O]bjects which stimulate the senses do not excite different passions in us because of differences in the objects, but only because of the various ways in which they may harm or benefit us, or in general have importance for us."[22] Being divides accordingly: the self-valuing cogito on one side, its utilities on the other.[23] Mind's freedom is all but entailed by this division. For acts impelled by thought or will are unconstrained if I exist though, possibly, nothing else does. Other things are mind's qualifications or instruments. Mind has no inhibiting respect for them.

This is the moral formula taught and affirmed as our natural right. Each of us is a self-elected good-in-itself; other things have instrumental value only. I can and should attend principally or only to my prosperity and well-being. Let the Prisoners' Dilemma be our example. This thought experiment supposes that two prisoners are interviewed separately. Each can confess the crime they have allegedly committed together, or remain silent. There are four possible outcomes: if either confesses (defects) while the other is silent (cooperates), the one confessing is freed while the other is sentenced to seven years in prison; if both remain silent (hoping for the partner's silence), each receives a two-year sentence; if both confess, each is sentenced to five years. (The relative magnitude of the payouts is essential to the puzzle; the particular values are arbitrary.) Cooperating has payouts of two and seven years; defecting pays zero or five years. Accordingly, cooperation is more expensive than egoism: only a fool risks cooperation and silence when egoism earns two years of freedom. What does this dilemma prove about moral life? Very little, because the dilemma is a game that expresses the moral sentiments of an atomist ontology and an egoist morality. The attention the dilemma receives is nevertheless testimony to the discomfort provoked by the game's moral cynicism. Why not respond by inventing games whose payouts illustrate the benefits of cooperation?[24]

The egoist message would be innocuous in the Garden of Eden, where everyone has ready access to goods and services. But egoism guarantees conflict where scarcity is commonplace, and wealth is unequally distributed. Hence this question: Should our social theory be predicated on idealized circumstances—the easy availability of instrumental goods—that are usually unachievable because of inadequate resources, incompetent management, or scarcity and crowding? Neither natural nor logical necessity justifies the priority we ascribe to self-sufficiency and self-regard. Indeed, the Cartesian preference for egoism would have seemed an odd quirk if Western economies had been less productive than they are. It is cruel to postulate self-sufficiency and self-concern where poverty, frustration, and inter-dependence characterize most lives.

How do I justify affirming that I am the final cause, and that other things are good or bad because of their utility for me? Living deep in the cave, my beliefs are opinions rather than knowledge: I could be deceived. Descartes acknowledges this possibility in *The Passions of the Soul*. Passion couples feeling and drive; but it is no kind of knowledge. Plato, Aristotle, and Kant distinguished reason from the passions, saying that the first rules the second in the character of the good man.[25] *The Passions of the Soul* perpetuates this tradition in the respect that reason rules passion by repressing its excesses. Yet, Descartes believed that passion, not reason, is responsible for the choice of ends.[26] We need only take prudent care that our choices have more good than bad effects on us. Hume, Mill, Nietzsche, and the emotivists side with him: goods are functions of prudent desire.[27] They encourage the belief, current among us, that there are only such goods as people individually choose and enjoy. Different lives, different values: we retreat into private pleasures, each of us distinguished by our hungers and ways of satisfying them. Base desires are easily satisfied, making us prey to all the suppliers of crude entertainments. Some people make a fetish of tastes that are hard to satisfy, but this is self-willed frustration.

Descartes would not have liked our vulgarity; yet he greased the slide, first by establishing the cogito as the final cause and self-elected good-in-itself, then by supposing that the value of other things is a function only of their utility for us. There are two questions. First, is there a sound basis for discerning among instruments? Is desire the only measure? Or should we distinguish with Mill among the utilities appropriate to animal, intellectual, and moral pleasures?[28]. Second, and more pressing, can we moderate the egoism of Descartes' formulation?

Egoism expresses the cogito's self-discovery and self-sufficiency. Knowing myself to exist when possibly nothing else does, wanting my good but having no partners for getting it, I choose myself.[29] Why should I do otherwise? This persuasion survives when the cogito has dissolved under criticism. For we continue to valorize ourselves and our instruments, but not public and corporate goods. This point of view is persistent, but anomalous, if we understand the terms of our integration into the physical, social world. For we are neither alone nor self-sufficient.

There are individual persons, but also families, friendships, neighborhoods, religious communities, companies, and states. These are higher-order systems having individual persons as their proper parts.[30] Organic analogies are useful. The human body is a corporate reality, a system created by the mutually sustaining—reciprocal—causal relations of its parts.[31] We idealize (and idolize) self-sufficiency, though each human body relies on its circumstances for everything that sustains it, including oxygen, food, information, and friendship. Families too are systems, and each has an internal economy that relies on its context for nourishment and information. There are many such higher-order systems; some endure for a long time, whereas others—conversations, for example—are ephemeral. Every system has corporate goods, including its survival and the satisfaction of its parts. One participates in a system by working with others to achieve its objectives. They may be consistent with one's own, so that working for the system requires no self-denial. Other times, conflicted aims force a choice between loyalty to the system and loyalty to oneself. This is everyone's experience. We sometimes fail to acknowledge it, because Descartes has convinced us that each person's reality and his or her personal goods are the only ones worthy of effort or notice.

This prejudice dies when we espouse a naturalism that acknowledges the systems formed by the reciprocal relations of their members. Before, our regard for social goods seemed sentimental and ungrounded: good members of the herd, we mouth the values that keep us in place. Now, our social ontology supplies a reasoned justification for attitudes we typically have. It explains and legitimizes our regard for the systems in which we participate. They engage and satisfy us; character is formed to qualify us for roles within them; we are responsible to them while valuing them and ourselves. Participation also explains familiar conflicts: systems compete for our time, resources, and approval. We don't solve these conflicts by retreating into our privacy, reaffirming with Descartes that I am, though nothing else may exist. For I am not free to think of my desires only, if they subvert the interests of systems that engage me, systems I value.

Associations that once seemed to have no value but utility come to be perceived as systems having value in themselves. Engaging us, making us worthy in our own eyes, we value them as we value ourselves.[32] Orchestras are an example: they are fellowships in which musicians gratify themselves while earning a salary. One may say that these effects have a merely instrumental value. But there is a difference between the utility value of a salary that supports members as they have been, and the value of a system that transforms its members and audience too, engaging them in itself, making of them something they value and would not otherwise be. This was Mill's point when he distinguished moral and intellectual from material pleasures: utilities have different effects; some sustain us, others elevate us.

We reduce the apparently rigid difference between these two kinds of value—my value as self-elected final cause and the instrumental value of other things—if preference for myself is a choice. For I may sacrifice myself for something else, be it another person or system. Doing this may seem unnatural, as sometimes it is. But it may also be reasonable and worthy, as when parents choose family interests over personal desires. Idealizing systems, believing that our value derives from our roles in systems and the qualities achieved therein, we often value them more than ourselves. We discover that there are more goods—more things worth valuing—than Descartes acknowledged. People who look within themselves for valorizing desires discover the basis for some of their values in systems that engage them. This encourages social responsibility and cohesion with no increase of compulsion. For we already participate in many systems. We need only realize that they have objectives—goods—of their own, and that some of them are good for us, their members. Change the ethos—including our metaphysical assumptions—and we learn to choose goods that were previously invisible.

The agenda for moral education is here. Do we say that virtue is unteachable (apart from laws that protect us from one another by prescribing minimum standards of civility), leaving individuals to discover it for themselves while pursuing their private goods? Or do we teach virtue by introducing people to roles in which they learn responsibilities to one another? Does a child's moral sense grow like a weed? Or is it nourished in contexts where selfhood is elaborated and deepened by the child's relations to others? Atomism makes short work of moral education by leaving virtue to chance, or by requiring that each of us be endowed with a God-given conscience. Communitarianism affirms that virtue is learned in contexts where affiliation is its necessary condition. It says that moral autonomy is a social achievement—not an act of will, or the effect of good genes.

People liberated from the myth of self-sufficiency dare to look beyond themselves to possibilities that were once unthinkable. Is there, for example, an overriding, common good? There could be such a good if one system dominated every other, either because of being the highest-order system of systems or because it earns distinction for another reason—beauty or power, for example. The state often claims this status; but its goods—the elevation of every citizen into the community of laws[33]—is only one of many systemic goods. The one, common good would be constructed presumably from the goods of the many human systems, all of them reconciled, all conflicts purged. This is an outcome each of us could prize—satisfaction of all goods where none conflicts with others. We never achieve this result, because the goods of disparate systems typically conflict (as the factory that employs us pollutes and makes us sick). The idea of a common good is a shifting target, one we specify by aiming for the maximum coherence possible among goods pursued by competing systems. There are many such corporate goods, each one dominated by its own conflict-resolving value.

This is where politics intrudes. Each political party is a system in its own right, and each has a strategy for promoting specific goods or for reconciling goods that are mutually inimical. Contemporary politics is distorted because of its individualist ontology: we ignore systems, though they produce or defend many things we value. This is an old prejudice: the *loi Chapelier*, passed by the revolutionary Committee of Public Safety in June, 1794, decreed that there were no systems intermediate between the French state and its citizens. Labor unions, religious orders, and other systems were thereby marginalized, their aims and conflicts suppressed or ignored: nothing was to mediate between individual thinkers and their state. The self-sufficient cogito still inspires the liberal thinking that postulates individuals and aggregates, but ignores these systems. Systems respond by turning this apparent liability to their advantage. Excluded from the forums where laws are made, businesses, schools, and religious sects are ontologically invisible, but politically potent. Never apologizing for their bulk because we see only their members, they work hard to assure that legislators will pass laws congenial to themselves. Wanting to avert the corruption this guarantees, we need to rethink the individualism that ignores systems while allowing them to dominate the choice, regulation, and distribution of goods.[34]

There is also this caveat: replacing social atomism with communitarianism is necessary but not sufficient if moral theory and practice are to be reconstituted. We need an alternative basis for dualism's positive moral role. It sacralized thinkers: man is made in the image of God; each of us has an immortal soul, one inscribed with God's laws. These religious precepts distinguished body from soul, while obliging us to treat others and ourselves with appropriate respect. Mind–body dualism abetted these principles by grounding the moral light and moral worth in the cogito. Now, with confirmation that we are only material, we lose the ontological status that justified our claim to intrinsic worth. We risk having no value apart from our utility for people or systems more powerful than ourselves: cynical practice reduces *ought* to *is* or *does*. We shall need to believe that we, together with vital social systems, are not less worthy of decent treatment for being self-valuing.[35] For there is no other plausible basis for our "intrinsic" value, and no other defense against the demoralized self-perception that dead bodies are "business waste," and living bodies, business costs.

The dead are a test of our self-perception. People treated badly in life won't be better treated when dead; devaluing the dead will likely encourage us to devalue the living. For there are only two choices if we believe that humans are natural creatures with no essential importance to any thing but themselves. Each person values only him or herself, or we value one another, our systems, environment, and selves. The second alternative averts distortions of the first: helping friends, harming enemies, invites a Hobbesian war, if each person is his only friend.

Afterword

It isn't news that we live in the midst of nature as its creatures. Many people have said as much. The cogito has nevertheless retained its authority through our time. Freudian analysis intensifies its self-concern. Novelists and playwrights emphasize its ruminations and anguish. Idealist philosophers are an enduring prop: there is no reality, they tell us, apart from minds that think. But slowly and steadily, the centrality and autonomy of the cogito give way to the conviction that mind is a complex of bodily activities. Sometimes, as when a chess-playing computer defeats a grand master, we reappraise our situation. My suggestions are a conservative response to the enthusiasm that would have us ditch the cogito and all its works.

Mind and self are more than philosophic inventions. They support our human undertakings and justify us in work we already do: Hamlet didn't need Descartes to reflect. Yet, nothing vital to mind or self has disappeared when their exclusively physical nature is confirmed. We require no magic to explain this. Properties emerge with complexity, as angularity emerges when line-segments are joined. Consciousness emerges when sufficient neurons are organized hierarchically, enabling some to take the measure of others. Supporting conditions for the emergent property are necessary and sufficient. It disappears in their absence: there is no mind in the absence of body.

Plato is blameless. His surmise, that Being is intelligible in itself and everywhere knowable, is still our best hypothesis about the world and our place in it. Descartes' leaner theory extracted being and intelligibility from the world, locating them within the cogito before Kant exaggerated mind's autonomy and powers beyond all plausibility. Mind's achievements remain when their psychocentrism is rejected: self and culture survive when mind proves to be the activity of body. We rediscover our circumstances, but lose the fiction that made us grandiose.

Philosophy has lost its anchor, almost without noticing. Want of interest in its history blinds us to the cogito's foundational role in our thinking, and to the effects of its demise. Discussion churns. One side describes experience, analyzes words or theories, promotes world-making, or alleges that worlds dissolve when the motives of the world-makers are exposed. This is traditional philosophic work, but it cannot be all that philosophy does. The other side—materialist naturalism—has a rare opportunity. It renews philosophic inquiry by invoking the questions that once directed us: What are we? What is our place in the world? What concerns are appropriate to being here? Descartes' cogito separated us from other things. What do we make of ourselves as we rediscover our place among them?

Notes

Introduction

1. Reported by the BBC, August 7, 1998.

2. Friedrich Nietzsche, *Beyond Good and Evil*, trans. Walter Kaufmann (New York: Vintage Books, 1989), p. 27.

3. Arthur O. Lovejoy, *The Great Chain of Being* (Cambridge, Mass.: Harvard University Press, 1964)

4. René Descartes, *Discourse on Method and Meditations on First Philosophy*, ed. David Weissman (New Haven: Yale University Press, 1996), p. 383.

Chapter One. Plato's Divided Line

1. Plato, *The Republic*, trans. Francis MacDonald Cornford (Oxford: Oxford University Press, 1945), pp. 227–230, 514a–516e.

2. Ibid., p. 224, 509d–511d.

3. Ibid., p. 219, 508c–d.

4. Aristotle, *Metaphysics*, in *Basic Works*, ed. Richard McKeon (New York: Random House, 1941), pp. 784–786, 1028b33–1029b13.

5. See Plato, *Republic*, pp. 221–223, for the diagram from which this one derives.

6. Plotinus, *Enneads*, trans. Stephen MacKenna, 2nd ed. rev. C. S. Page (London: Faber and Faber, 1956), p. 434.

7. Ibid., p. 548.

8. Ibid., p. 555.

9. Ibid., p. 529.

10. Ibid., p. 554.

11. Ibid., p. 538.

12. Ibid., p. 539.

13. Plato, *Timaeus*, in *Collected Dialogues*, ed. Edith Hamilton and Huntington Cairns (New York: Pantheon Books, 1964), p. 1176, 49a.

14. Plotinus, *Enneads*, p. 22.

15. Ibid., p. 26.

16. Plato, *Parmenides*, in *Collected Dialogues*, p. 925, 131a–d.

17. Plotinus, *Enneads*, p. 262.

18. Ibid., p. 415. Plotinus is not always so bold: "When we seize anything in the direct intellectual act there is room for nothing else than to know and to contemplate the object; the subject is not included in the act of knowing, but asserts itself, if at all, later and is a sign of the altered; this means that, once purely in the Intellectual, no one of us can have any memory of our experience here" (ibid., p. 288).

19. Ibid., p. 241.

20. Ibid., p. 245.

21. Ibid., p. 390.

22 René Descartes, *Meditations on First Philosophy*, in *Discourse on Method and Meditations on First Philosophy*, ed. David Weissman (New Haven: Yale University Press, 1996), pp. 69–70.

23. Plotinus, *Enneads*, p. 432.

24. Ibid., p. 28.

25. Ibid., p. 166.

26. Ibid., p. 226.

27. Ibid., p. 273.

28. Ibid., pp. 274–275.

29. Ibid., p. 279.

30. Ibid., p. 238.

31. Stephen Menn, *Descartes and Augustine* (Cambridge: Cambridge University Press, 1998), pp. 130–206.

32. Lucas Siorvanes, *Proclus* (New Haven: Yale University Press, 1996), pp. 247–256.

33. Augustine, *Confessions*, in *Augustine, Confessions and Enchiridion*, trans. Albert C. Outler (Philadelphia: Westminster Press, 1955), p. 151.

Chapter Two. Descartes' Revisions of the Line

1. René Descartes, *Meditations on First Philosophy*, in *Discourse on Method and Meditations on First Philosophy*, ed. David Weissman (New Haven: Yale University Press, 1996), p. 59.

2. Plato, *Letter VII*, in *Collected Dialogues*, ed. Edith Hamilton and Huntington Cairns (New York: Pantheon Books, 1964), pp. 1589–1591, 342b–344d; David Weissman, *Intuition and Ideality* (Albany, N.Y.: State University of New York Press, 1987), pp. 17–52.

3. Descartes, *Meditations on First Philosophy*, pp. 49-51.

4. René Descartes, *Treatise on Man* and *The Passions of the Soul*, in *Philosophical Writings*, vols. 1 and 2, trans. John Cottingham, Robert Stoothoff, and Dugald Murdoch, (Cambridge: Cambridge University Press, 1985), vol. 1, pp. 99–108, 314–324.

5. Descartes, *Meditations on First Philosophy*, pp. 67–69.

6. Ibid., pp. 90–91.

7. Plato, *Timaeus*, in *Collected Dialogues*, pp. 1176–1178, 49a–51b.

8. Plato, *Republic*, pp. 219–220, 508a–d.

9. Ibid., p. 143, 444c–e.

10. Descartes, *Passions of the Soul*, in *Philosophical Writings*, vol. I, p. 349. See also John Stuart Mill, *Utilitarianism* (Indianapolis, Ind.: Hackett Publishing Co., 1969), p. 7: "Pleasure and freedom from pain are the only things desirable as ends."

11. This was Descartes' principle before it was Berkeley's. Descartes, *Meditations on First Philosophy*, p. 150; George Berkeley, *The Principles of Human Knowledge*, *Berkeley's Philosophical Writings* (New York: Collier Books, 1965), p. 62.

12. Descartes' Dedication to the *Meditations* joins two issues: God and the soul, and his "Method for the resolution of difficulties of every kind in the Sciences" (Descartes, *Meditations on First Philosophy*, p. 50). It might seem that these concerns are mutually extraneous, one as it flatters theological prejudices, the other as it concern a procedure for discovering truths. Their relation is, nevertheless, critical for the richer theory. It supposes that truth claims—and the criteria for meaning and truth—inevitably make assumptions about the knower, the known, and their relation, as when God guarantees the truth of clear and distinct ideas. The leaner theory, approximated in Descartes' *Rules for the Direction of the Mind*, argues to the contrary that the criteria for meaning and

truth are a priori standards applied in every domain where knowledge claims are made, without reliance on a divine guarantor. This is a critical difference in the evolution of philosophic thinking about knowledge: is knowledge a function of the character and relation of knower and known. Or is it the a priori product of thinking that satisfies mind's own standards? See David Weissman, *Truth's Debt to Value* (New Haven: Yale University Press, 1993), p. 127.

13. Stephen Menn, *Descartes and Augustine* (Cambridge: Cambridge University Press, 1998), p. 262.

14. Descartes, *Meditations on First Philosophy*, p. 64. Also see Proclus, *The Elements of Theology*, trans. E.R. Dodds (Oxford: Clarendon Press, 1963), 2nd ed., p. 165: "*Every soul is self-animated (or has life in its own right)*. For if it is capable of reversion upon itself and all that is capable of such reversion is self–constituted, then soul is self-constituted and the cause of its own being."

15. René Descartes, *Philosophical Writings*, vol. 3, trans. John Cottingham, Robert Stoothoff, Dugald Murdoch, and Anthony Kenny (Cambridge: Cambridge University Press, 1991), p. 235.

16. Descartes, *Meditations on First Philosophy*, pp. 96–108.

17. Nicholas Malebranche, *Dialogues on Metaphysics and on Religion*, trans. Morris Ginsberg (London: George Allen & Unwin, 1923), pp. 195–199.

18. David Hume, *A Treatise of Human Nature*, ed. L.A. Selby–Bigge and P.H. Nidditch (Oxford: Clarendon Press, 1978), p. 75.

19. G.W. Leibniz, *Philosophical Essays*, trans. Roger Ariew and Daniel Garber (Indianapolis: Hackett Publishing Co., 1989), pp. 33, 179, 184–185, n.239.

20. Immanuel Kant, *Critique of Pure Reason*, trans. Norman Kemp Smith (New York: St. Martin's Press, 1965), pp. 67–74.

21. Weissman, *Intuition and Ideality*, pp. 29–42.

22. Descartes, *Philosophical Writings*, vol. 2, p. 139. Descartes thanked another correspondent who called his attention to this similarity:

I am obliged to you for drawing my attention to the passage of St. Augustine relevant to my *I am thinking, therefore I exist*. I went today to the library of this town to read it, and I do indeed find that he does use it to prove the certainty of our existence. He goes on to show that there is a certain likeness of the Trinity in us, in that we exist, we know that we exist, and we love the existence and the knowledge we have. I, on the other hand, use the argument to show that this I which is thinking is *an immaterial substance* with no bodily element. These are two very different things. In itself it is such a simple and natural thing to infer that one exists from the fact that one is doubting that it could have occurred to any writer. But I am very glad to find myself in agreement with St. Augustine, if only to hush little minds who have tried to find fault with the principle. (Descartes, *Philosophical Writings*, vol. 3, p. 159)

This response is disingenuous, given that Descartes too regards the cogito as self-valorizing. See the remark quoted previously from the *Passions of the Soul*, where the benefit or harm done us is the criterion for evaluating other things. Unequivocally presupposed is the idea that I am the self–valuing good for which their value is instrumental only. Did he get the idea from Augustine? We don't know.

23. Menn, *Descartes and Augustine*, pp. 130–206.

24. Lucas Siorvanes, Proclus, (New Haven: Yale University Press, 1996), pp. 225–226, alludes to this difference:

The general idea that properties can have both a mathematical and a physical aspect stems from the fusion of Neo-Pythagoreanism and Stoicism in Neo-Platonism. Iamblichus, rather than Plotinus, was the one whose established firmly the 'Pythagorean' interpretation characteristic of (late) Neo-Platonism. The Athenian School [Proclus] followed it, and so revitalized the intimate bond of these two philosophies which can be found in the later Plato and the early Academy.

25. Proclus, *The Elements of Theology*. trans. E.R. Dodds, 2nd ed., (Oxford: Clarendon Press, 1963), p. 11; Siorvanes, *Proclus*, pp. 82–84. For Descartes see *Meditations on First Philosophy*, pp. 64, 90–91.

26. Proclus, *Elements of Theology*, p. 151; Siorvanes, *Proclus*, pp. 168–169. For Descartes see *Meditations on First Philosophy*, p. 66.

27. Siorvanes, *Proclus*, p. 155; Proclus, *Elements of Theology*, p. 147. For Descartes see *Meditations on First Philosophy*, pp. 64–67.

28. Siorvanes, Proclus, p. 154; Proclus, *Elements of Theology*, p. 147. For Descartes see *Meditations on First Philosophy*, p. 66.

29. Proclus, *Elements of Theology*, p. 155. For Descartes see *Meditations on First Philosophy*, pp. 90–91.

30. Proclus, *Elements of Theology*, pp. 71–73; Siorvanes, *Proclus*, p. 77. For Descartes see *Meditations on First Philosophy*, p. 75.

31. Siorvanes, *Proclus*, p. 247. For Descartes see *Principles of Philosophy*, in *Philosophical Writings*, vol. 1, pp. 227–228.

32. Siorvanes, *Proclus*, p. 218. For Descartes see *The World*, in *Philosophical Writings*, vol. 1, p. 86.

33. Siorvanes, *Proclus*, p. 298. For Descartes see *Principles of Philosophy*, in *Philosophical Writings*, vol. 1, p. 247.

34. Siorvanes, *Proclus*, p. 226. For Descartes see *Principles of Philosophy*, in *Philosophical Writings*, vol. 1, p. 247.

35. Siorvanes, *Proclus*, p. 208. For Descartes see *The World*, in *Philosophical Writings*, vol. 1, pp. 89–90.

36. Siorvanes, *Proclus*, p. 208. For Descartes see *Principles of Philosophy*, in *Philosophical Writings*, vol. 1, pp. 245–246.

37. Siorvanes, *Proclus*, pp. 271–272. For Descartes see *The World* and *Principles of Philosophy*, in *Philosophical Writings*, vol. 1, pp. 91, 243.

38. Siorvanes, Proclus, p. 293. For Descartes see *Optics*, in *Philosophical Writings*, vol. 1, p. 152.

39. Proclus, *Elements of Theology*, p. xxvii, n.3.

40. Martin Heidegger, *Nietzsche*, vols. 3 and 4, ed. David Farrell Krell (San Francisco: Harper Collins, 1991), vol. 3, p. 19.

Chapter Three. Consequences

1. René Descartes, *Meditations on First Philosophy*, in *Discourse on Method* and *Meditations on First Philosophy*, ed. David Weissman (New Haven: Yale University Press, 1996), p. 64.

2. René Descartes, *Rules for the Direction of the Mind*, in *Philosophical Writings*, vols. 1 and 2, trans. John Cottingham, Robert Stoothoff, and Dugald Murdoch (Cambridge: Cambridge University Press, 1985), vol. 1, p. 20.

3. Ibid.

4. Ludwig Wittgenstein, *Tractatus Logico-Philosophicus*, trans. D.F. Pears and B.F. McGuiness (London: Routledge & Kegan Paul, 1963), pp. 15–19, paras. 2.15–2.225.

5. David Weissman, *Intuition and Ideality* (Albany, N.Y.: State University of New York Press, 1987), pp. 29–32.

6. Descartes, *Rules for the Direction of the Mind*, in *Philosophical Writings*, vol. 1, p. 33.

7. The status of the discursive knowledge acquired by dialectic is equivocal. Plato should locate it below the divided line because it is fallible. He puts it above the line, presumably, because its objects are the Forms.

8. Descartes, *Rules for the Direction of the Mind*, in *Philosophical Writings*, vol. 1, p. 21.

9. Ibid., p. 37.

10. Ibid., p. 44: "[W]e term 'simple' only those things which we know so clearly and distinctly that they cannot be divided by the mind into others which are more distinctly known."

11. Ibid., pp. 44–45.

12. Descartes, *Principles of Philosophy*, in *Philosophical Writings*, vol. 1, pp. 289–291.

13. Descartes, *Meditations on First Philosophy*, p. 60.

14. "But what am I? A thing which thinks." Being a *thing*, a substance, is the mark of unity. Descartes, *Rules for the Direction of the Mind*, in *Philosophical Writings*, vol. 1, p. 66.

15. Descartes, *Meditations on First Philosophy*, p. 65.

16. Parmenides, *Parmenides of Elea*, trans. David Gallop (Toronto: University of Toronto Press, 1984), p. 57.

17. Descartes, *Meditations on First Philosophy*, p. 64.

18. Ibid., p. 70.

19. Ibid., p. 66.

20. Descartes, *Passions of the Soul*, in *Philosophical Writings*, vol. 1, p. 349.

21. Descartes, *Meditations on First Philosophy*, p. 91.

22. Proclus, *The Elements of Theology*, trans. E.R. Dodds (Oxford: Clarendon Press, 1963), p. xxxiii. Coleridge seems awed. Gilson was annoyed:

We have here, indeed, one of the most extraordinary spectacles in the history of thought; the first act opened with Descartes and the play still proceeds. The Christian philosophers were certainly persuaded that nature was made for man, and in this sense it is true to say that man stands at the centre of the medieval world; but they recognized none the less, that since the universe was created by God it is endowed with an existence proper to itself, it is something that man can know but could never pretend to have created. Etienne Gilson, *The Spirit of Medieval Philosophy*, trans. A.H.C. Downes [Notre Dame, Ind.: University of Notre Dame Press, 1991], pp. 244–245.

23. John Locke, *An Essay Concerning Human Understanding* (New York: Dover, 1959), vol. 2, p. 253.

24. George Berkeley, *Three Dialogues between Hylas and Philonus*, in *Berkeley's Philosophical Writings* (New York: Collier Books, 1965), p. 170.

25. Descartes, *Meditations on First Philosophy*, p. 66.

26. Albert Einstein, *Relativity* (London: Routledge, 1960), pp. 155–156.

27. Descartes, *Rules for the Direction of the Mind*, in *Philosophical Writings*, vol. 1, p. 14.

28. René Descartes, *Philosophical Writings*, vol. 3, trans. John Cottingham, Robert Stoothoff, Dugald Murdoch, and Anthony Kenny (Cambridge: Cambridge University Press, 1991), p. 324.

29. Descartes, *Meditations on First Philosophy*, p. 65.

30. Nicholas Malebranche, *Dialogues on Metaphysics and on Religion*, trans. Morris Ginsberg (London: George Allen & Unwin, 1923), pp. 202-224; G.W. Leibniz, *Philosophical Essays*, trans. Roger Ariew and Daniel Garber (Indianapolis, Ind.: Hackett Publishing Co, 1989) pp. 35–41; Berkeley, *Three Dialogues between Hylas and Philonus*, in *Berkeley's Philosophical Writings* pp. 214–219.

31. Descartes, *Philosophical Writings*, vol. 2, pp. 69–71.

32. Descartes, *Meditations on First Philosophy*, p. 85.

33. Ibid., p. 86.

34. Kant described the transcendental ego's self-sufficiency as "spontaneity," thereby implying that understanding is exempt from the constraint of, and need for other things (*Critique of Pure Reason*, trans. Norman Kemp Smith [New York: St. Martin's Press, 1965], p. 93).

35. Descartes, *Meditations on First Philosophy*, p. 66.

36. Berkeley, *The Principles of Human Knowledge*, in *Berkeley's Philosophical Writings*, p. 62.

37. Leibniz, *Philosophical Essays*, p. 216.

38. Locke, *An Essay Concerning Human Understanding*, vol. 1, pp. 121–125.

39. Berkeley, *Three Dialogues between Hylas and Philonus*, pp. 193–194.

40. Kant, *Critique of Pure Reason*, p. 179.

41. Johann G. Fichte, *The Science of Knowledge*, trans. Peter Heath and John Lachs (Cambridge: Cambridge University Press, 1982), p. 97.

42. G.W.F. Hegel, *Phenomenology of Mind*, trans. J.B. Baillie, (New York: Harper, 1967).

43. Ibid., pp. 490–491.

44. Kant, *Critique of Pure Reason*, pp. 81, 132–133.

45. Descartes, *Meditations on First Philosophy*, p. 69.

46. Kant, *Critique of Pure Reason*, pp. 257–275.

47. Ibid., p. 59.

48. Rudolf Carnap, *The Logical Structure of the World*, trans. Rolf A. George (Berkeley: University of California Press, 1969), pp. 11–12; and W.V.O. Quine, *Word and Object* (Cambridge, Mass.: MIT Press, 1960), p. 271.

49. Alfred Tarski, "The Semantic Conception of Truth," in *Semantics and the Philosophy of Language*, ed. Leonard Linsky (Urbana, Ill.: University of Illinois Press, 1952), pp. 21–23. The relation of ordinary speech to its immanent, controlling grammar is a another example of such hierarchies. We rise from unconsidered uses to their justifying rules, rules that have no application apart from actual or possible uses. See the essays in J.L. Austin, *Philosophical Papers* (Oxford: Oxford University Press, 1970).

50. Tarski, "Semantic Conception of Truth," pp. 21–23.

51. Carnap, *Logical Structure of the World*, pp. 27–28.

52. Rudolf Carnap, "Empiricism, Semantics, and Ontology," in *Semantics and the Philosophy of Language*, pp. 219–221.

53. Plato, *Sophist*, in *Collected Dialogues*, ed. Edith Hamilton and Huntington Cairns (New York: Pantheon Books, 1964) pp. 957–1017, 216a1–268d5; David Hume, *A Treatise of Human Nature*, ed. L.A. Selby–Bigge and P.H. Nidditch (Oxford: Clarendon Press, 1978), pp. 1–17.

54. Leibniz, *Philosophical Essays*, p. 219.

55. Kant, *Critique of Pure Reason*, pp. 105–106, 180–187.

56. Descartes, *Meditations on First Philosophy*, p. 69.

57. Leibniz, *Philosophical Essays*, p. 325.

58. Kant, *Critique of Pure Reason*, p. 135.

59. Ibid., p. 113.

60. Ibid., pp. 180–187.

61. Hegel, *Phenomenology of Mind*, pp. 462–610.

62. Carnap, *Logical Structure of the World*, pp. 175–246.

63. Ludwig Wittgenstein, *Philosophical Investigations*, trans. G.E.M. Anscombe (Oxford: Basil Blackwell, 1953), p. 11, para. 23.

64. J.L. Austin, *How To Do Things With Words* (Oxford: Clarendon Press, 1962), pp. 4–7.

65. Alfred North Whitehead and Bertrand Russell, *Principia Mathematica* (Cambridge: Cambridge University Press, 1964); David Hilbert, *Foundations of Geometry*, trans. Leo Unger (La Salle, Ill.: Open Court, 1988); Arend Heyting, *Intuitionism, an Introduction* (Amsterdam: North Holland, 1956).

66. Descartes, *Philosophical Writings*, vol. 3, p. 235.

67. Descartes, *Meditations on First Philosophy*, p. 86.

68. Benedict Spinoza, *Ethics*, trans. by R.H.M. Elwes (New York: Dover, 1955), pp. 202–205.

69. Arthur Schopenhauer, *The World as Will and Representation*, trans. E.F.J. Payne (New York: Dover, 1966), vol. l, p. 58; Sigmund Freud, *The Ego and the Id*, trans. Joan Riviere (New York: W.W. Norton and Co., 1989, pp. 44–47.

70. Friedrich Nietzsche, *Beyond Good and Evil*, trans. Walter Kaufmann, (New York: Vintage Books, 1989), p. 48.

71. Friedrich Nietzsche, *The Will to Power*, trans. Walter Kaufmann and R.J. Hollingdale (New York: Random House, 1968), pp. 270–271.

72. Immanuel Kant, *Critique of Practical Reason*, trans. Lewis White Beck (Indianapolis: Liberal Arts Press, 1956), pp. 52–59.

73. Martin Heidegger, *Nietzsche*, vols. 3 and 4, ed. David Farrell Krell (San Francisco: Harper Collins, 1991), vol. 3, pp. 242, 243, and 250. The editor asks in his Introduction if Heidegger was a Nazi. He answers that, "Heidegger's resistance to the crude biologism, racism, and anti-Semitism of the Nazi Party cannot . . . be doubted." I doubt it. See Tom Rockmore, *On Heidegger's Nazism and Philosophy* (Berkeley: University of California Press, 1992).

74. Fichte, *Science of Knowledge*, pp. 232, 259.

75. Descartes, *The Passions of the Soul*, in *Philosophical Writings*, vol. 1, p. 350.

76. Ibid., pp. 350, 353–355.

77. Edmund Husserl, *Cartesian Meditations*, trans. Dorion Cairns (The Hague: Martinus Nijhoff, 1960), p. 84.

Chapter Four. Descartes' Heirs: Ontological Foundationalism and "The End of Western Metaphysics"

1. David Hume, *A Treatise of Human Nature*, ed. L.A. Selby–Bigge and P.H. Nidditch (Oxford: Clarendon Press, 1978), p. 172.

2. Ibid., p. 207.

3. Ibid., pp. 104, 179.

4. Immanuel Kant, *Critique of Pure Reason*, trans. Norman Kemp Smith (New York: St. Martin's Press, 1965), pp. 65–91.

5. René Descartes, *Meditations on First Philosophy*, in *Discourse on Method and Meditations on First Philosophy*, ed. David Weissman (New

Haven: Yale University Press, 1996), p. 69; G.W. Leibniz, *Philosophical Essays*, trans. Roger Ariew and Daniel Garber (Indianapolis, Ind.: Hackett Publishing Co., 1989), pp. 217–218.

6. Kant, *Critique of Pure Reason*, pp. 104–119.

7. Ibid., pp. 180–187.

8. Ibid., pp. 135–161.

9. Ibid., pp. 124–125.

10. Ibid., p. 292.

11. Ibid., pp. 142–143; J.G. Fichte, *Science of Knowledge*, trans. Peter Heath and John Lachs (Cambridge: Cambridge University Press, 1982), pp. 207–208, 275–276; F.W.J. Schelling, trans. Peter Heath, *System of Transcendental Idealism (1800)* (Charlottesville, Va.: University Press of Virginia, 1978), pp. 13–14, 72, 76; and G.W.F. Hegel, *The Phenomenology of Mind*, trans. J.B. Baillie (New York: Harper and Row, 1967) p. 792.

12. Immanuel Kant, *Critique of Judgment*, trans. W.S. Pluhar (Indianapolis: Hackett Publishing Co., 1987), pp. 16-18.

13. Leibniz, *Philosophical Essays*, p. 214; Kant, *Critique of Pure Reason*, p. 285.

14. Kant's moral theory—apply only those maxims which are universalizable without contradiction—does not mitigate this result. For universalization requires an act of imagination in which each thinker extrapolates from *its* experience. We may suppose that the extra-mental world imposes regularizing constraints on each one's experience—the Sun that shines on all of us, for example. But nothing in Kant justifies this assumption. Our experiences may be radically different, even incommensurable, so that only a mysterious harmony makes my experience consistent with yours.

15. Plato, *Theaetetus*, in *Collected Dialogues*, ed., Edith Hamilton and Huntington Cairns (New York: Pantheon Books, 1963), pp. 857, 152d–e; 887, 182d.

16. Kant, *Critique of Judgment*, p. 16, n.18.

17. Kant, *Critique of Pure Reason*, pp. 297–307.

18. Leibniz, *Philosophical Essays*, p. 219.

19. Kant, *Critique of Pure Reason*, p. 93.

20. Ibid., pp. 129–130.

21. Ibid., pp. 189–191.

22. Immanuel Kant, *Critique of Practical Reason*, trans. Lewis White Beck (Indianapolis, Ind.: Liberal Arts Press, 1956), pp. 52–59.

23. Hume, *Treatise of Human Nature*, p. 165.

24. Kant, *Critique of Pure Reason*, p. 147.

25. Descartes, *Meditations on First Philosophy*, pp. 195–209.

26. A.J. Ayer, *Language, Truth, and Logic*, 2nd ed. (London: V. Gollancz, 1967).

27. There are also eclectic analysts, many of them having no conscious or consistent historical allegiance. Analysts of all sorts should be distinguished from speculative thinkers who use formal arguments to justify their extra-philosophic beliefs—about God, for example. See Alvin Plantinga, *God and Other Minds* (Ithaca, N.Y.: Cornell University Press, 1990).

28. William James, "The Will to Believe," in *The Writings of William James*, ed. John J. McDermott (New York: Modern Library, 1968), pp. 717–735.

29. Friedrich Nietzsche, *Beyond Good and Evil*, trans. Walter Kaufmann (New York: Vintage Books, 1989), pp. 47–48.

30. Friedrich Nietzsche, *The Will to Power*, trans. Walter Kaufmann and R.J. Hollingdale (New York: Random House, 1968), pp. 420–421.

31. Friedrich Nietzsche, *On The Genealogy of Morals*, trans. Douglas Smith (Oxford: Oxford University Press, 1996), pp. 15–16.

32. Ibid., pp. 64–66.

33. Martin Heidegger, *Nietzsche*, vols 1 and 2, trans. David Farrell Krell (San Francisco: Harper Collins, 1991), vol. 2, p. 203.

34. Nietzsche, *Genealogy of Morals*, pp. 217–219.

35. Nietzsche, *Will to Power*, p. 17.

36. Nietzsche, *Beyond Good and Evil*, p. 2.

37. Ibid., p. 100.

38. Ibid., pp. 158–59.

39. Nietzsche, *Genealogy of Morals*, pp. 5–6, 8.

40. Nietzsche, *Beyond Good and Evil*, p. 161.

41. Ibid., p. 29.

42. Martin Heidegger, *Being and Time*, trans. James Macquarrie and Edward Robinson (New York: Harper & Row, 1962), pp. 67–90.

43. Edmund Husserl, *Cartesian Meditations*, trans. Dorion Cairns (The Hague: Martinus Nijhoff, 1960), pp. 9–11.

44. Kant, *Critique of Pure Reason*, p. 169, n.

45. Heidegger, *Nietzsche*, vol. 3, p. 222.

46. Ibid., p. 226.

47. Ibid., p. 70.

48. Ibid., p. 226.

49. Ibid., p. 242.

50. This allegation elides Kant's transcendental and empirical egos. The empirical ego—the way I appear to myself—is transformed as often as experience is schematized by the transcendental ego. The transcendental ego is the power for creating a thinkable experience; it never changes.

51. Heidegger, *Nietzsche*, vol. 3, p. 138.

52. Aristotle, *The Basic Works of Aristotle*, ed. Richard McKeon (New York: Random House, 1941), pp. 564–567, 417b32–418a7; John Locke, *An Essay Concerning Human Understanding*, vol. 1, (New York: Dover, 1959), p. 142.

53. Heidegger, *Nietzsche*, vol. 3, p. 129.

54. Ibid., vol. 4, p. 207.

55. Ibid., vol. 3, p. 141.

56. Ibid., p. 221.

57. Ibid., p. 154.

58. Kant, *Critique of Judgment*, p. 16, n.18; Fichte, *The Science of Knowledge*, p. 32; and Schelling, *System of Transcendental Idealism (1800)*, pp. 137, 171–176.

59. Heidegger, *Nietzsche*, vol. 4, p. 211.

60. Husserl, *Cartesian Meditations*, pp. 69–72.

61. Rudolf Carnap, *The Logical Structure of the World*, trans. Rolf A. George (Berkeley: University of California Press, 1969), p. 288.

62. Ibid., p. 15.

63. Ibid., p. 158.

64. Ibid., p. 101.

65. Ibid., p. 104.

66. Ibid.

67. Ibid., p. 288.

68. Rudolf Carnap, *Meaning and Necessity* (Chicago: University of Chicago Press, 1956), p. 248.

69. Carnap, *Logical Structure of the World*, pp. 233–234.

70. Rudolf Carnap, "Empiricism, Semantics, and Ontology," in *Semantics and the Philosophy of Language*, ed. Leonard Linsky (Urbana, Ill.: University of Illinois Press, 1952), pp. 209–210.

71. Carnap, *Logical Structure of the World*, pp. 233–234.

72. W.V.O. Quine, *Word and Object*, (Cambridge, Mass.: MIT Press, 1960), p. 272, n. 2.

73. Kant, *Critique of Pure Reason*, p. 137.

74. David Weissman, *Intuition and Ideality* (Albany, N.Y.: State University of New York Press, 1987), pp. 288–289.

75. W.V.O. Quine, *Ontological Relativity and Other Essays* (New York: Columbia University Press, 1969), p. 26.

76. Ibid., p. 84.

77. W.V.O. Quine, *The Ways of Paradox* (Cambridge, Mass.: Harvard University Press, 1976), pp. 246–254.

78. Quine, *Ontological Relativity and Other Essays*, p. 82. Quine emphasizes his naturalism in W.V.O. Quine, *Theories and Things* (Cambridge, Mass.: Harvard University Press, 1981), pp. 21-22; and he thanks Gibson for correctly describing his naturalistic views: "Reply to Roger F. Gibson, Jr.," in The *Philosophy of W.V. Quine*, ed. Lewis E. Hahn and Paul A. Schilpp (Chicago and La Salle, Ill.: Open Court, 1998), pp. 155–157. Quine's naturalism is, nevertheless, qualified: "Factuality, like gravitation and electric charge, is internal to our theory of nature" (Quine, *Theories and Things*, p. 23).

79. Quine, *Ontological Relativity and Other Essays*, pp. 125–126.

80. Quine, *Ways of Paradox*, p. 134.

81. Quine, *Ontological Relativity and Other Essays*, p. 91.

82. Quine, *Word and Object*, p. 271.

83. Ibid., pp. 9–13.

84. Ibid.

85. Ibid., pp. 31-35. Quine's behaviorism is oddly asymmetrical: we are stimulated—acted on by those I-know-not-whats that provoke sensation within us—but we do not act on other things, except to the extent of organizing sentences that express our thoughts about them. For we can't act on things that have no existence apart from the quantified variables used to talk about them.

86. Ibid., pp. 12–13.

87. W.V.O. Quine, *The Roots of Reference* (La Salle, IL: Open Court, 1974), p. 88.

88. Quine, *Ontological Relativity and Other Essays*, pp. 81–141.

89. Ibid., p. 94.

90. Quine, *Word and Object*, p. 24.

91. Ibid., p. 23.

92. For the rationale, see: W.V.O. Quine, "Existence and Quantification," in *Ontological Relativity and Other Essays*, pp. 91–113.

93. Quine, *Roots of Reference*, p. 138.

94. Quine, *Ontological Relativity and Other Essays*, pp. 126–127.

95. Charles Sanders Peirce, "The Fixation of Belief," in *Collected Papers of Charles Sanders Peirce*, vol. 5, ed. Charles Hartshorne and Paul Weiss (Cambridge, Mass.; Harvard University Press, 1965), pp. 223–247; David Weissman, *Hypothesis and the Spiral of Reflection* (Albany, N.Y.: State University of New York Press, 1989), pp. 92–96.

96. Quine, *Word and Object*, p. 12.

97. Quine, *Ontological Relativity and Other Essays*, p. 50.

98. Ibid., p. 83.

99. Heidegger, *Nietzsche*, vol. 4, pp. 97–98.

100. *Ibid.*, p. 100.

101. Ibid., vol. 3, p. 223.

102. Ernest Nagel, *The Structure of Science* (New York: Harcourt, Brace & World, 1961), pp. 151–152.

103. Thomas Kuhn, *The Structure of Scientific Revolutions* (Chicago: University of Chicago Press, 1962), p. 117.

104. Ibid., p. 171.

105. Ibid., p. 206.

106. Carnap, "Empiricism, Semantics, and Ontology," p. 211.

107. Nietzsche, *Will to Power*, p. 545.

Chapter Five. The *Cogito's* Demise

1. René Descartes, *Philosophical Writings*, vols. 1 and 2, trans. John Cottingham, Robert Stoothoff, and Dugald Murdoch (Cambridge: Cambridge University Press, 1985), vol. 2, pp. 122; 183–184; John Locke, *An Essay Concerning Human Understanding* (New York: Dover, 1959), vol. 2, p. 193.

2. Descartes, *Treatise on Man*, in *Philosophical Writings*, vol. 1, p. 99.

3. René Descartes, *Oeuvres de Descartes*, ed. Charles Adam and Paul Tannery, rev. ed., 12 vols. (Paris: Vrin/CNRS, 1964–76), vol. 11, p. 185; see also Descartes, *Philosophical Writings*, vol. 2, p. 161.

4. David Chalmers, *The Conscious Mind* (Oxford: Oxford University Press, 1996), pp. 150–160.

5. Aristotle, *De Anima*, in *Basic Works*, ed. Richard McKeon (New York: Random House, 1941), p. 555, 412a25.

6. Plato, *The Republic*, trans. Francis MacDonald Cornford (Oxford: Oxford University Press, 1945), pp. 219–220, 508b.

7. Descartes, *Treatise on Man*, in *Philosophical Writings*, vol. 1, p. 100.

8. Immanuel Kant, *Critique of Pure Reason*, trans. Norman Kemp Smith (New York: St. Martin's Press, 1965), pp. 92–93.

9. Ibid., pp. 74–80.

10. Descartes, *Philosophical Writings*, Vol. 2, pp. 122, 183–184.

11. See, for example, Chalmers's views about "property dualism," the irreducibility of phenomenal to physical properties (*Conscious Mind*, pp. 264–268).

12. Thomas Nagel, *The View from Nowhere* (New York: Oxford University Press, 1989), p. 29

13. Chalmers has little to say of the idea that mental states and activities are emergent:

> Sometimes it is argued that consciousness might be an *emergent* property, in a sense that is still compatible with materialism. In recent work on complex systems and artificial life, it is often held that emergent properties are unpredictable from low-level properties, but that they are physical all the same. Examples are the emergence of self-organization in biological systems, or the emergence of flocking patterns from simple rules in simulated birds. . . . If *all* the physical facts about such a system over time are given, then the fact that self-organization is occurring will be straightforwardly derivable. This is just what we would expect as properties such as self-organization and flocking are straightforwardly functional and structural. If consciousness is an emergent property, it is emergent in a much stronger sense. There is a stronger notion of emergence, used by the British emergentists . . . according to which emergent properties are not even predictable from the entire ensemble of low-level physical facts. It is reasonable to say (as the British emergentists did) that conscious experience is emergent in this sense. But this sort of emergence is best counted as a variety of property dualism. Unlike the more "innocent" examples of emergence given above, the strong variety requires new fundamental laws in order that the emergent properties emerge (Chalmers, *Conscious Mind*, pp. 129–130).

The last sentence is an opinion expressed without supporting evidence. The emergence of consciousness may require that many neurons be organized in particular ways, but not that there be new laws to regulate these formations. Or new laws emerge *with* consciousness, not as conditions required before it can emerge. So, the Pythagorean theorem emerges when three line-segments are joined to create a right triangle. But there is no categorial difference between the line segments and triangle. Moreover, the theorem cannot be a condition for the emergence of the triangle, because it emerges with the creation of the triangle.

Chalmers ignores emergence, because of his fundamental assumption. Taking consciousness seriously we notice, like Descartes, the apparent, categorial difference of physical and phenomenal properties. Chalmers' book is an extended defense of this observation: properties that appear categorially different are as they seem.

14. Descartes, *Description of the Human Body*, in *Philosophical Writings*, vol. 1, p. 315.

15. Eric Kandel, *Cellular Basis of Behavior* (San Francisco: W.H. Freeman, 1976).

16. Aristotle, *De Anima*, in *Basic Works*, p. 555, 412a15–21: "It follows that every natural body which has life in it is a substance in the sense of a composite. . . . Hence the soul must be a substance in the sense of the form of a natural body having life potentially within it."

17. See Daniel Dennett, *Consciousness Explained* (New York: Little, Brown, 1991).

18. Peirce anticipated this result when he described four methods for achieving belief—tenacity, authority, intuition, and hypothesis—and the trajectory in which each subsequent method supersedes the one or others before it. See C.S. Peirce, "The Fixation of Belief," in *Collected Papers*, vols. 5 and 6, ed. Charles Hartshorne and Paul Weiss (Cambridge, Mass.: Harvard University Press, 1935), vol. 5, pp. 233–247.

19. Ibid., pp. 32–40.

20. Ibid., p. 394.

21. W.V.O. Quine, *Word and Object*, (Cambridge, Mass.: MIT Press, 1960), p. 23.

22. David Weissman, *Hypothesis and the Spiral of Reflection* (Albany, N.Y.: State University of New York Press, 1989), pp. 34–40.

23. Henri Bergson, *Creative Evolution*, trans. Arthur Mitchell (London: Macmillan and Co., 1919), p. 381; Edmund Husserl, *Cartesian Meditations*, trans. Dorion Cairns (The Hague: Martinus Nihjoff, 1960), p. 78.

Chapter Six. Churning

1. David Lewis, *Parts of Classes* (Cambridge, Mass.: Basil Blackwell, 1991), pp. 79-81.

2. David Weissman, *A Social Ontology* (New Haven: Yale University Press, 2000), pp. 24–88.

3. W.V.O.Quine, "Epistemology Naturalized," in *Ontological Relativity and Other Essays* (New York: Columbia University Press, 1969), pp. 69–90. This essay expresses Quine's naturalistic inclinations. He amplifies them:

> I am of that large minority or small majority who repudiate the Cartesian dream of a foundation for scientific certainty firmer than scientific method itself. But I remain occupied, we see, with what has been central to traditional epistemology, namely the relation of science to its sensory data. I appropriate it as an input-output relation within flesh-and-blood denizens of an antecedently acknowledged external world, a relation open to inquiry as a chapter of the science of that world. To emphasize dissociation from the Cartesian dream I have written of neural receptors and their stimulation rather than of sense or sensibilia. I call the pursuit naturalized epistemology, but I have no quarrel with traditionalists who protest my retention of the latter word, I agree with them that repudiation of the Cartesian dream is no minor deviation. (W V.O. Quine, *Pursuit of Truth* [Cambridge, Mass.: Harvard University Press, 1990], p. 19).

How does this passage square with the claims, previously quoted and discussed, that objects are products of the conceptual system used to think them—that to be is to be the value of a bound variable? The two positions are irreconcilable. The realism expressed in the passage just cited is unstable, because of Quine's preoccupation with sensory data. Is it effects of extramental causes from which we abductively infer—from the voice on the phone to the person calling—or do the data "represent" just such objects as are schematized by the scientific theory used to interpret them? Does scientific theory comprise testable, revisable hypotheses about extra-mental states of affairs? Or is *scientific theory* the honorific phrase for Kant's empirical schemas? Quine implies the former, in the paragraph quoted above; his detailed arguments always promote the idealist alternative. The epistemology of his major work is Kantian, not naturalistic or naturalized.

4. Thomas Kuhn, *The Structure of Scientific Revolutions* (Chicago: University of Chicago Press, 1962), pp. 43–51.

5. Pierre Duhem, *The Aim and Structure of Physical Theory*, trans. Philip P. Wiener (New York: Atheneum, 1962), pp. 304–306.

6. See Ruth Millikan, *Language, Thought, and Other Biological Categories* (Cambridge, Mass.: MIT Press, 1984); and Peter Godfrey–Smith,

Complexity and the Function of Mind in Nature (Cambridge: Cambridge University Press, 1998).

7. W.V.O. Quine, *Word and Object* (Cambridge, Mass.: MIT Press, 1960), pp. 206–211.

8. Aristotle, *De Anima*, in *Basic Works*, ed. Richard McKeon (New York: Random House, 1941), pp. 564–581, 416b32–424b19; Alvin Goldman, "A Causal Theory of Knowing," *Journal of Philosophy* 64 (1967): 357–372.

9. René Descartes, *Rules for the Direction of the Mind*, in *Philosophical Writings*, vols. 1 and 2, ed. John Cottingham, Robert Stoothoff, and Dugald Murdoch (Cambridge: Cambridge University Press, 1985) vol, I, p. 21.

10. Gilbert Harman, *Explaining Virtue* (Oxford: Clarendon Press, 2000), p. 221.

11. John Searle, "End of the Revolution," *New York Review of Books* 49 (3): 36.

12. Ibid.

13. Ibid., p. 35. Classifying Searle with the dualists seems inappropriate, given his emphatic claim that "consciousness is an ordinary biological phenomenon comparable with growth, digestion, or the secretion of bile" (John Searle, *The Mystery of Consciousness* [New York: New York Review of Books, 1997], p. 6). Yet, he qualifies this view:

> There is an object of study for natural science, the human brain with its specific language components. But the actual languages that humans learn and speak are not in that way natural objects. They are creations of human beings. Analogously humans have a natural capacity to socialize and form social groups with other humans. But the actual social organizations they create, such as governments and corporations, are not natural, observer-independent phenomena, they are human creations and have an observer-dependent existence ("End of the Revolution," p. 34).

This seems to be, but is not Aristotle's distinction of natural things and artifacts. His artifacts depend on humans for their creation and use, but they are observer–independent objects in the respect that they are enmattered forms. Perhaps, Searle intends to distinguish structures from functions, brains being structures, linguistic usage being one of their functions. But it doesn't follow that structures are natural, while their functions—including attitudes and productive activities—are not. Is bird song other than natural when used to warn a flock of nearby predators? Are beaver dams other than natural because useful to beaver colonies? Or we concede that the behavior of beavers and birds is natural, so the significant difference is the one of formulaic animals and inventive, conscious humans. Searle would agree that post office buildings are natural objects. It is their use—their significance—that is other than natural. Why? Because the use of money or the postal service requires rules that could not be followed if we could not be conscious of them. This is the core of Searle's equivocation: why is the activity of a natural system—consciousness, for example—other than natural, if the system is natural? This is odd when Searle lumps consciousness with secretions of bile. Aren't both exhaustively material?

Searle hedges. Observer-dependent functions are not material, because the irreducibilty of consciousness sets it apart from nature:

> There are no purely physical properties that are sufficient to determine all and only sentences of English. . . . But why not, since all these are physical phenomena? Because the physical phenomena satisfy these descriptions only relative to some set of conventions and of people's attitudes operating within the conventions (Ibid., p. 35).

This distinction is "a fundamental distinction in ontology" (Ibid., p. 34)—though the only "ontological" difference specified is the one of things that are independent or observer–dependent. Hence the previous question: why are the uses of bile natural, while those of consciousness are not? Is this an expression of the deeply rooted Cartesian belief that conscious understanding is the difference that distinguishes mind, categorially, from body?

14. Ibid.

15. Antonio R. Damasio, *Descartes' Error* (New York: Putnam, 1994), pp. 155–158.

16. David Weissman, *Truth's Debt to Value* (New Haven: Yale University Press, 1993), pp. 160–162.

17. Ibid., pp. 199–202.

18. Ibid., pp. 286–287.

19. Ibid., pp. 170–174.

20. Immanuel Kant, *Critique of Pure Reason*, trans. Norman Kemp Smith (New York: St. Martin's Press, 1965), pp. 106, 191–194.

21. Ibid., pp. 645–652.

22. Paul Horwich, *Truth* (Oxford: Blackwell, 1990, p. 111.

23. Descartes, *Rules for the Direction of the Mind*, in *Philosophical Writings*, vol. 1, p. 13.

24. David Weissman, *Intuition and Ideality* (Albany, N.Y.: State University of New York Press, 1987), pp. 29–32.

25. Aristotle, *Posterior Analytics*, in *Basic Works*, pp. 111–113, 71b8–72b4.

26. Rudolf Carnap, *The Logical Structure of the World*, trans. Rolf A. George (Berkeley: University of California Press, 1969), pp. 87–88.

27. Quine, *Word and Object*, p. 12: "In an obvious way this structure of interconnected sentences is a single connected fabric including all sciences, and indeed everything we ever say about the world; for the logical truths at least, and no doubt many more commonplace sentences too, are germane to all topics and thus provide connections."

28. Godfrey–Smith, *Complexity and the Function of Mind in Nature*, p. 110.

29. Descartes, too, used hypotheses, but only in his scientific work. See Descartes, *Principles of Philosophy*, in *Philosophical Writings*, vol. 1 pp. 256–257; and Lou Massa, "Physics and Mathematics," in *Discourse on Method and Meditations on First Philosophy*, ed. David Weissman (New Haven: Yale University Press, 1996), pp. 272–274. Inspection and demonstration were the only methods he espoused when the objects of knowledge were mind's ideas, activities, or structure.

30. Ludwig Wittgenstein, *Philosophical Investigations*, trans. G.E.M. Anscombe (New York: Macmillan, 1953), p. 80, para. 199; p. 83, para. 202; pp. 92–94, paras. 258–265.

31. Kant, *Critique of Pure Reason*, p. 314.

32. Quine, *Ontological Relativity and Other Essays*, pp. 30–34.

33. Kant, *Critique of Pure Reason*, pp. 67–91.

34. Ibid., pp. 151, 153.

35. John Stuart Mill, *On Liberty* (New York: Macmillan, 1956), p. 16.

36. David Weissman, *A Social Ontology* (New Haven: Yale University Press, 2000), pp. 57–58.

37. Descartes, *Meditations on First Philosophy*, p. 66.

38. Robert Nozick, *Anarchy, State, and Utopia* (New York: Basic Books, 1974), p. 33.

39. Descartes crystallized this tradition, without being its founder. Hobbes and Nietzsche are also critical for contemporary libertarians.

40. Weissman, *A Social Ontology*, p. 69

41. Ibid., pp. 51–52, 119–120.

42. Thomas Hobbes, *Leviathan*, ed. Michael Oakeshott (Oxford: Blackwell, 1946), pp. 172–189; Nozick, *Anarchy, State, and Utopia*, pp. 23–25.

43. Michel Foucault, *The Order of Things* (New York: Vintage Books, 1973).

44. John Rawls, *A Theory of Justice* (Cambridge, Mass.: Harvard University Press, 1971), pp. 54–117; Jurgen Habermas, *The Theory of*

Communicative Action, vol. 1, trans. Thomas McCarthy (Boston: Beacon Press, 1884), pp. 8–42:

> [T]he knowledge embodied in normatively regulated actions or in expressive manifestations does not refer to the existence of states of affairs but to the validity of norms or to the manifestation of subjective experiences. With these expressions the speaker can refer not to something in the objective world but only to something in a common social world or in his own subjective world. For now I shall have to leave the matter with this provisional suggestion that there are communicative actions characterized by other relations to the world and connected with valididty claims *different* from truth and effectiveness (*Theory of Communicative Action*, p. 16).

45. Weissman, *A Social Ontology*, pp. 59–63.

46. Friedrich Nietzsche, *Philosophy and Truth: Selections from Nietzsche's Notebooks of the Early 1870's* (Atlantic Heights, N.J.: Humanities Press, 1993), p. 79.

47. John Lachs, *In Love with Life* (Nashville, Tenn.: Vanderbilt University Press, 1998).

48. This issue provokes Western philosophy from its inception. Plato's allegory of the cave and Hegel's *Phenomenology of Mind* are two high points. Contemporary disccusions include Thomas Nagel, *The View from Nowhere*, (New York: Oxford University Press, 1989), p. 5; and William Desmond's notion of the *between: Being and the Between* (Albany, N.Y.: State University of New York Press, 1995).

49. George Berkeley, *Three Dialogues between Hylas and Philonus*, in *Berkeley's Philosophical Writings* (New York: Collier Books, 1965), p. 170.

50. The ontological opacity of quantum theory differs from Quine's inscrutability of reference. Quine supposes that the want of isomorphism between or among languages makes it uncertain that the quantified terms of two or more languages have the same referents, even when tied directly to empirical data, *red* and *rouge*, for example. Ostensive terms may be correlated to subtly different data from language to language; rules for joining ostensive to theoretical terms vary among languages. It is undecidable and unlikely, therefore, that the bound variables of disparate languages have the same referents. Ontological opacity is a consequence of wave particle duality, the discovery that the character of a test determines the character of things tested, and the implications of regulative principles gleaned from some interpretations of quantum theory, especially the claims that something may come from nothing, and that electrons and photons don't exist until perceived.

51. David Finkelstein, *Quantum Relativity* (Heidelberg: Springer, 1996). For realist doubts see Andrew Whittaker, *Einstein, Bohr and the Quantum*

Dilemma (Cambridge: Cambridge University Press, 1996); and F. Selleri, *Quantum Paradoxes and Physical Reality* (Dordrecht: Kluwer, 1990).

52. Dennis Overbye, "Peering through the Gates of Time," *New York Times* 151 (52,055) Tuesday, March 12, 2002, p. F1.

53. David Hume, *A Treatise of Human Nature*, ed. L.A. Selby–Bigge and P.H. Nidditch (Oxford: Clarendon Press, 1978), p. 82.

54. Ibid., p. 79.

55. David Albert, *Quantum Mechanics and Experience* (Cambridge, Mass.: Harvard University Press, 1992), pp. 112–113.

56. Ibid., pp. 128–129.

57. Kant, *Critique of Pure Reason*, pp. 297–570.

58. Compare the operationalism of Finkelstein, *Quantum Relativity*, and the realism of Albert, *Quantum Mechanics and Experience*, pp. 47–60.

59. See Marshall Spector, "Mind, Matter, and Quantum Mechanics," in Patrick Grim, *Philosophy of Science and the Occult*, 2d ed. (Albany, N.Y.: State University of New York Press, 1990), pp. 326–349, for a sober view of quantum theory's implications.

Chapter Seven. Ideas to Reformulate and Save

1. David Weissman, *Truth's Debt to Value* (New Haven: Yale University Press, 1993), pp. 66–100; Friedrich Nietzsche, *Genealogy of Morals*, trans. Douglas Smith (Oxford: Oxford University Press, 1996), pp. 113–114.

2. Ludwig Wittgenstein, *Tractatus Logico-Philosophicus*, trans. D.F. Pears and B.F. McGuinness (London: Routledge & Kegan Paul, 1963), p. 115, para. 5.6.

3. Ibid., p. 15, paras. 2.15–2.1512.

4. Plato, *The Republic*, trans. Francis MacDonald Cornford (Oxford: Oxford University Press, 1945, pp. 9–10, 331e–332c.

5. David Weissman, *Eternal Possibilities* (Carbondale, Ill.: Southern Illinois University Press, 1977) pp. 115–126; *idem, A Social Ontology* (New Haven: Yale University Press, 2000), pp. 27–30.

6. Graham Nerlich, *The Shape of Space*, 2nd ed. (Cambridge: Cambridge University Press, 1994).

7. Stephen Gaukroger, "The Nature of Abstract Reasoning: Philosophical Aspects of Descartes' Work in Algebra," in *The Cambridge*

Companion to Descartes, ed. John Cottingham (Cambridge: Cambridge University Press, 1992), pp. 91–114.

8. Weissman *Eternal Possibilities*, pp. 57–58; *idem, Truth's Debt to Value*, pp. 262–272.

9. John N. Findlay, *The Discipline of the Cave* (London: George Allen & Unwin, 1966); and *idem, The Transcendence of the Cave* (London: George Allen & Unwin, 1967).

10. Ludwig Wittgenstein, *Philosophical Investigations*, trans. G.E.M. Anscombe (Oxford: Blackwell, 1953), pp. 125–127, paras. 416–426.

11. Norman Malcolm, *Dreaming* (London: Routledge & Kegan Paul, 1962)

12. Wittgenstein, *Tractatus Logico-Philosophicus*, p. 147, para. 6.43.

13. Weissman, *Eternal Possibilities*, pp. 57–107.

14. Weissman, *Truth's Debt to Value*, pp. 297–330.

15. Etienne Gilson, *The Spirit of Medieval Philosophy*, trans. A.H.C. Downes (Notre Dame, Ind.: University of Notre Dame Press, 1991), pp. 168–188.

16. David Weissman, *Hypothesis and the Spiral of Reflection* (Albany, N.Y.: State University of New York Press), pp. 187–197; *idem, A Social Ontology*, pp. 104–110.

17. Weissman, *A Social Ontology*, pp. 267–271.

18. Adolf Grünbaum, *The Foundations of Psychoanalysis* (Berkeley: University of California Press, 1985).

19. René Descartes, *Meditations on First Philosophy*, in *Discourse on Method and Meditations on First Philosophy*, ed. David Weissman (New Haven: Yale University Press, 1996), p. 86.

20. Immanuel Kant, *Critique of Practical Reason*, trans. Lewis White Beck (Indianapolis, Ind.: Liberal Arts Press, 1956), p. 45.

21. This is a surmise. Descartes' indifference to other people is implied when he fails to mentions them, social rules, or a common good, either while doubting "everything" or when describing the world recovered in the sixth *Meditation*. He wrote letters to many people, but relations with them and others seem to have been correct but distant.

22. René Descartes, *The Passions of the Soul*, in *Philosophical Writings*, vols. 1 and 2, trans. John Cottingham, Robert Stoothoff, and Dugald Murdoch (Cambridge: Cambridge University Press, 1985), vol. 1, p. 349.

23. Weissman, *A Social Ontology*, pp. 229–237.

24. Tit for tat is a strategy that promotes mutual loyalty and cooperation if the individuals are known to one another because they regularly interact, and if their interactions and choices come fast enough for each person to judge the costs and benefits of his or her strategy. Typical formulations of the Prisoner's Dilemma discourage this strategy, because they imply little or no knowledge of, or loyalty to, the other person, long jail sentences, and no prospect of subsequent interaction. Why risk a longer sentence by hoping your altruism is matched by that of someone you don't know?

25. Plato, *Republic*, p. 142, 443d-e; Aristotle, *Politics*, in *Basic Works*, ed. Richard McKeon (New York: Random House, 1941), pp. 1277–1279, 1323a15–1324a13.

26. Descartes, *The Passions of the Soul*, in *Philosophical Writings*, vol. 1, p. 349.

27. David Hume, *A Treatise of Human Nature*, ed. L.A. Selby–Bigge and P.H. Nidditch (Oxford: Clarendon Press, 1978) p. 415; John Stuart Mill, *Utilitarianism* (Indianapolis, Ind.: Hackett Publishing Co., 1969), p. 7; Nietzsche, *The Genealogy of Morals*, pp. 58–60, 73–74.

28. Mill, *Utilitarianism*, pp. 8–10.

29. Self-love is not a modern heresy. See Gilson, *Spirit of Medieval Philosophy*, pp. 269–270.

30. Weissman, *A Social Ontology*, pp. 147–148.

31. Ibid., pp. 101–104.

32. Ibid., pp. 229–235.

33. G.W.F. Hegel, *The Philosophy of Right*, trans. T.M. Knox (Oxford: Clarendon Press, 1952), pp. 122–155.

34. Weissman, *A Social Ontology*, pp. 164–178.

35. Ibid., pp. 229–235.

Index